Cataclysm: General Hap Arnold and the Defeat of Japan

Cataclysm

General Hap Arnold
and the Defeat of Japan

Herman S. Wolk

University of North Texas Press
Denton, Texas

10 9 8 7 6 5 4 3 2

Permissions:
University of North Texas Press
1155 Union Circle #311336
Denton, TX 76203-5017

The paper used in this book meets the minimum requirements of the American
National Standard for Permanence of Paper for Printed Library Materials, z39.48.1984.
Binding materials have been chosen for durability.

Library of Congress Cataloging-in-Publication Data

Wolk, Herman S., 1931-
Cataclysm : General Hap Arnold and the defeat of Japan / Herman S. Wolk. -- 1st ed.
p. cm.
Includes bibliographical references and index.
ISBN 978-1-57441-281-9 (cloth : alk. paper)
1. Arnold, Henry Harley, 1886-1950. 2. Arnold, Henry Harley, 1886-1950--Military
leadership. 3. Bombing, Aerial--History--20th century--Japan. 4. B-29 bomber. 5.
World War, 1939-1945--Aerial operations, American. 6. United States. Army Air
Forces. Air Force, 20th--History--20th century. 7. Air power--United States. I. Title.
UG626.2.A76W65 2010
940.54'4973092--dc22
2009053828

Dedicated with Much Love
to

My wife Sandy

Elliot, Vera and Henrietta
who lived through it all

Our children, Jill and Traci

And our grandchildren, Julie, Michael, Kelsea and Dalton

Contents

vii

List of Illustrations after Page 162

Acknowledgments

First and foremost, I am indebted to all the historians who have researched and written on the Pacific war. Their scholarship has thrown critical light on the end of the war in the Pacific and eased the path of this author.

Similarly, this book could not have been written without the help of the many dedicated archivists at the Manuscript Division of the Library of Congress. Their diligence and timeliness were greatly appreciated. Many archivists at National Archives II, College Park, Maryland, were indispensable to the author's sustained search through the enormous record collections. Timothy Nenninger helped with insightful comments pertaining to the records of the Headquarters, Twentieth Air Force. The author would like to thank John Taylor, a legend in his own time, for an all-too-brief chat which jump-started an especially flagging day of research.

Robert Clark, supervisory archivist at the Franklin D. Roosevelt Presidential Library at Hyde Park, New York, gave the author his unique expertise on President Roosevelt's records pertaining to air matters during World War II. Robert was unsparing in lending his time to this project. Archivists Virginia Lewick and Alycia Vivona eased the path through the Roosevelt collections for the author and his wife, Sandy, without whose research ability this project could not have been completed.

Ronald Chrisman, director of the University of North Texas Press, guided the author through the many demanding stages of publication. During crucial points in the long writing process, Ron's steadiness and enthusiasm carried the day. I owe a great debt to Karen J. DeVinney, managing editor of the UNT Press, for editing this book with discernment, knowledge, and rare ability to find the perfect word for any difficult situation. Many thanks to designer Steve Tiano for his imaginative work that set this book solidly in time and place. I am also deeply grateful for the support of Philip Meilinger and Dik Alan Daso in the early stages of conceptualizing this book.

Chancellor\President Emeritus of the University of North Texas, Alfred F. Hurley, friend and colleague, and one of the nation's great advocates of military history, provided important support to the author at critical junctures. Professor Eric Bergerud, with his keen knowledge of the war in the Pacific, gave especially insightful comments and observations on the manuscript.

Yvonne Kinkaid, director of the Library at the Office of Air Force History, Bolling Air Force Base, Washington, D.C., was indispensable with her knowledge of Air Force collections. On numerous occasions, she also answered questions and offered suggestions. At critical moments, she also came through as lending librarian. Also at the Bolling library, Terri Kiss was unfailing in answering inquiries.

George Watson and Roger Miller, historians of the Office of Air Force History, answered questions and helped with all manner of things. George saved the day many times with his deliveries of much-needed books. This work could not have been completed without Mary Lee Jefferson, senior editor in the Office of Air Force History, whose selective eye contributed photos for the centerpiece gallery. I want to express my great appreciation to my daughter Jill Kephart, who stepped in at a critical juncture to apply her technological knowledge to the photo gallery.

Jack Neufeld, superb editor of *Air Power History*, helped point to research materials and edited an article on General Arnold adapted from this book. Moreover, Jack proved to be an unflagging friend, who as a fellow retiree from the Air Force Historical Studies Office, always found time to be a morale-booster in so many ways.

I am indebted to Maj. Gen. John W. Huston, former Chief of the Office of Air Force History, for his many insightful observations during our telephone conversations about General Arnold's command of the Army Air Forces in World War II. Warren Kozak, author of *LeMay: The Life and Wars of General Curtis LeMay*, has been for several years a trove of information on LeMay and a true friend and supporter. Heartfelt thanks to Kreg Kephart and Dave Sheffer for being there.

My wife Sandy was a full partner in this book: researcher, trip arranger, and the editor who took the long legal pages and made them into manuscript. For this, and a thousand other courtesies and kindnesses, I give my love and admiration.

The attack on Japan by the B-29 from distant bases introduces a new type of offensive against the enemy. It also creates a new problem in the application of military forces.

—General George C. Marshall
U.S. Army Chief of Staff,
June 16, 1944

The surrender of Japan comes after the severest and most concentrated bombing campaign in history and without actual invasion of the homeland. Thus it is the first time a nation has capitulated with its major armies designed for defense of the homeland still intact.

—General H. H. Arnold
August 14, 1945

The most impressive lesson learned in this operation was the cataclysmic result of losing a modern war. Nothing could be more impressive than the utter destruction of the resources of this country, carrying with it the loss of all will to resist and ability to defend themselves.

—Rear Admiral M. L. Deyo
Commander, U.S. Navy
Task Force 55,
In REPORT, ON THE SURRENDER AND OCCUPATION
OF JAPAN,
February 1946

Introduction

There have been books on the B-29 and works on Gen. Henry H. (Hap) Arnold, but not an analytical work that binds these two together and gets into the mind of Hap Arnold. This is what this book is all about. In the massive literature on the end of World War II in the Pacific, much attention has been given to the dropping of the atomic bombs on Hiroshima and Nagasaki. The fact, however, is that prior to August 1945 Japan had been defeated militarily, but was politically unwilling to surrender. A significant share of the credit for the hopeless situation of the Empire of Japan in the summer of 1945 must go to General Arnold, Commanding General, Army Air Forces (AAF) and Commander of the Twentieth Air Force, the global B-29 force in the Pacific. Arnold was an American original. Impetuous, never adverse to risk taking, he set goals that associates thought outlandish. Impatient, he drove himself, without regard to his health, plunging ahead like the proverbial bull in the china shop. Although he would certainly plead guilty to not being especially articulate, he frequently outwitted his adversaries on the strategic level and was a master at playing his cards close to his vest. Arnold was not a master strategist; in the application of bombardment, he believed in getting out large numbers of sorties with heavier bombloads. He was however, a master builder who knew how to work with aircraft manufacturers and how to organize and control air forces. Thus, he became a builder and promoter of air power.

Arnold was a survivor of the interwar years; there was no inevitability about his succeeding to the AAF top command. Little known today, as early as the 1920s he was almost canned by Maj. Gen. Mason Patrick, head of the Air Service, over a messy contretemps that shed a bad light on Patrick. And prior to the U.S. entry into World War II, Arnold was close to being fired by President Franklin D. Roosevelt over the issue of the distribution of bomber production. Not only did Arnold persevere and survive in the interwar period, and in the air power buildup, 1938—1941, but it was his drive and determination that brought the B-29 into production and subsequently led to the strategic bombing campaign against Japan.

Criticized as parochial, a self-promoter, and a man of light intellect, he was, in fact, the indispensable leader who built the Army Air Forces and made possible the B-29 campaign that played a decisive role in ending the war in the Pacific. This book traces Arnold's thought from the prewar buildup through the war—culminating in the summer of 1945—and into his important postwar opinions wherein he takes a critical look at the wartime experience and offers his vision of the future of air power. Previous works have failed to clearly trace Arnold's thought on prewar doctrine; his specific part in bitter interservice debates; his relationships with President Roosevelt and Gen. Douglas MacArthur; the development of joint and combined operations; and Arnold's role in the abortive requirement for unified command in the Pacific. Also insufficiently illuminated is his constant hectoring of operational commanders in the field. Nor have the reasons for Arnold's determination to command the global Twentieth Air Force been clearly analyzed. For example, not traced previously, this question involved complex and sensitive theater issues between the U.S. Joint Chiefs of Staff, the British Chiefs of Staff, and Lord Mountbatten, Supreme Allied Commander, Southeast Asia. And contrary to the opinions of some historians, strategic bombing commanders in the Pacific received plenty of direction from Washington. They were under enormous pressure.

Unlike most books on the Pacific war, this work uses interrogations, not only of officials and the military, but of the *Taro Keda*, the so-called average citizens, to bring out that the B-29 attacks on Japanese cities were the primary factor stoking defeatism and plunging morale, resulting in enormous numbers of evacuees. Most works on prewar air doctrine stress the high-altitude precision bombing doctrine. In this regard, one of the major themes of this work is that attack on the enemy's morale—the civilian and workforce population—can also be traced back to the evolution of doctrine at the Air Corps Tactical School. It was always present in prewar and wartime air plans along with the doctrine of striking the enemy's industrial fabric. World War II was not fought by the western democracies with morality primarily in mind. President Roosevelt was all for strategic bombing, pressuring Arnold to deploy the B-29 against Japan and constantly urging him to bomb Tokyo and other Japanese cities. I emphasize that Arnold's insistence on incendiary raids caused a massive shift in the Japanese population and had a huge effect on the war production industries in urban areas. The realization in the general population that the massive air attacks could not be stopped proved fatal. When the attacks extended to even smaller towns the people became convinced that the entire country could be destroyed. The flight from the great cities was uncontrollable. In the greater Tokyo area alone, the population dropped over sixty percent during the spring and summer of 1945, all of this prior to the dropping of atomic bombs. I also believe that the evidence shows that the Japanese people were in fact relieved that the war was finally over. Japan gambled that after a year or two of limited conflict the U.S. would come to a negotiated settlement, as the United States would not have the staying power to force an unconditional surrender. This gamble utterly failed, the Japanese homeland ultimately coming under horrific air attack, culminating with the dropping of atomic bombs.

Generally unknown are Arnold's somewhat startling views on the post-World War II world. Given the many critics who considered him an intellectual lightweight, he surpassed most wartime military leaders with his vision of the future in the atomic era. Here was the leader who built and led the mightiest air force the world had seen, now stating after the war that air power could well become obsolete in the atomic age. High intellectual power and concomitant scientific thought with vision were required in the postwar world. Atomic weapons had made war unthinkable. It would be incumbent upon the fledgling United Nations organization, Arnold emphasized, to get nations to work together to prevent war.

Consequently, unlike many books on World War II in the Pacific, this is not an operational history that focuses on island campaigns or individual bombing missions. My emphasis is on Arnold, policy, strategy, and issues of command. As historian Ray S. Cline observed: "Some of the greatest generals in World War II, far from striking the classic posture of the man on horseback, issued their military orders from the quiet of their desks and fought their decisive battles at conference tables."[1] This was certainly true of Arnold. Thus, I have focused this study on what one might call "grand strategy," that is strategy at the highest level of decision-making. The approach here is primarily topical. No published work examines Arnold's thinking in-depth during 1944–1945, specifically in the context of planning for the defeat of Japan at the joint and combined levels, emphasizing connections among doctrine, organization, and command. I have attempted as much as possible to get inside Arnold's mind in the summer of 1945 although the narrative also necessitates some brief consideration of the earlier war years and even the pre-World War II period. The historian's task is made all the more difficult by the fact that Arnold, in his memoir and diaries, was so circumspect and obsessed with security on critical issues that both works are lacking in substance, even though the diaries have been meticulously edited, with insightful commentary, by Maj. Gen. John W. Huston.[2]

It is commonplace to point out that much controversy surrounds the end of World War II in the Pacific. The sweep of global operations in World War II was so immense, the strategic decisions so intense and critical, that debate and interpretations will always engage future generations of historians and observers. This is certainly true of the employment of strategic air power which, as Gen. George C. Marshall emphasized, evolved into a new and important element in the application of military force. In this work, I answer these questions: Was it necessary to drop the atomic bombs on Japan? After the atomic attack on Hiroshima, was it necessary to drop the atomic bomb on Nagasaki? What was President Truman's rationale? Did he pre-emptively attempt to deliver a message to the Soviet Union as some revisionist historians have charged? Should the United States have warned Japan specifically about the bomb before using it or actually conducted a demonstration of the new weapon before employing it? In the spring of 1945, was it absolutely necessary to ditch high-altitude precision bombing against the Japanese home islands in favor of area incendiary attacks? Was Hap Arnold the reluctant warrior when he established the Twentieth Air Force? Why was unified command never established in the Pacific? At the highest levels of the Army Air Forces' leadership, did serious concern exist over civilian casualties in the bombing of cities? Put starkly and simply, Arnold aimed to show that the B-29 strategic bombing offensive could knock Japan out of the war prior to the planned invasion of the Japanese homeland on November 1, 1945.

Thinking back over decades, it seems to me that perhaps initially I got the idea for this book in 1974 when I interviewed at length Lt. Gen. Ira Eaker, former commander of the Eighth Air Force, and a long-time associate of Arnold's, who knew him especially well, and who in the summer of 1945 was Deputy Commander of the U.S. Army Air Forces (AAF) under General Arnold. Eaker explained to me that no one in the top leadership of the AAF at that time thought that an invasion would be required to force Japan to capitulate.[3] However, in the spring and summer of 1945, Gen. George C. Marshall, Army Chief of Staff—President Truman's most trusted military adviser—held the view that blockade and air bombardment would not be sufficient to drive Japan out of the war. Air power had not been decisive in Europe, Marshall emphasized, and like Europe, in the Pacific an invasion of the enemy's homeland would be required as the fastest way to finish off Japan. This, despite the probability in July and August 1945, that the U.S. Joint Chiefs of

Staff and President Truman considered cancelling the invasion of Kyushu (OLYMPIC) due to the enormous buildup of Japanese forces on southern Kyushu. In early August, the Joint War Plans Committee recommended that alternatives to the Kyushu invasion be considered.

I bring out Arnold's relationship with Marshall, an important, sensitive combination during the entire war. Marshall's view that an invasion was the quickest way to end the war, expressed to President Harry Truman, presented a dilemma to Arnold, who was convinced that the air and sea blockade and the conventional B-29 bombing campaign could force Japan to surrender. It was Arnold pre-eminently among the Joint Chiefs who envisioned the air and sea blockades, *powerfully buttressed by the B-29 incendiary attacks,* as sufficient to bring the Japanese down prior to the invasion. In Admirals King and Leahy, however, Arnold had additional voices advancing the thesis that an invasion was not necessary. Even after the atomic bombing of Hiroshima, Marshall, as well as MacArthur, suggested other invasion locations in place of Kyushu, where the Japanese had conducted a huge force buildup. Arnold's long suit was, and always remained, perseverance. At times fighting long odds, and even defeated at the strategic table, he refused to waver in his convictions on doctrine, production, organization, and strategy. And if nothing else he was—as Marshall put it—"loyal," even though he and Marshall disagreed on the question of the necessity of an invasion. Arnold never brought the subject up directly in front of Roosevelt, Truman, or the Army Chief of Staff. Nor did Arnold direct his proxy, Lt. Gen. Ira C. Eaker, to initiate on his own such a discussion at the highest level at any time. This was made clear to Eaker by Arnold after Eaker's return to Washington from Europe in May 1945. At the highest policy level, Arnold did not want to oppose Marshall, to whom the AAF owed a great deal. Marshall, even prior to the war, had provided Arnold with the support and resources to build up the air forces. A sidelight to the Arnold-Marshall combination, Arnold's relationship with MacArthur was sensitive and fascinating, Arnold having to tread lightly in dealing with the Southwest Pacific theater commander.

In his introduction to R. Cargill Hall's (editor) *Case Studies in Strategic Bombardment,* the distinguished historian of air power, David MacIsaac, points to General Arnold's "ubiquitous" and important role "played from afar" in the B-29 campaign against Japan.[4] Arnold indeed, played the key role. Even prior to deployment of B-29s to the Pacific, he had driven—almost willed—the Superfortress into production. He fashioned the unprecedented command arrangement of the Twentieth Air Force reporting directly to himself, in Washington, as executive agent of the Joint Chiefs of Staff. Impatient and a driver, he selected—and relieved—operational field commanders. He intruded into targeting decisions and hectored commanders over sorties and bomb tonnage. He insisted that they provide him with hard evidence of accomplishments. Arnold went so far as to cable his B-29 commander that he was watching him on a daily basis, as indeed he was. Under great pressure from Roosevelt and Marshall, he was driven. He had rammed the B-29 Superfortress through the enormously difficult development and production cycles at great cost. Gen. Hap Arnold was the architect of the strategic bombing offensive against Japan that in the summer of 1945 brought the Pacific war to a close. The Japanese were forced to capitulate with a large army intact and without the necessity of an invasion of their homeland, a circumstance unprecedented in the history of war. According to the U.S. Strategic Bombing Survey: "The capability of very heavy bombardment was never fully recognized and was not given adequate weight in the plans established for conduct of the war against Japan. The Very Heavy Bombardment campaign against Japan was conceived in effect as a means to an end, namely invasion, rather than a decisive force within itself. ... "[5]

A strong supporter of a postwar United Nations force—including U.S. air contingents—Arnold came to believe that war had become so destructive that it could no longer serve as an option to resolve international issues. Arnold called for high intellectual leadership in postwar America to come to grips with the enormous issues attendant to the atomic age. Basically optimistic about the future, he nonetheless worried about the U.S. once again lapsing into technological unpreparedness in the postwar era. He realized that the triumph in World War II was at times a close affair that, as a result, now in peacetime called for a strategic vision far into the future.

The year 2010 marks the sixty-fifth anniversary of the end of World War II in the Pacific. The marking of this event presents an opportunity for scholars, students, and observers not only to assess General Arnold's role, but to once again reflect upon the enormously important and daunting issues that characterized the conflict and its sudden denouement with the dropping of atomic bombs on Hiroshima and Nagasaki.

Chronology

September 29, 1938

Appointed by President Franklin D. Roosevelt, Maj. Gen. Henry H. (Hap) Arnold becomes Chief of the Army Air Corps.

November 14, 1938

President Roosevelt calls for a massive air power buildup.

November 10, 1939

Maj. Gen. Arnold, Chief of the Army Air Corps, initiates B-29 development program.

December 7, 1941

Japanese aircraft attack the U.S. Pacific fleet and facilities at Pearl Harbor, Hawaii, bringing the United States into World War II.

April 18, 1942

Lt. Col. James H. Doolittle leads raid of B-25 bombers against Tokyo, Japan, from the aircraft carrier *Hornet.*

June 3–6, 1942

In the battle of Midway Island, U.S. Navy aircraft put four Japanese aircraft carriers out of action.

January 14–23, 1943

At Casablanca conference, President Roosevelt vows to pursue the "unconditional surrender" of Japan.

January 23, 1943

The final report of the Casablanca conference by the U.S. and British Combined Chiefs of Staff states the importance of land-based air attacks against Japan from China.

August 1943

Gen. Arnold introduces "Air Plan for the Defeat of Japan" at the Quadrant conference.

November 11, 1943

Gen. Arnold's Committee of Operations Analysts (COA) emphasizes Japan's vulnerability to incendiary bombing.

April 4, 1944

The Twentieth Air Force is activated, commanded by General Arnold, reporting as executive agent directly to the Joint Chiefs of Staff.

June 1944

Start of B-29 Operation Matterhorn from Chengtu valley of western China.

October 1944

Brig. Gen. Haywood S. Hansell, Jr. initiates XXI Bomber Command operations against Japan from the Marianas.

January 20, 1945

Maj. Gen. Curtis E. LeMay replaces Hansell as commander of XXI Bomber Command.

March 9–10, 1945

    B-29 low-level incendiary attack on Tokyo, the most destructive bombing raid of the war.

April 12, 1945

    Death of President Franklin D. Roosevelt; Harry S. Truman becomes president.

April 25, 1945

    Secretary of War Henry L. Stimson informs President Truman of Manhattan Project on the atomic bomb.

May 8, 1945

    Germany surrenders.

May 25, 1945

    Joint Chiefs of Staff direct invasion of southern Kyushu (OLYMPIC), November 1, 1945.

June 1945

    On Guam, LeMay informs Arnold that Japan cannot hold on past October 1945.

June 18, 1945

    At key White House meeting with Joint Chiefs of Staff, President Truman approves planning for invasion of Kyushu (OLYMPIC), target date November 1, 1945.

July 16, 1945

    Successful atomic bomb test in New Mexico desert (Trinity).

July 25, 1945

    Gen. Thomas T. Handy issues order to employ atomic bombs "as soon as weather would permit visual bombing after about 3 August."

July 26, 1945

    The Potsdam Declaration, signed by the United States, the United Kingdom, and China, calls on Japan "to proclaim now the unconditional surrender of all Japanese armed forces."

August 6, 1945

Atomic bomb dropped on Hiroshima.

August 8, 1945

The Soviet Union declares war on Japan.

August 9, 1945

Atomic bomb dropped on Nagasaki; Emperor Hirohito informs cabinet and Supreme Council that Potsdam Declaration should be accepted provided the imperial institution be retained.

August 10, 1945

Japanese communicate offer to surrender if the emperor is retained.

August 12, 1945

Response by United States to Japanese offer is unclear.

August 14, 1945

Japanese cabinet and Supreme Council accept Emperor Hirohito's request to agree to U.S. surrender terms.

August 15, 1945

Emperor Hirohito broadcasts message to Japanese people that the war has ended.

September 2, 1945

The surrender documents ending the Pacific war are signed aboard the battleship USS *Missouri* in Tokyo Bay.

1

Roosevelt and Arnold

The roots of the strategic bombing offensive of the Twentieth Air Force against Japan can be traced to the prewar doctrinal struggles at the Air Corps Tactical School and debate within the War Department itself. Despite the twists and turns in the evolution of doctrine, a clear strain can be illuminated between prewar evolution and wartime development and prosecution.

Arnold did not attend the Tactical School, but in the 1930s the struggle by the school's faculty to define air doctrine held great import for the air forces that Arnold would lead in World War II. Instructors at the ACTS—including Muir Fairchild, a future Air Force vice chief of staff—evolved the precision bombing doctrine, aimed to destroy the enemy's war-making industrial base. What has been overlooked however, and will be pointed out in this chapter, is the emphasis the Tactical School also placed on morale or population bombing. It was the targeting of civilians and the workforce in 1945 by the Twentieth Air Force that played a major role in forcing the Japanese surrender. Thus, there is a clear connection between the prewar evolution of doctrine and the morale attacks by the B-29 campaign, culminating in the dropping of atomic bombs on Hiroshima and Nagasaki. Viewed doctrinally, the atomic bombings were not an over-turning of the precision bombing doctrine, but rather the reflection of a constant thread in the development of air doctrine going back to the Tactical School. The B-29 force in the Pacific at the start—under Hansell—inherited the precision doctrine that was subsequently over-turned by LeMay's population bombing, under pressure from Arnold and his staff in Washington.

Doctrine however, did not evolve in isolation, but was integral to building an air force. Here President Roosevelt and General Arnold needed to find an accommodation over how and in what numbers to conduct an air power buildup. Although anxious to gear up and produce big numbers of aircraft, especially bombers, the president had a major interest in distribution of production aircraft. He determined that the British required a high priority in the fight against Nazi Germany while Arnold made the case for structuring an American air force.

No delivery weapon has generated more awe and terror than the strategic bombing plane. Yet, in the history of warfare the strategic bomber has enjoyed a relatively short period of dominance. Employed by Germany in World War I, it is most commonly associated with the American and British bombing offensives of World War II. However, tracking down the history of the strategic bombardment idea and the evolution of doctrine are difficult and chancy tasks at best. "Strategic" refers to long-range air attacks conducted independently of ground and naval forces, i.e., against industry, sources of the enemy's military power, and against his population. By "tactical" is meant strikes against ground or naval forces and their supporting elements. Absolute precision recreating the doctrinal tensions of the times almost always proves to be problematical at best. Strategical concepts evolve from the circumstances of a period and are usually developed independently, if not simultaneously, by theorists and military officers.

During World War I, on November 28, 1917, Lt. Col. Edgar S. Gorrell, chief of the Strategical Aviation Branch of the Air Service in France, described the first American plan for a strategic bombing campaign, a recommendation to bomb the German industrial centers of Dusseldorf, Cologne, Mannheim, and the Saar Valley. "The object of strategical bombing," he observed, "is to drop aerial bombs upon the commercial centers and lines of communication in such quantities as will wreck the points aimed at and cut off the necessary supplies without which the armies in the field cannot exist."[1] Significantly, during World War I, Lt. Gen. Jan C. Smuts recommended to the British War Cabinet formation of what subsequently became the Royal Air Force and he also proved visionary about air operations by observing that "there is absolutely no limit to the scale of its future independent war use. And the day may not be far off when aerial operations with their devastation of enemy lands and destruction of industrial and populous areas on a vast scale may become the principal operations of war, to which the older forms of military and naval operations may become secondary and subordinate."[2]

After World War I, the development of air doctrine proceeded in concert with advancing aircraft technology and the breakdown of diplomacy in Europe. Significantly also, the American public's opposition to bombing became more intense. World War I, marked by trench stalemate and bombing of civilians in London, had made a lasting impression and the nation's mood grew increasingly isolationist. In 1926, the Air Corps Tactical School (ACTS) published *Employment of Combined Air Force*—subsequently revised under the title, *Air Force*—which for the first time articulated the idea that the basic air objective was the enemy's "vital centers," population, and air force. *Air Force* borrowed from Italian General Giulio Douhet, whose seminal work, *Command of the Air* (1921 edition), was translated into English. Douhet emphasized that an attack on morale should be made at the outset of hostilities.

It is, however, not possible precisely to trace the intellectual twists and turns that mark the evolution of the strategic bombardment idea. Nonetheless, one can attempt to discover the major developmental lines. Not all of Douhet's concepts were original. In World War I, Germany led the way in strategic bombing and before it ended the British and Americans developed strategic formulations. But Douhet became the first to put these concepts into coherent form. Although he was especially interested in alleviating Italy's military problems, he structured a total war scenario universal in its application. *Command of the Air* reveals Douhet's total disenchantment with the Allied war strategy. He abhorred the casualties attended by no clearly articulated political objectives, save to press on to victory. His harsh indictment of wartime superiors resulted in his serving a year in prison; in 1920, a military court reversed this verdict.[3]

Aerial duels appalled him. Airplanes were offensive machines; no effective defense against them existed. Effective military action depended on mastery of the air and the major objectives should be industry and population, not military forces. Equally important, air units should strike first and in mass without waiting to declare war formally. It was not necessary to engage and defeat the enemy's air force. The same objective could be accomplished by striking factories and air bases. To Douhet, the airplane was unique. It could reach the enemy's vitals without being stopped. Attacking the enemy heartland required an independent air force functioning completely independent of the army and navy. It would command the air and exploit it "to crush the material and moral resistance of the enemy." Thus, surface forces were relegated to a defensive role and they would hold the line while the air offensive destroyed the enemy's ability to continue.[4]

For the air strike force he foresaw a "battle plane" that could bomb but also defend itself. Bombers might be lost, but they would not be turned back. Because the airplane was radically different from other weapons, wars would be total in scope. Douhet's conception of air warfare and the organization of air forces provided a model on which later ideas could be grafted. His emphasis upon an independent air arm and the aerial offensive and his downgrading of the pursuit plane were welcomed in other air services including the American. Despite the fact that time revealed Douhet to have badly underestimated the ability of civilians to stand up under bombing and to have greatly misjudged the tactical utility of aircraft (he had plenty of company), his early framework remains impressive given the status of technology at the time.

Distinguished British and American air officers, Sir John Slessor and Generals Laurence Kuter and Curtis E. LeMay among them, have disparaged Douhet's influence, but not his ideas. This difference is worth noting. Their adherence to "principles" strongly suggests Douhet; it must be noted that air advocates have never been quick to credit their intellectual predecessors. Because Douhet may not have been widely read by air officers does not mean that his views failed to influence them. And although he may not have had a great deal to do with the way air forces developed or were equipped, his ideas were relevant to air strategy, to the way in which air forces were later used. Aside from the question of influence, the fact remains that on the basis of the warfare he prophesied, his reputation as the foremost of early air theorists remains unchallenged.

After World War I, the development of air doctrine proceeded in concert with advancing aircraft technology and the breakdown of diplomacy in Europe. Brig. Gen. William (Billy) Mitchell considered the "bombardment airplane" as the foundation of air power. In his book, *Skyways* (1930), he emphasized that combat was the attempt to control "vital centers," the cities "where the people live, areas where their food and supplies are produced and the transport lines that carry these supplies from place to place."[5]

> The advent of air power which can go straight to the vital centers and entirely neutralize or destroy them has put a completely new complexion on the old system of war. It is now realized that the hostile main army in the field is a false objective and the real objectives are the vital centers. The old theory that victory meant the destruction of the hostile main army, is untenable. Armies themselves can be disregarded by air power if a rapid strike is made against the opposing centers, because a greatly superior army numerically is at the mercy of an air force inferior in number.[6]

Thus, between the wars, the advanced ideas of Mitchell and his followers set up a long-running clash with the War Department over the role of the Army's air arm.[7] The War Department General Staff insisted that the function of the air arm was to support the ground army: the so-called close support mission. The airmen advocated the independent air mission, following Mitchell's primary concept of striking the "vital centers."

They also put forward the idea that airmen knew best how to organize and employ air forces.[8]

Mitchell's thinking evolved through several phases. He came out of the war an advocate of the tactical use of aviation. Bombing was a means of keeping the enemy's reinforcements from the battlefield. He was neither a champion of strategic bombing nor of aviation support for the Army and Navy. Pre-eminently, he thought military aviation indispensable to the nation's security, its first line of defense. Later, Mitchell argued for a strategic concept of air power, for striking the enemy's air force on the ground. Also, industry would be the target, especially aircraft production. However, Mitchell's tour of the Far East in 1923–1924 convinced him that Japanese cities were "highly inflammable." In 1923, the great Tokyo fire had killed over 100,000 people. Mitchell informed the Navy's General Board that Japan was more vulnerable to air attack than any country in the world. He still believed in pursuit aviation and in the utility of the long-range escort. Mitchell later supported formation of a Department of Aeronautics and a Department of National Defense to supervise the three services. He was supported by Maj. Gen. Mason Patrick, Chief of the Air Service, and Major Carl Spaatz, but the War Department General Staff and Navy Department noted indisputably that aviation had never decided a war. On the other hand, they recognized the airplane's capacity for reconnaissance and ground support.

Emblematic of the temper of the times, the Morrow Board report of November 30, 1925, came out squarely against formation of a Department of Aeronautics, observing that air power had not yet proved its value for independent operations. Such missions could "be better carried out under the high command of the Army or Navy. ... " The United States had no reason to fear an enemy air attack:

> No airplane capable of making a transoceanic flight to our country with a useful military load and of returning to safety is now in existence. ... With the advance in the art it is to be expected that there will be substantial advance in the range and capacity of bombing airplanes; but, having in view present practical limitations, it does

not appear that there is any ground for anticipation of such development to a point which would constitute a direct menace to the United
States in any future which scientific thought can now foresee. ... The
fear of such an attack is without reason.[9]

Mitchell's vituperative attacks resulted in his court martial in October 1925. Mitchell was particularly adept at recognizing promising ideas
to develop and publicize. He was ahead of his time, one of America's
most brilliant technologists, impatient because others could not share
his enthusiasm and confidence in machines that had yet to demonstrate
their capacity. Mitchell's influence on Arnold was beyond question.
Arnold's confidence in technology, his belief in publicity, and his faith in
unified air power could all be traced to Mitchell. But Mitchell's vindica-
tion awaited the development and production of planes not yet on the
drawing board. With the energy of a crusader, he had been driven by
issues that, when aired publicly, could only arouse discord. Not willing
to compromise, he became isolated. After Franklin Roosevelt became
president, he hoped to influence a change in air policy, but he couldn't
turn the tide alone and soon became disenchanted. He died in February
1936, a proud zealot to the end.

In the mid-1930s, advent of the GHQ Air Force gave the Army airmen
a striking force as concern over hemispheric defense accelerated. This
reflected the danger that a foreign nation might gain air bases in Latin
America from which to attack the United States. The leadership of the Air
Corps reasoned that long-range reconnaissance bombers were required
to be capable of offensive action. Concomitant with establishment of the
GHQ Air Force on March 1, 1935, the B-17 bomber arrived on the scene
and in the mid-1930s events in Europe began to energize the Roosevelt
administration toward the path of rearmament. Specifically, in 1937, the
creation of the Axis alliance of Germany, Italy, and Japan began to tilt
American rearmament toward aircraft and offensive concepts.

In the meantime, the Air Corps Tactical School evolved theories of
air doctrine based on advancing technology and offensive air concepts
and tactics, which by the late 1930s would form at least a theoretical

foundation for the Air Corps going into World War II. The primary objective in war, the school's theorists emphasized, was to break the enemy's will to resist, forcing him to capitulate. Air forces would not attack armies, but nations themselves. This kind of advanced concept depended on using aircraft offensively. The ability to attack the enemy's vital points depended upon accurate intelligence to pinpoint the enemy's critical industrial, economic, and social centers. This was the genesis of the high-altitude "precision" daylight bombardment air doctrine. Theoretically, it also stressed the counter-air force mission, attacking the enemy's air forces. All of this, as indicated, was dependent upon timely, accurate intelligence.

Maj. Gen. Frank M. Andrews, commanding GHQ Air Force and supporting the evolving air doctrine, noted on October 1, 1938, that the nation's defense of its borders could best be accomplished by attacking the enemy. "I do not minimize the importance and value of reconnaissance, pursuit, and attack aviation," Andrews stressed, "but bombardment aviation is and always will be the principal striking force in air operations. Air power is measured in terms of bombardment aviation."[10] Even Maj. Gen. Oscar Westover, Chief of the Air Corps, who had his differences with Andrews over whether to push for greater air arm independence from the War Department, supported production of long-range bombers. Westover emphasized to the Secretary of War that the Army required bombers to defend the United States as well as to reinforce Hawaii, Panama, and Alaska.

Interestingly, the Tactical School theorists who evolved the doctrine of the Air Corps—Robert Olds, Kenneth Walker, Donald Wilson, Robert M. Webster, Haywood S. Hansell, Muir Fairchild, and Harold L. George, *et al.*—ignored the limitations of aircraft range and location of bases in propounding their concepts. And as far as enemy targets were concerned, they reasoned that other nations were like the United States, so they analyzed critical points in U.S. industry, as an overlay on foreign countries. Among critical targets, they identified electrical power, transportation, oil refineries, steel manufacturing, and food distribution. As to the need for bases, the theorists counted on allies providing the appropriate operating locales which would support a sustained attack against the enemy's industrial fabric.[11]

As noted, the prime objective was the "enemy's will." The question of how this comported with the goal of smashing the industrial web has remained an intriguing and sensitive topic, especially when considering strategic bombing in World War II, both in Europe and over Japan. There is no doubt that the bombardment theorists, looking ultimately for bombers capable of long-range and heavy loads, had evolved the idea to attack war-making industry and, if necessary, "morale." Development of the daylight, precision bombing concept naturally flowed after Mitchell's demonstration against obsolete warships in the Virginia capes. Also, aircraft were not yet able effectively to bomb at night. Air historians have frequently observed that the precision concept owed much to the American tradition of marksmanship. This may well have been a factor, but a far more persuasive case needs to be made for the general climate of opinion in the 1920s and 1930s, which was strongly opposed to bombing cities. At the time, Arnold, an especially sharp judge of prevailing opinion, was clearly impressed with this public feeling.

Born in Gladwyne, Pennsylvania, on June 25, 1886, Arnold's upbringing as a young lad is relevant to a number of traits that in later years marked his military career. His father, an authoritarian physician, ruled with an iron hand. Hap Arnold subsequently developed a stubborn streak, tenacity, and impatience with those who failed to measure up to his expectations. He frequently failed to control his temper and drove himself without regard to his health. He developed real affection for his mother and Arnold's broad outlook can reasonably be traced to her influence.[12]

He graduated from the U.S. Military Academy at West Point in 1907, sixtieth out of one hundred ten in academics, resulting initially in an assignment to the infantry. Arnold, however, was attracted to flying and in 1911 took pilot training with the Wright brothers in Dayton, Ohio. Subsequently, he received pilot license number 29 and became one of two active pilots in the U.S. Army. Flying was a dangerous occupation. Of the first twenty-eight pilots, ten were killed in accidents, fourteen quit flying, and four died of natural causes while serving in the Army.

Arnold became an authentic air pioneer. In 1911 and 1912 he set world altitude records. On October 9, 1912, he earned the first Mackay Trophy for outstanding aeronautical achievement by flying a triangular course from

College Park, Maryland, to Washington Barracks, D.C., to Fort Myer, Virginia, and then back to College Park. However, after a traumatic close call on November 5, 1912, in which he lost control of his plane and almost dived into the ground, he developed a case of fear of flying. He could not look at a plane in the air without thinking that it would crash.

Between 1913–1918, he served in various posts in the Philippines, Washington, D.C., and California. On August 5, 1917, he became the youngest colonel in the Army at age thirty-one. Arnold never saw combat service in World War I—or, of course, World War II when he commanded the Army Air Forces—and this left him with a feeling of incompleteness. He served in a number of important positions in the 1920s and early 1930s including as commander of the air depot and logistics complex at Fairfield, Ohio. In 1928–1929, Arnold attended the Army Staff College at Fort Leavenworth where he subsequently taught classes on air power and thus influenced the Army's ground students in the classes. He also commanded March Field, California, converting it from a training facility to an operational base. Arnold commanded the 1st Wing, the west coast's operational combat unit at Riverside, California. As it turned out, his varied experience at March Field in the early 1930s provided him with an important foundation for wartime leadership of the Army Air Forces. It was here in California that he also made important contacts with Donald Douglas, the aircraft manufacturer, and scientist Robert A. Millikan of the California Institute of Technology.

The operations that Arnold's wing carried out gave him a great appreciation of the importance of logistics in fielding an operational force. In the winter of 1932–1933, the First Wing dropped food to Indian settlements. And in 1933 Arnold helped to organize relief for victims of the Long Beach earthquake. As officer-in-charge of the California branch of the Civilian Conservation Corps, he benefitted from his relationship with Harry L. Hopkins, director of the Civil Works Administration and advisor to President Roosevelt. This connection subsequently proved crucial to influencing FDR on the importance of air power.

Perhaps most important of Arnold's work at March Field was the division of labor that he established between himself and Carl (Tooey)

Spaatz. As commander of the Wing, Arnold was responsible for personnel, buildings, and maintenance, and Spaatz, his executive officer, took charge of all flying operations. Thus, this organization would come to reflect the command relationship between Arnold and Spaatz during World War II.

When the Air Corps carried the mail in the difficult winter of early 1934, Arnold commanded the western air mail routes, and took fewer casualties than other regions in the country. One of the highlights of his career occurred in July–August 1934, when, after overcoming his fear of flying, he led a historic round-trip flight of ten B-10 bombers between Bolling Field, Washington, D.C. and Alaska. This event, which received a great deal of publicity, demonstrating the reach of long-range bombers—of great significance to Arnold—earned Arnold his second Mackay Trophy and also a Distinguished Flying Cross. Despite Arnold's entreaties, none of the additional crew received awards, resulting in years of bad feeling.

On February 11, 1935, Arnold took command of the newly created 1st Wing of GHQ Air Force, under Maj. Gen. Frank M. Andrews, Commanding General of GHQ Air Force. Continuing to climb the Army Air Corps career ladder, on December 24, 1936, Arnold became the Assistant Chief of the Air Corps under Maj. Gen. Oscar Westover. On September 21, 1938, Westover was killed in an air crash and Arnold succeeded him as Air Corps Chief upon the approval of President Roosevelt. As Chief of the Air Corps, Arnold's earlier flying and educational experience helped him in building the air forces. Although he did not attend the Air Corps Tactical School, his time as a student at the Army Industrial College gave him an understanding of how the Army worked with manufacturers. Arnold became an advocate of nurturing aircraft companies for potential mass production. Concomitantly, he was refining his understanding of the application of logistics to building operational air forces.[13]

As noted, the Tactical School instructors evolved theory that predated technology and clearly promulgated concepts that targeted the "hostile will." The faculty emphasized that "no barrier can be interposed to shield the civil populace against the airplane." The instructors described war as a consequence of conflicting national aims. The objective of conflict, emphasized Maj. Muir S. Fairchild, Tactical School instructor in the late 1930s, and a future four-star general, was "to force an unwilling enemy government to accept peace on terms which favor our polices. Since the actions of that hostile government are based on the will of the people, no victory can be complete until that will can be molded to our purpose."[14] In most cases, having little special training in history or geopolitics, the air instructors never described exactly how "the will of the people" could be bent to our purpose, whatever that might be. Nor did they think it necessary to explain how the policies of a hostile, totalitarian nation somehow reflected the aspirations of its people. Their logic was not always above reproach and often it seemed that their conclusions were insufficiently thought out and jarringly out of touch with the state of technology. Yet, despite these crucial omissions (or because of them?), one finds references to these ill-defined ideas in high-level air planning documents of World War II and postwar years. The key to all this was the "peculiar power" of the air arm, the ability to strike a crushing blow. Could the air forces win a war on their own? Whether or not they could, the point remained that "sound strategy" demanded at least that the effort be made. This called for using air power for a strategic end; it did not mean support missions, considered a misuse of air power.[15] This was pure Douhet with its emphasis on total war, smashing industry, and breaking a nation's will to fight.

Fairchild made clear that air power opened avenues for a new method of waging war. His lectures in 1939, congruent with President Roosevelt's calls for a massive buildup of air forces, described the ultimate goal of military operations as "to destroy the will of the people at home." Fairchild—who during World War II was a key member of the important Joint Strategic Survey Committee—differentiated between military and civilian morale: "None of the props which bolster the soldier's morale are present to the same degree to support the will of the civilian. And yet loss of that morale in the civilian population is far more conclusive than the defeat of the soldier."[16] Thus, the argument that the Tactical School evolved a precision bombing doctrine that failed to consider "morale" bombing—area strikes upon cities—is false. In retrospect, this can be seen as a harbinger of what happened over Japan in the spring and summer of 1945. "The aim in war," Fairchild stressed, "is to force an unwilling enemy government to accept peace on terms which favor our policies."[17] Fairchild's thinking in the late 1930s could in fact be projected to a press conference by Maj. Gen. Lauris Norstad in March 1945, in the wake of the landmark incendiary attack on Tokyo on March 9–10, 1945, which turned around the entire B-29 strategic campaign against Japan. Norstad pointed to the connection between attacking industry and morale and the importance of the population's morale in forcing the enemy to capitulate.[18]

General Spaatz brought up the matter of population bombing many times, usually in opposition to British proposals for all-out area attacks against Germany. General Arnold at the time thought the American public would not stand for city-bombing. As Ira Eaker recalled: "Arnold feared the reaction of the U.S. public to the urban area bombing of women and children."[19] But he and others continued to say that not only would the air offensive wreck Germany's industry, but it would also break down morale to the point where resistance would crumble.[20] At any rate, as to how the school's instructors could promulgate an air doctrine that featured the strategic offensive and yet depended on aircraft without sufficient range, they were counting on better airplanes and overseas bases being made available by potential allies.[21]

With Roosevelt's call on January 12, 1939, for a buildup, instructors at the Air Corps Tactical School also kept a close eye on events in Europe indicating that new forms of warfare were coming to the fore. Col. Donald Wilson of the faculty noted that "The military high command must learn from the fatal mistakes of defense-mindedness and ground-mindedness; the new kind of warfare called for flexible thinking and a high degree of air-mindedness."[22] Major Fairchild emphasized the objective of imposing policies on the enemy nation by shattering its will. Historically, ground armies defeated the enemy, but air power now provided a new method of conducting warfare, striking directly at the enemy's will, his social fabric. In this regard, the Tactical School instructors remained sensitive to the ability of air power to accomplish political objectives, in this case, the goals of Hitler's Nazi state. Again, the key was target selection, which depended upon timely intelligence. Unfortunately, during World War II timely intelligence on critical enemy target sets was frequently not available. This was especially the case with Japan. While the enemy's national structure was the ideal target, other objectives might be more appropriate in any given situation.[23]

In an important report of September 1939, the Air Board, chaired by General Arnold, emphasized the critical importance of air power, particularly in the early stages of conflict, and noted that the bomber aircraft was the foundation of air forces. Range was stressed as well as the need for bases, which should be located so that aircraft could blanket land and sea areas from which a decisive strike might be launched.[24] This called for employment of strategic air power, not close support missions, considered a misuse of air power. Again, as in Fairchild's lectures, this idea was straight out of Douhet. Thus, the air theorists declared: "We have here, not a useful new weapon to be used as an adjunct to the old, not a new projectile to be included in the family of supporting fire weapons; but an instrument which allows us to adopt a new method of waging war."[25]

The period between the wars was distinguished by a debate between the Army airmen and the War Department staff over how to organize and employ air forces. Did the airplane offer a way to minimize battlefield casualties, avoiding a bloodbath like World War I? Or did the ground forces still hold the key to victory? Haywood S. Hansell, Jr., who was associated with the Tactical School, and subsequently became a major air planner and World War II bomber commander, retrospectively commented that "Proponents of the two ideas soon lost all sense of proportion in the very intensity of their zeal. There was a tendency of the airmen to advocate strategic bombing to the exclusion of all else; and of the ground soldiers to view bombardment simply as more artillery." Hansell also observed that if the General Staff belittled the airmen's claims, "it must also be admitted that at least in some very small measure we may possibly have overstated our powers and understated our limitations."[26]

In the late 1930s, the onset of war in Europe, the signing of the Munich pact, seen by airmen as blackmail based on the might of German air power, quickened refinement of the Air Corps' doctrine. In light of these events, the Tactical School sharpened its thinking pertaining to the nature of warfare and the role of air power. As described by Fairchild, the aim of conflict was to support national policy by overcoming the will of the enemy. AWPD-1 stated that "if the morale of the people is already low ... then heavy and sustained bombing of cities may crush that morale entirely."[27] Air power formed a new way of waging war, striking directly at the enemy's ability to wage war. Fairchild specifically pointed to the Munich pact which he considered as an example of forcing political compliance.

Although in the late 1930s the Air Corps doctrine as taught at the Tactical School emphasized offensive air warfare, a large gap remained between what the school had promulgated and the officially approved doctrine as developed in Army field manuals. The Tactical School emphasized air warfare, primarily against the enemy's heartland. Fairchild sounded the theme: "Let us make our preparations now—in advance—to wage Air Warfare, rather than to employ our valuable Air force to reinforce the supporting fires of the artillery."[28] This connected to the question of target selection, which the air theorists had been refining in the 1930s. Their conclusion was that bombardment strategy should feature the attack on the enemy's national economic structure with the aim of reducing his war-making capacity and simultaneously applying pressure on the civilian population.

The official air force history of the evolution of doctrine noted that the "dark question mark" that hung over bombardment theory related to whether bombers could survive over enemy skies. Could they accomplish precision attacks in daylight without prohibitive attrition? The theorists on the faculty of the Tactical School reasoned that daylight bombing was essential, that bombers would have to fly without escort, and that they could sustain themselves with defensive fire power. As we now know, this concept proved untenable over Europe during World War II when bomber formations without fighter escort suffered unacceptable attrition at the hands of the Luftwaffe's strong fighter defense.

The autumn of 1938 proved to be a major turning point in American rearmament, especially as it concerned the Army Air Corps. President Roosevelt had become increasingly concerned about events in both Europe and the Far East wherein the German Luftwaffe had been active in the Spanish Civil War and the Japanese Air Force had attacked cities in China. This prompted Roosevelt to suggest that peaceful nations might have to "quarantine" the aggressors. Although concerned over Japanese aggression against China, the president's primary attention focused on Europe. On September 12, 1938, while in Rochester, Minnesota, and able to understand German, he had listened to Hitler's Nuremberg speech, in which the German dictator, ranting and raving, indicated clearly that he was determined to go to war to achieve his objective of a greater Europe under the hegemony of the Fatherland. As a result, Roosevelt had sent Harry Hopkins secretly—and without Arnold's knowledge—to the western United States to gauge the readiness of the aircraft industry to produce large numbers of airplanes. Hitler's Nuremberg address proved a forerunner to the September Munich conference of the four major European powers (Germany, England, France, Italy). Hitler bullied the British and French, telling them that peace was up to Czechoslovakia, and then getting them to agree to give Germany the Sudetenland. As a result, British Prime Minister Neville Chamberlain returned to England proclaiming "peace for our time." Thus on September 29, the signing of the Munich pact resulted in consternation in both the United States and Great Britain. In the face of Hitler's bullying tactics, Winston Churchill, then a member of Parliament, noted "the blackmailing power of air-bombing."

Roosevelt was well aware of Hitler's use of the Luftwaffe as a weapon of blackmail. The president's sensitivity was further heightened on October 14, 1938, by a report he received from William C. Bullitt, U.S. Ambassador to France. Bullitt reported that French military authorities were absolutely convinced that Hitler's supreme confidence at Munich was due to the buildup of the Luftwaffe. According to the official U.S. Army history: "The French military chiefs attributed Hitler's confidence to his possession of an air force already large and still capable of rapid expansion by means of the huge German airplane factories already in operation. What impressed the French most was the existence of a German bomber fleet much larger than that of France and Britain combined, and what the French military now wished ardently was a rapid increase of French air resources of every kind, for the defense and for counteroffensive. They (and the British as well) knew that a rapid increase could come about only from American factories and they urged upon the United States a development of American airplane production for Anglo-French purchase."[29]

Thus, Roosevelt became convinced that the American aircraft industry needed to be geared up—and fast. Much of the potential production, at least in Roosevelt's mind, would be headed for Britain and France. As the president viewed it, his goals dovetailed nicely, the foreign orders buttressing the fight against the fascists and concomitantly expanding American aircraft manufacturing. Government funds however, could not be used to build production plants "whose product was declared to be for immediate benefit to foreign countries." This issue gained prominence when an observer of the French Air Ministry was injured in an air crash of a new U.S. light bomber, triggering charges that the French had been provided access to U.S. military aviation data. Arnold subsequently informed a Congressional committee that he had granted permission to the French "upon request of the Secretary of the Treasury and by direction of the Secretary of War; whereupon I was asked by the Senators, 'Who is running your Air Force: the Secretary of the Treasury or the Secretary of War?'"[30] Roosevelt then announced that he had approved the French purchase of various aircraft and Army General Malin Craig commented that no "secret devices" were shown to the French.

Meanwhile Arnold, whom Roosevelt had appointed Chief of the Air Corps on September 28, 1938, sent Secretary of War Stimson a long-range plan for expanding the Air Corps by 4000 planes. And in late October and early November additional initiatives were taken by Roosevelt and the Chief of the Air Corps. On October 24, the president appointed a committee to investigate ways to increase the production of military aircraft. Arnold, on November 10, sent a memorandum to the Assistant Secretary of War, laying out "our personal ideas of a method of establishing an Air Force objective and an indication of what such an objective might be." He described a major new goal of 7000 aircraft.[31] And Assistant Secretary of War Louis Johnson, in the *Report of the Secretary of War for 1938* noted that "our former technical superiority in aeronautical development is no longer clearly apparent. Recent advances in other countries have equaled if not exceeded our efforts. We have known for some time that foreign nations far surpassed us in the number of military aircraft at their disposal but we also knew that we led the field technically. It now appears that our research and development programs must be accelerated if we are to regain our position of technical leadership."[32]

This set the stage for what the official U.S. Army history of the prewar period called "the momentous White House meeting of 14 November 1938."[33] President Roosevelt took the lead in addressing the critical requirement to greatly accelerate production of aircraft, especially bombers. Alarmed by the report from U.S. Ambassador to France William C. Bullitt, Roosevelt convened a meeting at the White House that marked the start of a major buildup of U.S. air power. And despite the "fits and starts," the required interplay with Congress, and the subsequent friction between Arnold and Roosevelt, the plain fact was that the primary promoter of this program for the Air Corps was none other than the president himself, a really historic moment in the evolution of air power. This marked the beginning of the nation's rearmament, especially as it pertained to the Army air arm. Present for this meeting, among others, were Roosevelt, Secretary of the Treasury Henry Morgenthau, Harry Hopkins, Assistant Secretary of War Louis Johnson, Army Chief of Staff Gen. Malin Craig, Army Deputy Chief of Staff Brig. Gen. George Marshall, and Arnold, Chief of the Air Corps.

Roosevelt took over the meeting, emphasizing expansion of the Air Corps. Arnold, in his memoir, delightfully describes his own reaction: "To the surprise, I think of practically everyone in the room except Harry (Hopkins) and myself, and to my own delight, the president came straight out for air power. Airplanes—now—and lots of them!"[34] According to Arnold, to the Army and Navy representatives this was undoubtedly "a bolt from the blue," but Roosevelt was determined to discuss air expansion. Arnold was convinced that Roosevelt had put a great deal of thought into his proposals, "not made up on the spur of the moment."[35] Arnold claimed that FDR's "forceful way" of stating his view was based on a great deal of thought, familiar to Arnold from "long conversations" that he had with Harry Hopkins. Roosevelt emphasized aircraft standardization and faster aircraft production "for our friends abroad and for ourselves." He wanted 10,000 planes per year production with an annual capacity of 20,000 aircraft. Arnold reiterated his lack of surprise over the president's ideas for increasing production as "they had been talked over time and time again" with, among others, Assistant Secretary of War Louis Johnson, and had been discussed on many occasions between Arnold and Hopkins.[36]

Britain and France lagged in aircraft production capacity, the president emphasized, and concomitantly, the United States must be ready to defend the Western Hemisphere. The weakest link in the American defense setup was the Air Corps. The United States needed to produce large numbers of planes—now! The War Department needed to develop a 10,000-plane program of which 2500 would be trainers, 3750 combat, and 3750 reserve aircraft. Roosevelt's overall objective was production over a two-year period of 10,000 planes of which 8000 would come from existing plants and 2000 from new plant capacity. Roosevelt solely focused upon airplane production at the meeting. He was not concerned at this time with building an air force, an entity that would include bases, pilots, equipment, crews, and maintenance personnel. Observers, if not actually some participants in the meeting, noted that it appeared that Roosevelt's objective was to provide planes for purchase by Britain and France. Arnold, as noted, was elated, and wrote in his memoir that he immediately gave Gen. Malin Craig, Army Chief of Staff, "a get-rich-quick course" in how to build an air force: "He was a very apt pupil, and from then on until his tour was completed, fought for our program."[37]

The obvious significance of this meeting, Roosevelt's determination to build up the air arm, prompted Arnold to write that he had the feeling that the Air Corps "had finally achieved its Magna Carta."[38] It was the first time in history, he stressed, that the air arm actually had a program.

"A battle was won in the White House that day," he wrote, "which took its place with ... the victories in combat later, for time is a most important factor in building an Air Force."[39] The Air Corps Chief was certainly correct to emphasize the importance of Roosevelt's call for production of an unprecedented number of aircraft, for it amounted to a significant policy change at the highest level of government. Not only did the president issue the call to build an air force, but his action simultaneously sidelined the Army's long-considered plans for accelerating the buildup of the ground forces. Roosevelt emphasized the air forces, which had been a secondary consideration in Army planning. Despite delays and changes to the program that subsequently transpired, it was in fact a case of the president, as Commander-in-Chief, over-ruling prior recommendations of the War Department that emphasized the re-arming of ground forces. At this meeting, Roosevelt threw his weight and credibility behind Arnold and the air forces and moreover, insisted on a quick-start program. Army Deputy Chief of Staff George Marshall immediately supported the new program, informing Chief of Staff Malin Craig in late November that B-17 long-range bombers should be procured in maximum numbers to meet Roosevelt's objectives. Historian DeWitt Copp described Roosevelt's air-power initiative: "It was as though an aircraft with a 65-horsepower engine were to be converted almost overnight to two thousand horsepower, and in the metamorphosis its pilot, its equipment, its maintenance and its base of operations were to be updated accordingly."[40] This buildup signaled a significant change in U.S. foreign policy. Beginning in early 1939, America began to re-arm, a move unprecedented in peacetime. The U.S. tradition had been "first declare, then prepare." Now through the expansion of war production facilities, the United States aimed to become "the arsenal of democracy." There were difficulties, among the most important being the allocation of production aircraft, frequently to the detriment of the Air Corps' own expansion.

President Roosevelt followed up on January 12, 1939, with a special message to Congress, asking for increased defense funding, especially at it pertained to air power. He referred to the "increased range, increased speed, increased capacity of airplanes abroad" that "have changed our requirements for defensive aviation." Our air forces, he stated, "are so utterly inadequate that they must be immediately strengthened." In early April, Congress passed legislation authorizing $300 million for an air arm not to exceed 6000 aircraft. The air arm actually adopted a program for 5500 planes. Here the president was seen as advocating production of B-17s, which in the mid-1930s had been slowed by the War Department, only fourteen having been delivered up to September 1939. Roosevelt's actions in late 1938 and early 1939 recalled Harry Hopkins' comment that the president was "sure then that we were going to get into war and he believed that air power would win it."[41] As Assistant Secretary of the Navy in World War I, Roosevelt had certainly not been an aviation sup-porter. In retrospect, however, he became an air power advocate in the backwash of Hitler's rampage, the defining events being Hitler's Nurem-berg speech and the Munich pact. During 1938, the president had also received ominous reports on the buildup of German air power. As a result, as noted, he had sent Harry Hopkins on a crash tour to assess the capabilities of U.S. aircraft manufacturers.

Responding to Roosevelt's thrust, and a recommendation from Sec-retary of War Henry L. Stimson, Arnold, on May 5, 1939, had established the Kilner Board to make recommendations for future development and procurement programs. The board's report, issued at the end of June 1939, outlined aircraft and equipment to be procured by 1944, includ-ing a very long-range (VLR) heavy bomber.[42] This was a landmark report for, in effect, it was the beginning of the B-29 program. Arnold took the lead, alerting American aircraft manufacturers to tool up for expansion, buttressed by his long association with the leaders of America's aircraft industry. He promoted standardization of equipment. In the three years prior to Pearl Harbor, the Air Corps was authorized to spend about eight billion dollars and to procure about 37,500 aircraft.

Nazi Germany, on September 1, 1939, unleashed an onslaught against Poland, initiating World War II in Europe. Subsequently, Secretary Stimson emphasized that "air power today has decided the fate of nations. Ger-many with her powerful air armadas has vanquished one people after another. On the ground, large armies have been mobilized to resist her, but each time it was that additional power in the air that decided the fate of each individual nation. As a consequence, we are in the midst of a great crisis. The time factor is our principal obstacle."[43]

As noted, although in a real sense pre-occupied with events in Europe, the Roosevelt administration was also much concerned with Japanese aggression against China. Well before the attack on Pearl Harbor, the Japanese had been bombing China, including Chungking in western China, the capital of Chiang Kai-shek's Nationalist government. The U.S. protested bombing attacks on civilians, but the Japanese claimed they were only targeting military sites. On January 27, 1940, U.S. Secretary of State Cordell Hull declared that the Japanese "have in large number of instances resorted to bombing and machine-gunning of civilians from the air at places near which there were no military establishments or organizations. Furthermore, the use of incendiary bombs has inflicted appalling losses on civilian populations. Japanese air attacks in many instances have been of a nature and apparent plan which can be comprehended only as constituting deliberate attempts to terrorize unarmed populations."[44]

Hull's statement formed an important backdrop to the U.S. surge in aircraft production. In 1939–1940, Arnold opposed Roosevelt over the specific allocation of aircraft production, opposing Roosevelt's plan to give the British more planes, putting him in a precarious position with the president. Arnold was determined to build up the air forces when it seemed inevitable that America would ultimately enter the conflict. Roosevelt, like Arnold, was committed to production of heavy bombers. The year 1941, prior to the Pearl Harbor attack, marked the transition to a wartime economy, when preparedness gave way to the requirements of global war. In May 1941, FDR wrote to Stimson that the "effective defense of this country and the vital defense of other democratic nations required a substantial increase in heavy bomber production."[45] Roosevelt emphasized that "I know of no single item of our defense today that is more important than a large four-engine bomber capacity." Robert Lovett, Assistant Secretary of War for Air, termed Roosevelt's desired production figures a "fantasy, utterly unattainable."

Roosevelt, who saw aircraft shipments to the Allies as part of the lend-lease program, determined to keep the British in the war, demanding that production line aircraft be sent to them. It is certainly conceivable that when Roosevelt directed the re-arming of America, with emphasis on aircraft production, that he envisioned much of this production going to Britain and France to stem the Nazi tide. This presented Arnold with a large problem as he desperately attempted to build an air force: "The world situation demanded it," he emphasized. It wasn't that the Air Corps Chief failed to understand or sympathize with Roosevelt's view— Arnold at heart certainly wanted to support the British—but he felt strongly that "my obligations to my own country and my own Corps were definite." Between helping our allies, he emphasized, "and giving everything away, a realistic line must be drawn, or there would never be a United States Air Force except on paper."[46]

The AAF, he emphasized, "was rapidly changing its status from one of peace to one of war." General Marshall noted that the attempt to fill British aircraft requirements presented "a tremendously complicated task here in Washington." And Arnold emphasized that

> on top of other headaches there was the daily business of satisfying White House, Congressional, and War Department superiors who were constantly receiving phone calls, visits and letters from people, official and unofficial, American, British, French, Dutch, Chinese, Polish, Russian ... and what not, criticizing the Air Force's procedures, offering free advice and recommendations, or demanding a priority share of our equipment.[47]

As one historian commented, "American air power was getting strangled in the cradle by an excess of Presidential generosity." Arnold thought that he was about to lose his job. He was especially perturbed at Secretary of the Treasury Henry Morgenthau, noting it was not Morgenthau's responsibility to build up the air forces. This was Arnold's responsibility: "To build up our Air Force was an obligation that I had to Congress, to the president, to the people of the United States. It was a job that was still ahead of me, for we had no Air Force." Arnold noted that "it was the rosy dream of some Americans that we could save the world and ourselves by sending all our weapons abroad for other men to fight with. If this priority thus deprived our own air power of even its foundation stones, certain people seemed to take the view that it was just too bad."[48] Morgenthau himself recalled a two-and-a-half-hour meeting in mid-March 1940 when Roosevelt admonished Arnold "on the airplane thing." According to Morgenthau, the president looked directly at Arnold and said: "When people can't control themselves and their people under them, you know what we do with those kind of people? We send them to Guam." Morgenthau claimed that Roosevelt told Assistant Secretary of War Louis Johnson that "either Arnold cut it out or he would be removed as head of the Air Corps."[49]

In late 1940 and early 1941, Robert A. Lovett—to become Assistant Secretary of War for Air in April 1941—was convinced that air power would play a crucial role in the coming conflict and he agreed with Arnold that the air forces needed to be brought up to at least minimum strength as quickly as possible. Lovett knew how to get things done. With his perception and dry sense of humor, he was a perfect fit with Hap Arnold. "I found in Bob Lovett," Arnold emphasized, "a man who possessed the qualities in which I was weakest, a partner and teammate of tremendous sympathy and of calm and hidden force."[50] In the spring of 1941, he emphasized that it was time to allocate the majority of U.S. aircraft production to Arnold's forces rather than to the British. One of Lovett's toughest challenges was to keep Arnold and Roosevelt moored to reality. The president's and the Air Chief's insistence upon vastly unrealistic production goals frustrated Lovett. Lovett was appalled at what he considered FDR's casual production targets. "It is a little bit like asking a hen to lay an ostrich egg." Lovett told Arnold. "It is unlikely that you will get the egg and the hen will never look the same." Arnold did not flinch, replying that "if we can induce her to lay it, I, for one, feel that we must accept the wear and tear on the hen."[51] This was typical of Arnold, who often exhorted all—especially the aircraft manufacturers—to redouble their efforts. Like Roosevelt, he hated self-imposed obstacles. He reminded Lovett that "the negative assumption that requirements cannot be met, supported by facts as they are and not as we are capable of making them, too often has characterized thinking on this subject."[52] It was a program that Lovett felt he could not support because it was "likely to cause false hopes initially and bitter disappointment later."[53]

Marshall, Army Chief of Staff, found himself in the middle of this controversy between FDR and Arnold. Forrest Pogue, Marshall's biographer, wrote that to Marshall, "the President's requirements were almost more than he could bear."[54] Like Arnold, Marshall informed Roosevelt that it was not possible at that time to give the British (and the Soviets, the French, and the Chinese) everything they wanted and at the same time to build an American air force. Marshall finessed the situation by saving as much of the aircraft production as he could for Arnold while giving the Allies whatever he could. It was a fine line that FDR did not always appreciate. The fact was that in 1940, for the first time in its history, the United States was attempting to discern major wartime requirements and whether it had the capacity to fulfill these requirements. As noted, in Arnold's view, the British were the major problem. In July 1940, the British already had on order in the United States 8,275 aircraft, almost four times the number the U.S. had on order. As of December 1940, these early plans called for an 82,890-plane program, to be completed by the end of June 1943, of which by mid-1940 only about 3,000 had been delivered. Of the approximately 80,000 remaining to be delivered, almost 26,000 were for the British. Roosevelt had initially indicated to Stimson that he wanted 60,000 aircraft produced in 1941 and 125,000 in 1943.[55] Lovett thought that this level of production was not possible. Reluctantly, Arnold later gave ground and approved a production figure of 82,000 aircraft (vice 125,000) for 1943, which in retrospect proved to be wholly realistic for the "arsenal of democracy."

An example of Roosevelt's insistence and enthusiasm for aircraft and bombing, concerns his approval for a scheme—never consummated—to send B-17s to China. In late 1940, the president, outraged at the bombing, rape, and pillaging committed by the Japanese Imperial Army in East Asia, expressed the desire that Tokyo should be bombed to teach the Japanese a lesson. Morgenthau recalled that Roosevelt mentioned "to me that it would be a nice thing if the Chinese would bomb Japan." Morgenthau discussed this subject with Chinese officials including Foreign Minister T. V. Soong. In November and December 1940, General Claire Chennault and the Chinese Air Force were brought into the discussions. Chennault told Morgenthau that the goal was to "burn out the industrial heart of the Empire with firebomb attacks on the teeming bamboo ant heaps of Honshu and Kyushu."[56] The Chinese, as well as Roosevelt, were enthusiastic about the plan. However, in late December, Stimson had second thoughts, and finally, Marshall, on December 22, 1940, sunk the plan, emphasizing that the Air Corps did not have enough B-17s for its own purposes and thus could not afford to send these aircraft to China. Instead of B-17s, the Americans at the time agreed to send the Chinese 100 P-40 fighter aircraft, subsequently part of the American Volunteer Group, "the Flying Tigers."[57]

The British, according to Arnold, desired just about all of the American production. Well aware of the situation, Stimson and Lovett suggested to Arnold that he visit the United Kingdom to see first-hand what the British were up against. In April 1941, Arnold flew to England and spent two weeks talking with British leaders, civilian and military, and every top military official as well as Prime Minister Churchill and King George. Arnold was much impressed with British fortitude. He cemented a relationship with Air Chief Marshal Charles "Peter" Portal, head of Air Staff of the Royal Air Force. Upon his return, Arnold in early May 1941 briefed President Roosevelt. It was a comprehensive presentation and the Air Chief noted that it may have been the first time that the president and cabinet members had received a complete report on the European situation from the point of view of the British military. Roosevelt was duly impressed, and according to Stimson, the presentation marked Arnold's exit from FDR's doghouse.

Thus, the president continued to call for accelerated war preparations—dragging along a reluctant American public—and on July 9, 1941, almost three weeks after Germany had stunned the world by invading the Soviet Union with 160 divisions, he asked the Army and Navy for an estimate of the "overall production requirements needed to defeat our potential enemies."[58] Arnold received approval from the War Department to have the new Air War Plans Division of the Air Staff—created when the AAF was established in June 1941—prepare the requirements, known as Air Annex. The plan, called AWPD-1, was developed and refined during nine days in August 1941, under enormous pressure, day and night. In many ways, the United States already was at war. The plan was drawn up by Lt. Col. Harold L. George (head, Air War Plans Division), Lt. Col. Kenneth N. Walker, Maj. Laurence S. Kuter, and Maj. Haywood S. Hansell Jr. (recently returned from England with folders on German targets). It identified the following major target systems: aircraft assembly plants, electric power, transportation, and synthetic oil. This became the blueprint for the conduct of the air war against Germany in the early months of conflict. However, Imperial Japan struck on December 7, and the U.S. entered the war before Roosevelt ever received the briefing. In late December 1941, an Anglo-American conference in Washington endorsed the plan's concept, although it never did reach the president's desk.

Even prior to American entry into the war, the virtual equality of the Army Air Forces with the Army and Navy manifested itself in Arnold's presence on the Joint Chiefs of Staff and the Combined Chiefs of Staff and in AAF representation on the Joint Staff committees. Arnold had taken his place at the "high table" of Allied policy formulation. The January 29–March 27, 1941, American-British talks in Washington (ABC-1), led to creation at the Arcadia Conference in January 1942 of the Combined Chiefs of Staff (CCS) representing both British and American military forces with Arnold sitting in for U.S. air power. Although Arnold was subordinate to Marshall, the Army Chief of Staff insisted that he be present with his "opposite number," Air Chief Marshal Charles "Peter" Portal of the RAF, when the CCS considered grand strategy.

Meantime, Roosevelt took seriously his role as Commander-in-Chief and he acted upon it. In July 1939, he brought the Joint Army-Navy Board into his newly created Executive Office. President Roosevelt as Commander-in-Chief of the nation's armed forces, exercised a most important influence upon General Arnold, and thus on U.S. air power. There exists a consensus among historians, based on the record of

World War II, that Roosevelt aggressively used his authority as Commander-in-Chief. "Every President," historian Mark Skinner Watson has observed, "has possessed the Constitutional authority which that title indicates, but few Presidents have shared Mr. Roosevelt's readiness to exercise it in fact and in detail and with such determination."[59] When the Japanese Empire attacked United States forces at Pearl Harbor on December 7, 1941, the U.S. was unprepared for a two-front war in Europe and the Pacific, but did possess a firm foundation in strategy and war production due to Roosevelt's prewar efforts. In the fall of 1941, the "Victory Program" of war production was established and the "Rainbow 5" strategic plan went into effect on December 7, 1941.

In February 1942, the Joint Board was superseded by the Joint Chiefs of Staff. And although the service secretaries, Stimson (War Department) and Frank Knox (Navy Department), headed their respective departments, the military service chiefs reported directly to the president. The U.S. Joint Chiefs of Staff was never formally established; the JCS just came into being in February 1942 as an organization to coordinate policy to present to British counterparts. The British had a well-established joint committee system. With the enormous pressure that built up immediately after Pearl Harbor, it became necessary for the military to present common positions to the president for his approval. Along with Prime Minister Churchill, the British Chiefs of Staff arrived in Washington in December 1941 to attend the Arcadia Conference. It was here that the British proposed to leave a team in Washington to attend meetings with the Joint Chiefs.

The terms "Joint" and "Combined" reflected the thought of the British Chiefs of Staff, with the former referring to interservice affairs in either country and the latter used as a term for British-American collaboration. The CCS deliberations were meant to frame broad requirements reflecting strategic policy. These combined discussions framed the strategic direction of Allied forces. The British and Americans never expanded the combined system to include the military staffs of other nations. However, the Anglo-American military staffs consulted with representatives from other Allied nations on military issues being considered by the American and British Chiefs of Staff.

It is significant to note the role of President Roosevelt as Commander-in-Chief in relation to the American Joint Chiefs and the Combined Chiefs. Although he rarely, if ever, interfered in strictly tactical decisions, Roosevelt played a significant part in overall strategy. It will be recalled that in late 1938 he called for production capacity of 10,000 combat planes annually and in May 1940 accelerated this to 50,000 planes a year. In July 1942, he strongly backed "Torch," the invasion of North Africa, thus diverting air forces from Europe to North African operations. This decision for Torch over-rode the direction of previous U.S. military policy. In April 1942, over Marshall's objections, Roosevelt also called for deployment of two Army divisions to Australia.

Arnold coveted his role in formulating policy and strategy at the highest levels. "The Army Air Forces," he emphasized, "are being directly controlled by the Joint Chiefs of Staff and the Combined Chiefs of Staffs more and more each day. Consequently, AAF representation in the Joint and combined planning staffs has become a position of paramount importance to me."[60] Roosevelt underscored this by noting that "My recognition of the growing importance of air power is made obvious by the fact that the CG, AAF is a member of both the Joint and Combined Chiefs of Staff. The Air Forces, both in the Army and in the Navy, have a strong voice in shaping and implementing our national military policy." Control of long-range air operations was of great importance to Arnold. As the official U.S. Army history noted: "The success of the makeshift organizational arrangements in World War II did not conceal the ultimate importance in future national defense at arriving at a clear-cut definition of the functions and status of the Air Forces in relation to both the Navy and the rest of the Army."[61] According to historian Ray S. Cline: "It was clearly in the interest of the common military effort, as it was clearly the intent of General Marshall, to preserve the system whereby the Army Air Forces exercised great influence in determining the way in which U.S. Army air units were employed, but whereby OPD [the War Department's Operations Division] monitored air plans and operational orders in the interest of the ground-air team as a whole."[62]

Following the surprise attack on Pearl Harbor, crippling the U.S. Pacific fleet, Japanese planners posited that several crucial battles would ensue, followed by critical negotiations in which most Japanese demands would be satisfied. The Japanese high command thought that in effect the United States could be surprised and that it would ultimately take America years to power up from luxury goods to effective war production. The Japanese badly underestimated the U.S. productive capacity to rapidly manufacture war weaponry, thinking that Americans were decadent and would welcome peace. "The act of Japan at Pearl Harbor," Roosevelt emphasized in his January 6, 1942, State of the Union address, "was intended to stun us—to terrify us to such an extent that we would divert our industrial and military strength to the Pacific area, or even to our own continental defense. ... The plan has failed in its purpose."[63] The Japanese planners failed to foresee a war in which they would lose the initiative and be pushed back by U.S. military power. In this regard, they also failed to understand how vulnerable the homeland was to sea and air blockade. From the start of the war, American planners considered Japan to be as vulnerable to blockade as any nation in modern history. Surrounded by water, with a huge population, Japan remained dependent upon the importation of raw materials and a significant amount of food. Nor did the Japanese understand the potential of the long-range strategic air offensive which ultimately destroyed her cities. Japan saw air power in a tactical mode, as support for ground and naval forces. Nonetheless, at the time of Pearl Harbor, the U.S. remained unprepared for global war. Of some 900 combat aircraft overseas, fewer than 300 were in the Philippines and only about 200 in Hawaii. The Japanese homeland lay far beyond the range of U.S. bombers based in the Philippines.

Several months after the attack on Pearl Harbor, Arnold informed Stimson that the time was past for a complete turn-around in the development of the air arm. Stimson did not need to be convinced. Although Stimson was in poor health during much of the war, the Secretary made timely, important contributions to the aircraft buildup. He and Arnold had talked at length and in fact had been thinking along the same lines: specifically, that a "complete redistribution" of aircraft production was required to build up U.S. air power to meet strategic objectives.[64] President Roosevelt, however, had continued to press Stimson to allocate more bomber aircraft to the British, writing to the Secretary of War that it was more important "to have the British flying these planes in combat" than to strengthen U.S. units.[65] Stimson wrote on April 12, 1942, to Roosevelt, that "a complete reorientation of our thought" was desperately needed in order to build as quickly as possible a "powerful" air force. Stimson zeroed in on the question of production, mincing no words to the president, admonishing that all requests for aircraft "not essential to our own plans must be refused." He warned that "not a plane can be unnecessarily given away. We are so far behind that it will require herculean efforts to catch up." Stimson noted that U.S. air forces were now "a more prominent factor than either the Navy or the ground forces." "We are," Stimson emphasized, "no longer a mere arsenal for other nations. We are ourselves in desperate danger. Nothing but our own power will suffice to meet that danger."[66] Arnold had estimated a shortfall of 9000 planes by the end of 1942. Stimson informed Roosevelt that increasing production must be aimed at "establishing as quickly as possible a powerful American Air Force." This meant a "redistribution" from allocations to the British to the now-primary goal of building the American air force.[67]

Having now entered the conflict, Arnold and Stimson knew that the nation faced the difficult challenge of a global war, the necessity of military action in widely dispersed territories. Before major ground forces could be trained and deployed, air power was the primary force to be deployed into action. Even in the South Pacific, the Navy requested support from the air forces. However, the structuring of an American air force required more than airplanes. As Arnold had pointed out for years, it meant bases, logistical support, equipment, and training thousands of airmen. Stimson carried the message to President Roosevelt. After individual pilot training, it took six more months of unit training for a group to be prepared for combat. Almost a year's training was required for a four-engine bomber pilot. The strategy of "holding and striking" during 1942 depended upon a major effort to train airmen. The time had arrived to refuse all requests from other nations for aircraft essential to U.S. objectives.[68]

Arnold appeared confident that the AAF could be built up provided that aircraft production was given top priority. However, he brought to

Roosevelt's attention that in order to be decisive, air power must be employed in massive numbers against carefully selected targets; "half measures would not do." In the war against Japan, joint action with surface forces could gain appropriate bases from which the AAF could strike the Japanese home islands. "Air action as the dominant factor," Arnold wrote to FDR, "properly supported and extended by the action of surface forces, will win the war."[69] As noted, Roosevelt agreed, but his early fixation on providing a large percentage of America's production aircraft to the British fueled the tension with Arnold. Even after the air chief's removal from the president's doghouse, FDR closely followed the distribution of planes.

Pre-eminently however, after Pearl Harbor, Roosevelt, Hopkins, Stimson, Arnold, and Lovett agreed on the over-arching objective of building a powerful American air force. Here it is relevant to note Arnold's relationship not only with Roosevelt, Stimson, and Lovett, but also with Hopkins. Harry Hopkins enjoyed a unique influence with Roosevelt and Arnold enjoyed a very special rapport and relationship with Hopkins. Arnold called him "one of the most enthusiastic supporters of American Air Power," a man he had worked closely with for almost a decade in a relationship that played a large role in building the Army Air Forces.[70] Hopkins remained Arnold's entree to Roosevelt during the entire war. Most importantly, when a cabinet-level official, or even a Prime Minister, lined up against Arnold on a particular point, and the air chief required help, Hopkins would jump in and level the playing field, usually successfully. Discussions between Arnold and Hopkins frequently took place during breakfasts, luncheons, and in the evening. The subject always touched on air power, its organization, control, and employment. The specifics of the topics discussed between them reveal an extraordinarily broad agenda, ranging from aircraft production to strategy and employment. What is required for the United States to get the most effective use of its air forces? How to accomplish the overall mission? Fundamental to this special relationship was Arnold's rock-bound confidence in the integrity and judgment of Harry Hopkins, who fortunately had the ear of the president.

While Arnold maintained his fruitful relationship with Hopkins, the fact remained that no formal administrative organization integrated the flow of policy information and decisions from the president to the Joint Chiefs and the military planners. Thus, while Roosevelt relied on the Joint Chiefs for military advice, he himself coordinated policy by working with Hopkins, the cabinet secretaries, and the Joint Chiefs of Staff. The president kept the reins of national policy in his own hands and his cabinet secretaries conferred with him as individuals. This lack of systematic policy integration manifested itself at the wartime international conferences where the British were clearly better prepared. Here Churchill relied on his War Cabinet Defense Committee, which integrated national policy under his personal direction.

In the later war years, coordination of national policy improved due to the increasing prestige and influence of the JCS and the ability of Admiral Leahy, the president's chief of staff, to bring Roosevelt's views and desires to the Joint Chiefs on a daily basis. General Marshall noted that sometimes the Joint Chiefs were unaware of policy decisions until well after they were made. After cabinet meetings, varying impressions remained as to precisely what the president desired.[71]

During the war, Stimson remained a strong supporter of Arnold and the Army Air Forces. He rather liked Arnold's frequent lack of tact, as opposed to Marshall, whom Stimson characterized as "over-diplomatic." Stimson found that Arnold possessed a "quick mind" and did not hesitate to make his opinions known. Upon occasion however, the Secretary of War had to intercede to cut off some of the Air Chief's "half-baked actions."[72]

Lovett remained a leading proponent of the long-range bomber during all of this. Arguing that the war made the case for offensive weapons, he pressed his case to Stimson, Marshall, and Roosevelt through Hopkins. "At irregular intervals in history," Lovett pointed out, "some new development has altered the art of war and changed the fate of peoples and the world." The evolution of the long-range bomber, he emphasized to Stimson, amounted to a "watershed" in the history of warfare. In 1942, the major disagreement was over how many planes the U.S. industrial machine could produce in the year ahead. President Roosevelt was dissatisfied with the aircraft production objective for 1943 of approximately 70,000 tactical planes furnished by Donald M. Nelson, chairman of the War Production Board although Nelson made clear he could increase the total to 82,000 if given a "green light." The president supported Arnold's statement of 1943 aircraft requirements, which called for over 100,000 planes for the AAF, the Navy, and the allies. "I am of the opinion," Roosevelt emphasized, "that these requirements are essential if we are to secure and maintain unquestioned air superiority over the Axis powers in 1943." Roosevelt hurled the problem to the Joint Chiefs in October 1942, noting that he considered Nelson's 1943 production schedule "totally inadequate." He was determined that his goal, based generally on Arnold's 100,000-plus objective, should remain in effect for 1943. Roosevelt requested the JCS to promulgate specific monthly production schedules, and reenforced his opinion: "I mean 100,000 tactical combat planes delivered during the calendar year 1943, *not* 100,000 rate of delivery at end of that year."[73] The 100,000 figure was stressed by Harry Hopkins, who pointed out to the president that the total original requirement of 107,408 for the AAF, Navy, and allies could "not possibly be built in 1943 without such serious repercussions on escort vessels, ammunition, and anti-aircraft guns as to make the proposal an untenable one." He consequently recommended to Roosevelt that he stick with the 100,000 production goal to forestall any "inordinate delay" in the process. The president then requested Donald Nelson to take the necessary steps to allocate materials and machine tools to make certain that the production goal would be met.[74] As it turned out, due to pressure from Lovett, who emphasized realistic production goals to Arnold, Stimson, and Hopkins, the figure of 82,000 production aircraft for 1943 (what Nelson said could be accomplished) proved to be realistic.

On March 23, 1943, Roosevelt called Marshall and Arnold to the White House for an update on the distribution of American-made aircraft throughout the world. He requested the distribution of all combat planes delivered in 1942 and in the early months of 1943.[75] To those who contend that FDR was not involved in strategy and overall conduct of the war, a study of the documentary evidence points to an opposite conclusion. First of all, Roosevelt constitutionally was Commander-in-Chief of the armed forces. He did not hesitate to use this authority; in fact, he did so consistently throughout the war, especially prior to 1945. He seemed to relish the levers of power and insistently pursued them on a personal level. Note his direction in November 1938 to increase production of combat aircraft to 10,000, increased in May 1940 to a goal of 50,000 annually; he hounded Arnold to get the B-29s operating out of China; and he insisted on funneling aircraft to Britain when Arnold, Marshall, and Stimson thought more of these planes should go into building an American air force. Among large strategic decisions, he set the table, directing early on that the defeat of Germany came first with a holding operation in the Pacific. He also made the early, big decision to invade North Africa. On air matters, the president was also involved. In addition to championing the operational deployment of B-29s, Roosevelt maintained a keen interest in the air war over Europe, following its progress in detail. He frequently asked questions about radar, munitions and aircraft distribution. He kept informed about air operations over the Hump.

On March 16, 1942, Roosevelt jumped into an argument between the Army and Navy in the Southwest Pacific over the use of aerial torpedoes. He admonished his Secretaries of War and the Navy to get together quickly and work this issue out. "I do not care who fires the torpedoes—Army fliers or Navy fliers. The point is that they must be fired at Japanese ships. ... I do not give a continental about the use of these torpedoes after the next ninety days." The president added: "I am sending this as Commander-in-Chief of both services and I require that it be carried out by both Services ... this is a directive for joint action."[76]

Roosevelt even offered Arnold advice on targeting. Chinese ambassador T. V. Soong informed him that the Japanese were producing large amounts of war equipment in Shanghai. This production was dependent upon the sole power plant in the city which, if destroyed, would slow production for six months. Soong suggested bombing the power plant with aircraft operating from India. At the president's request, Arnold's office completed a study on the matter and determined that the industry in Shanghai—compared with Taiwan and Kyushu—did not afford a high priority. Arnold smoothly noted to FDR that he had forwarded this study on the question to General Stilwell for decision "in the light of such additional information as may be available to him."[77]

From time to time, Roosevelt would ask Arnold to follow up on somewhat more bizarre suggestions. In late May 1942, John Franklin Carter, whom Roosevelt had made a personal intelligence agent, reported that Harvey Davis, director of the Stevens Institute, had suggested that bombs be dropped in the craters of some of Japan's semi-active volcanoes, thereby igniting a lava flow. The president forwarded this suggestion to Arnold. The idea cannot "be dismissed without serious consideration," Arnold informed Roosevelt, but critical military objectives now deserved higher priority. The suggestion would be reconsidered "at such time as the extent of our bombardment effort against Japan warrants directing our efforts toward anything but the most critical military objectives."[78]

Roosevelt, as well as Arnold, followed reports of Japanese atrocities closely. The Japanese Imperial Army was an army out of control. According to Werner Gruhl, who has spent years analyzing the East Asian holocaust perpetrated by Japan's Imperial Army, during 1931–1945 there were 23,877,000 total Allied deaths from all war causes in East Asia. Survivors numbered in the tens of millions: "Those severely affected included the wounded and maimed, the raped and tortured, maltreated forced labor, massive numbers of destitute and despairing refugees and homeless, war orphans and widows." Additional victims included POWs and civilian internees who suffered from horrific treatment by the Japanese military. The number "of dead and severely affected" equaled the population of the United States at the time.[79] The Japanese also employed biological warfare, postwar research uncovering the grisly atrocities perpetrated by the infamous Unit 731, headed by General Shiro Ishii, and termed "the death factory."

The Japanese abuse of POWs and civilian internees is another horrific example of the Imperial Army out of control. These crimes were well known to Roosevelt, Marshall, and Arnold. The Japanese made it a practice to routinely violate the accepted rules of war. Gruhl estimated that the Japanese army took approximately 750,000 Chinese soldiers as prisoners and killed at least 267,000. As for American and Allied POWs, the Japanese beat them, starved them, and conducted medical experiments on them. Prisoners, called "marutas," were bitten by cholera fleas and were victims of vivisections. And at the end of the war, prisoners were killed and their bodies incinerated. The Bataan Death March is only the best known of the Japanese forced marches of the sick and malnourished. The POWs were also used in forced labor. Of 145,200 American and Allied POWs, 41,600 or twenty-nine percent were killed or died in captivity. In contrast, the death rate of U.S. and Allied prisoners held by the Germans was four percent.[80] As to civilian internees, of approximately 190,000 to 240,000 Western internees in Japanese-occupied Asia, 30,000 to 35,000 men, women, and children lost their lives.[81]

Roosevelt, outraged, kept up-to-date on Japanese atrocities. He would frequently release an official statement or mention the subject at a press conference or in a radio address. Upon learning of the "barbarous execution" of a number of American fliers who had participated in the April 1942 Doolittle raid on Tokyo, Roosevelt met with Arnold and announced publicly on April 21, 1943, that he had sent a formal condemnation to the Japanese government. The U.S., he said, would hold responsible the officers of the Japanese government who participated in these executions.[82]

The previous year's Doolittle raid on Tokyo, April 18, 1942, initially conceived by two Navy officers, Captains Francis S. Low and Donald B. Duncan, proved to be of primarily symbolic importance. Low and Duncan proposed a strike on Tokyo with Army medium bombers launched from an aircraft carrier approximately 500 miles from the Tokyo target. Arnold approved, pointing to Roosevelt's role: "Immediately following Pearl Harbor, the president was insistent that we find ways and means of carrying home to Japan proper, in the form of a bombing raid, the real meaning of war. We thought that out for some weeks. I talked it over with some key members of my Air Staff and then with Mr. Roosevelt."[83]

Flying a heavily loaded B-25 medium bomber from the rolling deck of an aircraft carrier presented a large challenge. After hitting the target, plans called for the aircraft to continue to airfields in China. To head the mission, Arnold chose Lt. Col. James H. Doolittle, a crack pilot and outstanding leader, who trained the crews to fly sixteen B-25Bs off the carrier *Hornet* with the carrier *Enterprise* and its aircraft defending the task force. On April 18, the mission launched from the *Hornet* into forty-mile-per-hour winds, thirteen of the planes bombing Tokyo, the remaining three striking Kobe and Nagoya. After bombing, Doolittle's flyers headed for China, but weather and lack of fuel forced them to crash or abandon their planes, except for one aircraft that managed to land in Vladivostok, in the Soviet Union. The attack actually caused little damage in Tokyo.

Of a total of eighty airmen in the raid, three died in crash landings or parachuting, while the Japanese took eight prisoner. Of those taken by the Japanese, three were executed by firing squad and another died in confinement. Four survived imprisonment.[84] Arnold described Roosevelt's reaction to the Doolittle raid: "The President was, of course, overjoyed by the news, He knew the heartening effect it would have on American morale and the morale of our Allies, and the blow to the prestige of the Japanese, to have American bombers over Tokyo even for a short, fleeting time. That is why he ordered the raid."[85]

Arnold was correct, for the attack on Tokyo amounted to a significant morale boost to the American people. As Samuel Rosenman emphasized, "the greatest of the propaganda exploits in the dark days of 1942 was the first bomber raid over Tokyo."[86] The Doolittle raid amounted to an early signal that the precision bombing doctrine espoused in the 1930s at the Tactical School would ultimately be ditched in the strategic bombing campaign against Japan. As noted, bombing of the enemy's population was always part of the doctrinal corpus at the Tactical School.

The subject of atrocities committed by the Japanese Imperial Army remained difficult throughout the war because of the American and Allied prisoners being held by the Japanese. This was an issue that always remained uppermost in Arnold's mind.[87] And Roosevelt in 1943 asked the Joint Chiefs for a recommendation as to when the nation might be officially informed "of the mistreatment of our nationals," as related by reports from escaped prisoners.[88] American escapees from Japanese prison camps emphasized that terrible conditions obtained and that over time few prisoners could survive. The Joint Chiefs informed the president on September 22, 1943, that release of such information might well increase the mistreatment of American POWs in Japanese hands. The Chiefs pointed out that it remained difficult to gauge specifically how the Japanese might react to the U.S. release of information obtained from escaped prisoners.[89]

International Red Cross shipments of food and supplies were on the way in September 1943 and the Joint Chiefs informed Roosevelt that no public statements should be made in the near future that might jeopardize the Red Cross mission. Roosevelt however, continued to speak out in general terms about "the systematic torture and murder of civilians," as well as military personnel, by the Japanese.[90] A public protest by the president was viewed as counterproductive in that it might indicate to the Japanese that atrocities were undermining U.S. Army morale.

Fervent over China's military and humanitarian difficulties long before the attack on Pearl Harbor, Roosevelt kept up-to-date on the air war over China and corresponded directly with Maj. Gen. Claire L. Chennault. To Chennault's suggestion on January 26, 1944, that the B-29 Matterhorn project be integrated into Fourteenth Air Force operations,[91] Roosevelt exhibited a characteristic smoothly worded evasion. Indicating that "people here" in Washington required command of the B-29s, the president added that once in China the planes would be assigned to Chennault for operational command. This, of course, never materialized. As to Chennault's recommendation that air attacks on Japanese shipping and air bases be assigned priority over bombing Japan proper, Roosevelt, on March 15, 1944, tried to have it both ways: "You are the Doctor and I approve your treatment. Nevertheless, as a matter perhaps of sentimentality, I have had a hope that we could get at least one bombing expedition against Tokyo before the second anniversary of Doolittle's flight. I really believe that the morale effect would help!"[92] This was characteristic of Roosevelt, for he remained a strong public supporter of strategic bombing throughout the war, a major departure from the American policy of the interwar period. He frequently reiterated his desire to see the Axis powers bombed "heavily and relentlessly ... they have asked for it and they are going to get it." He implored Marshall and Arnold to turn the B-29s loose on the Japanese home islands. There is no doubt that had Roosevelt lived, he would have approved dropping atomic bombs on Japan, consistent with his policy of ending the Pacific war as soon as possible with the least loss of American lives. Throughout the war, the president remained fearful of a long, drawn-out island campaign in the Pacific. He stated that he wanted to avoid a campaign that "would take about fifty years before we got to Japan."[93]

Airmen who discussed war plans and operations with FDR during the war came away impressed. These included not only Arnold and AAF leaders in Washington, but also operational commanders like General George Kenney, who headed the Allied Air Forces in the Southwest Pacific, under MacArthur. Kenney made the trip to Washington several times to meet with the AAF leadership and the Joint Chiefs and each time was afforded an opportunity to discuss operations in the Southwest Pacific with the president. He always found the Commander-in-Chief exceptionally knowledgeable about operations and equipment in the Pacific.[94]

Thus, going into World War II, the Army air arm possessed at least a foundation in both doctrine and technology. Significantly, its aspiration to build a viable air force was supported at the highest level of the U.S. government. In his memoir, Arnold pointed to the importance of the prewar buildup:

> The resourcefulness and energy of our people would have been of little avail against our enemies if the Army Air Forces had not begun preparations for war long before Pearl Harbor. By December 7, 1941, we were in low gear, and were shifting into second. That we were rapidly building up our strength at that time has been erased from the minds of many people by succeeding events. But due in large part to the initiative of our Commander-in-Chief, we did not start this war from scratch. When the conflict was thrust upon us, we were already exploiting our national war resources and we were exploiting them despite handicaps and obstacles.[95]

Arnold, of course, immediately picked up on Roosevelt's drive, crafting plans across the board to implement the building of a major air arm. This task proved to be difficult, featuring complex organizational and planning initiatives. Pre-eminently however, the U.S. Joint Chiefs of Staff, including Arnold, needed to craft a comprehensive strategic plan for the defeat of Japan. This was not a totally new exercise, as strategic planning designed to oppose Japanese moves in the Pacific pre-dated even Billy Mitchell's prognostications of conflict between the U.S. and Japan.

2

Planning for the Defeat of Japan

American war planning designed to oppose Japanese aggression was nothing new. Early in the twentieth century, the Joint Army and Navy Board had promulgated a series of color designations for various countries. Japan was assigned the code color Orange. Over the years, these Orange plans were revised, outlining strategies by which Japan could be defeated. Between the wars the Navy took the lead, with help from Army planners, to evolve theoretical plans to defeat Japan. Despite this early concern about Japan with its threat to American interests, corroborated in the 1930s by virulent Japanese aggression against China, it should be emphasized that Anglo-American planning in World War II rested on the firm, early decision—made in the ABC-1 discussions in January–March 1941, well before the United States entered the war—that Nazi Germany was the main enemy, Europe the decisive theater: "It should be a cardinal principle of American-British strategy that only the minimum of force necessary for the safeguarding of vital interests in other theatres should be diverted from operations against Germany."[1] Thus, the U.S. and British Chiefs of Staff took the view "that Germany is the prime enemy and her defeat is the key to victory. Once Germany is defeated, the collapse of Italy and the defeat of Japan must follow."[2]

In the Pacific, the United States, at least initially, would fight a defensive, holding action against the Japanese. "I am convinced," said Lieutenant General Arnold, "that a blow against Germany is of first importance. The strength of Japan is relative, the strength of Germany is absolute."[3] He felt that the air offensive should quickly be directed against the critical objectives of Germany's internal structure for these reasons:[4] help the Soviets by diverting German air strength; support the invasion of the Continent; impair Germany's ability to wage war by striking her industry and communications; and protect the "only existing base from which we can launch air or ground attacks directly against Germany." Precision daylight bombing, according to Arnold, "as planned by the Eighth Air Force and which it is equipped and trained for, can be estimated conservatively as having twice the effectiveness of the broad, area-target, night bombing for which the RAF is equipped and trained."[5] He firmly believed (and Spaatz and Eaker concurred) that German morale could be broken with the result that Allied troops would have a comparatively easy time applying the final touch. After Germany fell, Japan could be knocked out without great difficulty.[6] Considering Allied global requirements, U.S. air leaders realized that a simultaneous air campaign against Germany and Japan would be impossible. On May 6, 1942, President Roosevelt reiterated the over-arching Allied strategy of a defensive holding operation in the Pacific, emphasizing that this was the responsibility of the United States. The exceptions to this defensive posture, according to Roosevelt, were interdiction of Japanese lines of communications and the bombing of Japan's home islands. Here it is appropriate to note the JCS-approved strategy of the Pacific war that has been described as "island hopping," with Army ground forces, Navy, and Marine forces taking the lead. MacArthur and FDR, however, had a most willing collaborator in Hap Arnold. Early in the war, Arnold had been quick to recognize the importance of combining surface action with air strength in order to "apply direct pressure" against Japan. Arnold emphasized to the president that in his view the strategic plan was to capture bases "from which air power can hit at the heart of Japan." The advancing of bases, according to Arnold, "must be relentless and must be limited only by the availability of forces not required to crush Germany."[7] Here Arnold emphasized the approved strategy of defeating Germany first. He realized, he informed Roosevelt, "the drain of this plan on the Nation's productive capacity, but I have every confidence in it."[8] It was important to destroy more enemy ships and planes than the Japanese could replace. The president stressed that "combat against Japanese ships and planes must be sought out in order to hasten the attrition of Japanese arms."[9] It was also important to keep as many Japanese forces as possible occupied in China. Roosevelt's emphasis on bombing the Japanese home islands should be noted here; he kept coming back to it throughout the war, up until his death in April 1945. Although he did not live to witness the surrender of either Germany or Japan, he did indicate his satisfaction with the incendiary bombing of Japan, which commenced with the massive attack on Tokyo on March 9–10, 1945.

Almost simultaneously with the president's direction, the United States fought two naval and air battles in the Pacific in May and June 1942 that began to turn the tide against the Japanese. The Battle of the Coral Sea, May 7–8, 1942, was a conflict between American and Japanese carrier planes. In this action, the U.S. Navy suffered losses of more than sixty planes, a carrier, a destroyer, and a tanker. Naval aviators, however, sank a light carrier and damaged a large carrier, resulting in the Japanese aborting plans to attack Port Moresby.

Immediately following the Coral Sea struggle, decoded Japanese message traffic indicated plans to assault Midway Island, thus extending the Japanese defensive perimeter. Adm. Chester W. Nimitz, Commander-in-Chief, Pacific, directed three carriers, plus B-17s and B-26s of the Seventh Air Force, all under Navy command, to oppose the Japanese force in the Battle of Midway, June 3–6, 1942. The land-based Seventh Air Force planes did little damage to the enemy warships, but Navy dive bombers put three Japanese carriers out of action in just three minutes on June 4. Later the same day, Navy aircraft took out a fourth enemy carrier and on June 6 they sank a cruiser. U.S. forces lost the carrier *Yorktown*, but the defeat of the Japanese fleet at Midway proved crucial, for the enemy could not replace these staggering losses in both warships and pilots.

Nonetheless, in the wake of Midway, on July 16, 1942, in the face of renewed pressure from the Joint Chiefs, especially Admiral King, the president stated unequivocally his opposition to an "all-out effort against Japan."[10] Until the defeat of Germany was accomplished, U.S. planners were to hold the objective of maintaining defensive pressure on Japan. After Germany's defeat, the Joint Chiefs would look to a full-scale offensive against Japan, culminating in an invasion of the home islands: "Since the invasion of Japan is a vast undertaking, it should not be attempted until Japanese power and will to resist have been so reduced that favorable conditions for invasion obtain. Under these conditions the invasion of Japan is considered feasible." Prior to an invasion, it would be necessary to conduct what the Joint Chiefs termed "an overwhelming air offensive against Japan."[11] As seen in the spring of 1943, this would of necessity materialize ultimately from bases in China.

Japanese war planning, on the other hand, did not envision a long, total war calling for a limited conflict with the United States. Consequently, the war against the United States evolved into something far different from these assumptions of Japan's war planners. Contrariwise, the United States and its allies declared total, unlimited war on its enemies in Europe and the Pacific. Japan thought that America ultimately would accept a war with limited aims in the Pacific and come to terms. As it turned out, the Japanese made a fateful mistake. Japan attacked the United States bereft of any plan to end the war. Some Japanese officials however, entertained the idea that if the U.S. suffered great casualties, Japan could negotiate a peace allowing it to retain its far-flung conquests. In fact, some within the Japanese government thought that Japan should aim for early peace negotiations while it was winning the war. This proved unrealistic for two reasons: Japan's string of early military successes, which dictated continuing aggression; and the U.S. and Allied insistence on unconditional surrender, pursued without revision throughout the war. The original Japanese plan would have permitted Japan to maintain a defensive perimeter around conquered territories, providing her the resources to become self-sufficient. However, unless the Japanese could negotiate during the first two years of war and the longer the conflict dragged on, the less chance for success, dependent upon maintaining effective transportation and lines of communication. As time went on, the U.S. and the Allies pushed the Japanese perimeter backward, confirming the worst fears of some Japanese that the Empire was overextended.

While it intensified efforts to sustain England with the tools of war, the Roosevelt administration was well aware of the threat to American interests posed by Japan in the Pacific. In the summer of 1941, the Far Eastern situation had turned ever more dangerous. The Japanese had moved south, occupying French Indochina. As a result, the administration placed a freeze on Japanese assets in the United States, in effect creating an economic blockade of Japan. Also, the need for improved air defenses in Hawaii and the Philippines was in fact a requirement of exceptionally long standing and had been emphasized by Brig. Gen. William "Billy" Mitchell in his 1924 report on his Far Eastern trip. Mitchell suggested that it seemed inevitable that at some point in the future Japan and the United States would be at war with each other.[12]

Japanese aggression in East Asia and the worsening diplomatic situation in 1941 between the U.S. and Japan prompted Stimson to warn that "all practical steps" needed to be taken to increase defensive strength in Hawaii and the Philippines. Stimson was also much concerned about a secret letter he had received in early 1941 from Secretary of the Navy Frank Knox, who pointed out that the Navy had re-examined the security of the Pacific fleet at Pearl Harbor. Knox emphasized "the increased gravity of the situation with respect to Japan and by reports from abroad of successful bombing and torpedo plane attacks on ships while in bases." Knox added: "If war eventuates with Japan, it is believed easily possible that hostilities would be initiated by a surprise attack upon the fleet and the naval base at Pearl Harbor."[13] And, after the victory at Midway in June 1942, the U.S. Joint Chiefs of Staff directed Adm. Chester Nimitz, in the Pacific Ocean Areas, and Gen. Douglas MacArthur, in the Southwest Pacific, to conduct limited offensive action. This marked a departure from the Anglo-American decision made in the ABC-1 discussions to contain the Japanese until the defeat of Germany became imminent.

Early in the war, Arnold was already becoming frustrated over what he considered a lack of understanding about what air power could accomplish. To Harry Hopkins, on July 15, 1942, he reiterated the fundamental principles of air warfare: First, that critical objectives be selected only after deliberate study including intensive review of intelligence data on targeting. Second, he emphasized that air forces be employed massively, with "determined persistence" until the objectives were destroyed. Air forces had been dispersed rather than concentrated and consequently, air power had not been properly used against the Axis powers. The major problem, as Arnold viewed it, was "multiple military command," a lack of unity of command. He recommended appointment of an American as Supreme Commander of the Armed Forces of the United Nations. The Supreme Commander and staff "must have undisputed authority to determine objectives, select theaters, and to dispose and to control" the operations of the UN forces.[14]

The JCS directive for unified command for U.S. Joint Operations described it as

> that command organization in which a force composed of units of the Army and of the Navy operates as a single command unit under an officer specifically assigned by higher authority to the command thereof.

> A commander for U.S. Joint Operations, with appropriate title, is designated by and is responsible to the Joint Chiefs of Staff. His selection from the ground or air arm of the Army, or from the Navy by the Joint Chiefs of Staff will be guided by the nature of the contemplated operation and by the end to be attained.

> When the Joint Force Commander has been designated and the units composing his force assigned, his command responsibilities are the same as if the forces involved were all Army or all Navy. He will exercise his command of the Army and Navy forces assigned, through the commanders of these forces or of the task forces concerned.[15]

Arnold had long fought for unified command in the Pacific. Among the Joint Chiefs, Arnold stood out in 1942 as a blunt voice calling for unified command in the Pacific. With his strong views, he went directly to Marshall, who also wanted to establish a truly unified command, preferably under an Army overall commander, if not in the entire Pacific, at the least in the South and Southwest Pacific. In the autumn of 1942, Arnold

—back from an inspection trip in the Pacific—informed Marshall that Army forces in the South and Southwest Pacific could only be "properly employed" under an overall commander for the Pacific theater. Moreover, the AAF commander emphasized that the theater commander should be an Army officer, since the Navy "had not demonstrated its ability to properly conduct air operations," especially land-based operations. Also, the Navy's logistics operations had not properly supplied the Army's operations "and as a consequence operations to date have lacked continuity by reason of the shortage of essential supplies and installations to support military operations."[16] To Marshall, Arnold recommended three Army officers who, in his judgment, could properly exercise theater command: MacArthur, Lt. Gen. Joseph T. McNarney, and Lt. Gen. Leslie J. McNair.[17] Arnold's thoughts here reflected what he had heard from airmen on his trip to the Pacific as well as from a lengthy visit with MacArthur in Brisbane in September 1942. MacArthur's biographer, D. Clayton James, noted that Arnold's opinions were "strikingly similar" to MacArthur's own. Nonetheless, James noted: "Unity of command was never to be achieved in the Pacific, but if MacArthur learned of Arnold's support of him … it must have been of some consolation to the troubled SWPA commander during this critical period. Of course, he probably wondered why Arnold would have nominated McNarney and McNair also."[18]

Marshall, in turn, asked the War Department's Operations Division to consider Arnold's ideas. Gen. Albert Wedemeyer stated that such a theater commander must come "from that service which will exercise the strongest influence in the consummation of our plans for the entire area."[19] Wedemeyer suggested General Arnold. Brig. Gen. St. Clair Streett, Chief of the Theater group in the Operations Division, concluded that General MacArthur was the major problem to a "sane" military solution. He suggested appointing MacArthur ambassador to the Soviet Union, replacing him with Gen. Robert L. Eichelberger, and combining the South and Southwest Pacific under Nimitz or McNarney.[20] No action was taken on Streett's suggestion. In October 1942, Marshall recommended to Roosevelt that the South and Southwest Pacific should be unified, but the question was not presented at this time to the Joint Chiefs.

Arnold saw himself in a running battle with the Navy throughout the Pacific war. And yet at times when he seemed really literally to explode, he would have the opportunity to meet with Nimitz and the admiral would calm the air chief's fears. Arnold, especially later in the war, came to realize that not all his control and supply difficulties could be laid at the Navy's door. At heart however, Arnold could not overcome his feeling that the Navy, with its rigid procedures, would not allow sufficient flexibility to Army units in the Pacific. Arnold spelled out his view in detail:

> There was no doubt, the Navy was following out its approved policy with regard to the Pacific. Accordingly, we had to accept Navy control, command, and administration, when from a cold-blooded point of view, from a paramount interest point of view, and from the operational point of view, the Army should have had full control of some of the islands. Another thing—the War Department, for many years, had seemed to have the attitude that we shouldn't try to obtain unification of command in the Pacific. We must not bring the facts out squarely. We must not get the Navy mad at us right now. We must accept things as they were, even though we thought a change might be for the best; and we must not criticize the Navy. So we continued operating in our inefficient way, with first three, then two commands—MacArthur's and Nimitz'—both working toward the same end—the defeat of Japan, with overlapping lines of communication, overlapping air operations, overlapping sea operations, and finally, overlapping land Army operations.[21]

In the Pacific, where unified command was never established—Nimitz and MacArthur each conducting their campaigns—no final strategic calculus was determined. In addition to the two primary offensives conducted by Nimitz and MacArthur, the naval blockade and the strategic air bombardment of Japan were prosecuted until the dropping of the atomic bombs in August 1945. Importantly, both politically and militarily, the Joint Chiefs and the Combined Chiefs of Staff crafted into their strategy for the defeat of Japan, the planning for invasion of the Japanese homeland. These decisions during 1941–1945 paved the way in the summer of 1945 for the race to force Japan's surrender prior to the Kyushu invasion scheduled for November 1, 1945.

Roosevelt and Churchill had agreed in January 1943 at the Casablanca conference that a policy of "unconditional surrender" of Japan would be vigorously pursued. Indeed, the term itself was first used publicly by the president at Casablanca. Roosevelt had asked the press to describe Casablanca as the "unconditional surrender conference." He subsequently stated: "We mean no harm to the common people of the Axis nations. But we do mean to impose punishment and retribution in full upon their guilty, barbaric leaders." This policy, Roosevelt emphasized, "is precisely the same as our policy toward our Nazi enemies; it is a policy of fighting hard on all fronts and ending the war as quickly as we can on the uncompromising terms of unconditional surrender."[22] The president's announced policy came as a surprise to Secretary of State Cordell Hull who was opposed to it: "it might prolong the war by solidifying Axis resistance into one of desperation."[23] In early April, the Joint Chiefs clarified Allied strategic objectives as outlined at Casablanca. This "clarification" called for maintaining and extending "unremitting pressure" against Japan and in cooperation with allies, and possibly Russia, "to combine the full resources of the United States and Great Britain to force the unconditional surrender of Japan."[24] As was the case with President Roosevelt's use of the term "unconditional surrender" at Casablanca, in this statement of the Joint Chiefs there was no clear definition of the term. At Casablanca, the Combined Chiefs had "noted" that the defeat of Japan would be accomplished by methods that resembled those that might be effective against the British Isles: "blockade (attack on ships and shipping), bombing (attack on forces, defenses, industries, and morale), and assault (attack via the sea)." The CCS also noted that "it is our purpose during 1943 to work toward positions from which Japan can be attacked by land based air; assault on Japan is remote and may well not be found necessary."[25] In addition to Roosevelt's intense interest in supplying the British and Chinese and keeping them engaged in the war, there is another strain in his early thinking. In the period between his call for enormous aircraft production in

November 1938 and the Casablanca conference in January 1943, Roosevelt consistently made clear his desire to bomb Japan. At Casablanca, he emphasized the importance of deploying more planes to China and suggested to the Joint Chiefs of Staff that for psychological reasons it would be advisable to double General Chennault's force in China and also to bomb Japan proper. At a plenary session with Prime Minister Churchill, Roosevelt again brought up the subject of sustaining the Chinese war effort. He also made the point that an island-to-island campaign across the Pacific would be excessively time consuming. An offensive against Japanese shipping would go a long way toward reducing Japan's power. In addition to submarine operations, aircraft could be based in China or India to strike enemy shipping and also conduct attacks on Japan.[26]

The British were not especially concerned about more planes for China. Although the desire to send more planes to China was an issue for the Americans, Churchill endorsed the idea, in support of Roosevelt. Churchill was not about to get contentious over an issue that he knew FDR felt strongly about. Both Arnold and King thought along the same lines as Roosevelt. Arnold proposed sending more aircraft to Chennault and preparing to start a bombing offense against the Japanese home islands from bases in China and the Maritime Provinces. He was, however, concerned about major logistical difficulties attendant on maintaining more planes in China. Admiral King supported the concept of additional planes to China as part of the overall strategy for defeating Japan. On January 23, 1943, the final report of the Casablanca conference by the Combined Chiefs to Roosevelt and Churchill included a statement of principle supporting a buildup of U.S. air elements in China: "In order to ... strike at Japan herself when opportunity offers ... we hope that more sustained operations with increased Air Forces may begin in the spring (1943), and we regard this development as of great importance in the general scheme."[27]

Arnold had thought about the role of the strategic air forces in forcing the defeat of Japan. Even prior to securing B-29 bases in the Marianas, he had envisioned a phase of intensive air bombardment and sea and air blockade against Japan prior to an invasion of the home islands, "should that prove to be necessary." Arnold was thinking of "selected elements of Japanese industry," which would undermine the Japanese war machine until it was fatally weakened. This selective bombing doctrine had not only been studied at the Tactical School, but Arnold had likely spent some time with it when attending the Industrial College. Arnold pointed to the work of the Committee of Operations Analysts (COA), which he had established in December 1942, to formulate target lists for strategic bombardment. The Committee of Operations Analysts, reporting directly to Arnold, comprised representatives from the several military services, civilian agencies, and also a number of special consultants. This committee had been influential in 1943 in evolving target sets in Europe for the Combined Bomber Offensive. On March 13, 1943, Arnold directed the COA to analyze potential strategic targets in Japan, the destruction of which would force Japan to capitulate. The COA, in its report of November 11, 1943, described six preferred target systems: Merchant shipping, steel production, urban industrial areas vulnerable to incendiary bombing, aircraft manufacturing, anti-friction bearing industry, and the electronics industry. Two-thirds of Japanese steel was produced from coke coming from ovens in Kyushu, Manchuria, and Korea. Japan's steel industry was considered a critical target.[28]

Perhaps most interesting was the attention given by the committee to incendiary bombing of Japanese cities, a subject that in fact had been studied at the Tactical School prior to the war. The committee noted that less than 2000 tons of incendiaries dropped within critical areas of twenty cities would result in uncontrollable conflagrations in each of the urban areas. This, according to Arnold, contrasted with the Royal Air Force's attacks on Hamburg, Germany, where it took almost 5000 tons of incendiaries and a similar weight of high explosive bombs to destroy seventy percent of the city. The vulnerability of Japanese cities, compared to Germany's, was due to building materials and the congested nature of Japan's urban centers. Arnold also pointed to Japan's so-called "cottage industry," dispersed shops pock-marking the urban areas. The Japanese cities, Arnold emphasized, were "profitable targets, not only because they are greatly congested, but because they contain numerous war industries, large and small, particularly vulnerable to fire. The Japanese have adopted a widespread practice of sub-contracting to many small handicraft and domestic establishments." Also, Arnold noted Japan's industrial isolation, cut off from other industrial countries. Germany, on the other hand, could make up for critical shortages by tapping into industries in Sweden, Switzerland, Italy, Czechoslovakia, and France.[29]

In mid-May 1943, the Combined Chiefs approved a JCS memorandum stating that upon the conclusion of the war in Europe, the United States and Britain, along with other Pacific nations and possibly Russia, would direct their full resources to force an unconditional surrender of Japan. However, if "conditions develop which indicate that the war as a whole can be brought more quickly to a successful conclusion by the earlier mounting of a major offensive against Japan," then present strategical concepts might have to be reconsidered. Here, in the spring of 1943, the Joint Chiefs and the Combined Chiefs were counting on conducting "an overwhelming bombing offensive against Japan" from bases in China. Describing a potential invasion of Japan as "a vast undertaking," they noted that "it should not be attempted until Japanese power and will to resist" have been reduced sufficiently to produce favorable conditions. It was deemed "probable that the reduction of Japan's power and will to resist may only be accomplished by a sustained, systematic, and large-scale air offensive against Japan itself."[30]

In August 1943, at the QUADRANT conference in Quebec, the Combined Chiefs stated the objective of defeating Japan within twelve months of Germany's surrender. By late December 1943, the Combined Chiefs were still considering that an invasion might not be necessary, but at the same time vowed to press ahead with potentially intensive air bombardment and sea and air blockade. They looked forward to the defeat of Germany and to very long strategic bombing operations against Japan by the new B-29s, an intensive study of which was now underway to determine "the best employment of the B-29 aircraft against Japan."[31]

As noted, the "Air Plan for the Defeat of Japan," introduced by Arnold at QUADRANT in August 1943, discussed the eventual employment of the long-range B-29s. This was the first time that such a plan had been submitted to the Combined Chiefs of Staff. It concluded that "The destruction of Japanese resources to such a point that the enemy's capacity for effective armed resistance is substantially exhausted can be accomplished by sustained bombing operations of 10–20 B-29 groups based in an area of unoccupied China within 1500 miles of the center of the Japanese industrial zone."[32] The plan assumed that Germany would collapse in the autumn of 1944 and consequently planning for Japan's defeat should aim for a period within twelve months of Germany's surrender. The strategic bombing campaign against Japan should thus start not later than the fall of 1944. The question of potential bases for the B-29s was critical. The probability of gaining bases in Siberia was discounted and it was assumed that island bases in the Pacific would not be available in 1944 or early 1945, thus, the concentration on potential bases in China.

In this plan presented at QUADRANT, the AAF sketched out a potential B-29 bombing offensive between October 1944 and April 1945 that would "accomplish the destruction of selected strategic Japanese industrial systems, including aircraft factories and shipyards." Between May and August 1945, a sustained attack on additional objectives would bring about "the destruction of Japanese resources which are an essential preliminary to an occupation of the Japanese homeland by United Nations forces." Air planners believed that such a campaign would strengthen the Chinese military effort and "bring about a decisive defeat of Japan within twelve months after the defeat of the Axis powers in Europe." The role of American air power in supporting Chiang Kai-shek was something that President Roosevelt was intent on promoting.

The Joint Staff planners, as well as the British, harbored serious reservations about the plan, centering on logistical difficulties. Subsequently however, General Stilwell—who himself doubted the plan—forwarded an alternative written by Maj. Gen. George E. Stratemeyer, Stilwell's air deputy in the China-Burma-India theater. The Combined Chiefs directed their planners to look into the feasibility of Stratemeyer's option, which called for B-29s to be maintained at secure rear bases in the Calcutta, India, area. Bombs and supplies for the bases in China would be hauled by converted B-24s and C-54s.

Stratemeyer's plan, with slight modifications, was presented to the Joint War Plans Committee in October 1943. Air planners noted that the strategic bombing offensive from China would "constitute the major United Nations air offensive in the period immediately following the defeat of Germany, unless relations between Russia and Japan alter. Strategic and transport air forces required can be provided, the logistic needs come within the capacity of the facilities available, and the operations contemplated would contribute heavily to accelerating the collapse of Japan." The plan estimated that twenty-eight groups of B-29s would be operating by August 1945. This meant that additional bases would be required in the Pacific, within range of the Japanese homeland. At QUADRANT, planning had moved forward for occupation of the Mariana Islands by the close of 1944 to secure bases for the long-range bombers. It was possible that this schedule might be accelerated.

In late 1943, Arnold's air planners intensified their interest in the Marianas, recommending to the Joint War Plans Committee that the Marianas should be taken as early as possible, "with the establishment of heavy bomber bases as the primary mission." At the same time, it should be noted that the air planners emphasized that these strategic bomber forces, no matter where based, would require "cohesive over-all control." This command and control concept was directly in line with Arnold's thinking. The historian of the Joint Chiefs of Staff wrote that "Like the Navy, the Air Forces did not look with favor upon dispersing their components under a variety of unsympathetic commands."[33]

Meanwhile, the air planners modified Stratemeyer's plan, which was code-named "Twilight." In late 1943, they submitted to the Joint Staff planners the concept to attack Japan's coke industry to curtail the enemy's steel production. The B-29s would operate from the Chengtu, China, area, within the B-29 radius of the targets. These "limited" operations, combined with strikes against other critical resources, "may well accelerate the collapse of that country." As mentioned, Roosevelt was intensely interested in this project, and he asked Churchill to intercede with India in order "to render every possible assistance" to building bases in the Calcutta area. The president also asked Chiang Kai-shek to provide labor and materials for the Chengtu bases, while the U.S. provided funds under the lend-lease program.[34] In late 1943, the Joint Chiefs noted that the bases should be completed not later than May 1944 and at the SEXTANT conference the Combined Chiefs agreed to expedite construction. Still, at SEXTANT in late 1943, the Combined Chiefs emphasized that an invasion of the Japanese home islands would be necessary to force an unconditional surrender. It was doubtful, the CCS noted, that this could be accomplished by the fall of 1945. And despite obvious logistical difficulties, Brig. Gen. Haywood S. Hansell informed the Joint planners that the B-29 could be maintained in China and that he was not sure that an invasion was necessary to accomplish Japan's defeat.

Planning for the defeat of Japan accelerated in December 1943 when the "Overall Plan for the Defeat of Japan" was approved at the SEXTANT Conference in Cairo and remained the basic plan for the rest of the Pacific war. The Combined Chiefs agreed that the major effort against Japan should be made in the Pacific as opposed to the Asian mainland, specifically China and Burma. They also reiterated that Japan should be defeated within twelve months after the defeat of Germany. During 1944, however, Army planners were convinced that an invasion of Japan would be necessary. In March 1944, the Joint Chiefs of Staff (JCS) issued directions to General MacArthur to advance toward the southern Philippines and to Admiral Nimitz to move to the Marianas and Palaus, pointing toward an operation in the Formosa-Luzon area by February 1945. On April 24, 1944, War Department planners emphasized the necessity of an invasion: "The collapse of Japan as a result of blockade and air bombardment alone is very doubtful. The collapse of Japan can be assured only by invasion of Japan proper."[35]

General Arnold's staff vigorously opposed the view that Japan could be defeated only by invasion. The AAF argued that the potential effects of blockade and strategic air bombardment could force the enemy's collapse. Nonetheless, the Joint War Plans Committee on June 6, 1944, promulgated a study emphasizing a series of campaigns leading to an invasion of the Tokyo Plain by the close of 1945. This study noted that while blockade and bombing would have a "considerable effect" on the ability of Japan to continue the war, "there is little reason to believe that such action alone is certain to result in the early unconditional surrender of Japan." The study, however, went on to note that although it was possible that bombing and blockade could defeat Japan, it would probably involve "an unacceptable delay."[36] Thus, the crux of the problem was laid bare. The *quickest* way to force a surrender was by invasion of the Japanese homeland. This conclusion primarily reflected the view of General Marshall and the Army staff and it was maintained until July 1945 when several factors cast doubt on it.

In late 1944, the tide having turned in Europe, the American military turned its attention to planning for the defeat of Japan. The momentous question of how to decisively crush Japan involved politics, resources, strategy, logistics, and the ever-present issues of command and organization. Planning in 1944 and 1945 brought out divergent approaches among the Army, the Army Air Forces (AAF) and the Navy. To further complicate military planning, a major new factor appeared in late 1944 and 1945: the inception of the long-range B-29 bombing campaign against the Japanese home islands. By the end of 1944, War Department planning had crystallized around the necessity, as General Marshall put it, "to invade the industrial heart of Japan." At the OCTAGON conference in Quebec in September 1944, the Combined Chiefs had formally approved for planning purposes the invasion of Kyushu in October 1945 and the Tokyo Plain in December 1945. At this conference the Combined Chiefs of Staff re-stated their strategic concept and overall objective for the defeat of Japan. The Allies would "maintain and extend unremitting pressure against Japan with the purpose of continually reducing her military power and attaining positions from which her ultimate surrender can be forced." During the war, this or similar quotations are written repeatedly into plans by the Joint Chiefs at various junctures. Such repetition of the exact phrasing indicates that JCS had not and would not revise their determination to force an unconditional surrender of Japan. The exact phrasing throughout the war is very important. Sea and air blockades would be established and an "intensive" air bombardment campaign would be prosecuted along with "ultimately invading and seizing objectives in the industrial heart of Japan."[37] Along with Arnold and the Air Staff, King and Leahy went along with planning for invasion, but they viewed it more as contingency planning. Like Arnold, Admiral King saw a potential invasion of southern Kyushu as an opportunity to gain naval and air bases to intensify the blockade and bombing. Similarly, in 1944 Arnold strongly supported King and Nimitz in their push to capture islands in the Marianas that would be used to base B-29s.[38]

Meanwhile, Hansell was preparing to start B-29 operations from the Marianas. Perhaps with this in mind, among other things, the Combined Chiefs at OCTAGON emphasized that planning should feature flexibility with an eye to taking full advantage of strategic developments "which may permit taking all manner of short cuts. We propose to exploit to the fullest the Allied superiority of naval and air power and to avoid, wherever possible, commitment to costly land campaigns." The striking words, "taking all manner of short cuts," led the Combined Chiefs to note the importance of continuing submarine warfare and very long-range bomber operations from bases in China. However, they also noted that B-29 operations would soon begin against Japan proper from bases in the Marianas. The Combined Chiefs also stated that every effort should be made to bring the Soviet Union into the war against Japan "at the earliest practicable date." At ARGONAUT at Malta-Yalta, in January–February 1945, Marshall and King approved a planning paper stating the objective of forcing the unconditional surrender of Japan by sea and air blockade, intensive air blockade, and bombardment, the destruction of enemy air and naval strength, and finally, an invasion of the industrial center of Japan.[39]

In March 1945, top-level Army planners continued to believe that an invasion would be required in two stages: the invasion of Kyushu (OLYMPIC) by December 1, 1945, and an invasion of the Tokyo Plain (CORONET), March 1, 1946. However, the planners thought it critical to intensify the blockade and bombardment so that massive ground forces would not be sent ashore prior to prosecuting the full weight of the naval and air campaigns. At the same time, as noted, AAF and Navy leaders thought that the air and naval campaigns could force Japan's surrender. Arnold and the AAF at this time pointed to the shattering success of the March 9–10, 1945, attack on Tokyo by B-29s, the most destructive air attack of the war. This divergence of opinion as to whether an invasion would be required was highlighted in early 1945 by a study of the Joint Intelligence Committee, which noted that although Japan's "will" to continue might be broken by air and sea blockade along with strategic bombing,

> The Japanese "will" to continue the war maybe expected to weaken progressively. Entirely apart from the physical results obtained by air-sea blockade combined with strategic bombing, the psychological effects upon the Japanese people as a whole will be most detrimental and will progressively undermine their confidence in victory or even confidence in the hope of avoiding complete and inevitable defeat. Thus we believe that under the full impact of air-sea blockade combined with strategic bombing, Japan's "will" to continue the war can be broken.[40]

The problem, according to the Intelligence Committee, remained that it was not possible to determine whether an unconditional surrender might occur within a reasonable length of time. "Estimates," it noted, "vary from a few months to a great many years."[41] In June 1945, the Joint Chiefs of Staff directed MacArthur, Nimitz, and Arnold to plan for "potential favorable circumstances," such as a sudden collapse or surrender of Japan.

At Potsdam in July 1945 (TERMINAL Conference), planning for the defeat of Japan centered on the Kyushu and Honshu invasions. The "overall strategic concept" was described as follows:

> In cooperation with other Allies to bring about at the earliest possible date the defeat of Japan by: lowering Japanese ability and will to resist by establishing sea and air blockades, conducting intensive air bombardment, and destroying Japanese air and naval strength; invading and seizing objectives in the Japanese home islands as the main effort. ... The invasion of Japan and operations directly connected therewith are the supreme operations in the war against Japan.[42]

Prosecuting the B-29 offensive from the Ryukyus as well as the Marianas, Arnold noted, could achieve disruption of the Japanese military, industrial, and economic systems before the planned invasion. Japan, Arnold insisted, would "become a nation without cities, with her transportation disrupted and will have tremendous difficulty in holding her people together for continued resistance to our terms of unconditional surrender."[43]

In his own mind, although Arnold did not attend the Tactical School, he saw the potential success of the B-29 campaign in knocking Japan out of the war as the ultimate fulfillment of the strategic concept of defeating a nation without having to employ a ground invasion. The lifeblood systems and the morale of a modern, industrial nation could be shattered to the point of total collapse. The initial major task however, was to get the B-29 operational and deployed to the Pacific.

3

Arnold Forms the Twentieth Air Force

During the war, no other project exemplified Arnold's determination and drive like the B-29 and his concerted attempt to make the revolutionary big bomber operational in the Pacific. He was determined to employ the Superfortress against the Japanese homeland, thus writing "a new chapter in the history of the Army Air Forces." The B-29 program has been called the greatest gamble of the war, greater than the Manhattan project that developed the atomic bomb, an investment of $3 billion compared to $2 billion for the bomb. Here Arnold enjoyed the firm support of President Roosevelt who during 1943 promised Premier Chiang Kai-shek of China that the long-range B-29s would be deployed to China to undertake the bombing of Japan.

The development of the B-29 strategic bomber began prior to World War II and continued during the war under the so-called Very Long Range (VLR) project. The grave difficulties experienced by the Army Air Forces in the development and production of this revolutionary aircraft, together with Arnold's own iron determination to deploy this weapon against Japan, are the keys to understanding Arnold's insistence that it was not necessary to drop the atomic bomb. Arnold, as Chief of the Army Air Corps, initiated the B-29 development program on November 10, 1939, two months after Nazi Germany's invasion of Poland. Arnold's move came in response to a recommendation of the Kilner Board to request authority of the War Department to let contracts to develop a four-engine bomber superior in range, speed, and bomb load to the B-17 and the B-24. Boeing's design for the XB-29 was judged to be superior by the Air Corps, and the XB-29 contract was let in September 1940.[1] On October 17, 1940, Arnold wrote to Louis Johnson, the Assistant Secretary of War, that the B-29 was the only weapon with which the Army Air Forces "could hope to exert pressure against Japan without long and costly preliminary operations."[2]

Beginning in November 1939, thus began four years of frustration in engineering, testing, and production, during which a number of AAF leaders doubted that the program would succeed. Although the first production models were completed in July 1943, severe problems would be encountered well into 1944. Arnold took the risk of cutting developmental and procurement corners in order to accelerate production. Under increasing pressure from Roosevelt and Marshall to deploy and produce results quickly, Arnold ordered the new bomber into production before it had been properly tested. He directed that the experimental and production phases be simultaneously carried out. Even so, planning called for the first experimental B-29 to fly in 1941, but major problems delayed the initial flight until September 1942. One of the most serious difficulties with the entire project was the acute lack of machine tools. Arnold emphasized that everything about the B-29 project was new, untried: "Few aircraft developed by the aviation industry and the AAF ever posed more problems than the B-29." The pressure of time was enormous. This meant tamping down "second-guessing and redesign." He informed Maj. Gen. Kenneth B. Wolfe that speed was imperative. Wolfe went about working the "bugs out" simultaneously with production and training.[3]

Some officers in the Air Corps Materiel Division doubted that the radical project would succeed. General Wolfe, chief of B-29 development and subsequently the first commander of the XX Bomber command, noted in retrospect that "within the Air Force itself there were certain people who didn't think that we should spend our time and effort on a bomber that far advanced."[4] The B-29 was the first super-charged bomber and the first with automatic fire control. There were officers in the Production Engineering Division at Wright Field who remembered their experience with the B-26 medium bomber. Its high wing loading ratio led them to believe that the B-29 might be dangerously heavy for the wing area. A committee, including Generals George C. Kenney and Wolfe, and other technical and materiel experts at Wright Field, concluded that no design change needed to be made.[5]

It took all of Arnold's determination and daring—and the firing of some key officers—to drive the B-29 program to completion. As Maj. Gen. Lauris Norstad described it: "Arnold's life was that B-29 ... he was into every damn detail of that B-29."[6] Several special plants were built for the production of the gigantic bombers with their three-story tail assemblies and 2,200-horsepower Wright Cyclone R-3350 turbo-supercharged engines. Among other firsts that the Superfortress featured were a radar navigation system and pressurized crew compartments. The Army Air Corps originally planned to buy 250 B-29s, but after the Japanese attack on Pearl Harbor, the order increased to 500 and, following a February 10, 1942, production meeting in Detroit, to more than 1,600. This meeting marked the formation of the B-29 Liaison Committee, headed by Wolfe, who was to become the key official in the developmental program and in 1944 would lead the B-29 into combat from Chinese bases in Operation Matterhorn.

For more than two years following the Detroit meeting, grave difficulties were encountered in the VLR program, prompting some to call it "the three-billion-dollar gamble." Between September and December 1942, test flights indicated trouble with the aircraft's engines, which frequently failed or caught fire.[7] On February 18, 1943, disaster struck. With Boeing test pilot Edmund T. Allen at the controls, two engine fires broke out during a test flight from Seattle, the fire spreading into a wing. This second prototype plane crashed into a meat-packing plant three miles from the end of the Boeing runway, killing Allen, his entire crew of ten, nineteen people in the building, and one fireman. Investigations ordered by Arnold and Harry Truman (at the time a U.S. Senator) determined that the engines were defective and that the manufacturer's quality control was unsatisfactory. This shocking development resulted in Arnold's creation of the B-29 Special Project, under Wolfe and Col. Leonard Harman, to supervise all testing, training, and production. Incredibly, a third prototype almost crashed because of crossed aileron control cables, another disaster and the potential end of the program barely being averted. Arnold however, was not about to be deterred: "We could not and must not be stopped in our production."[8] As noted, Arnold figured that the B-29 could best be used against Japan and he thought that one hundred of them could be ready by January 1944. He was determined to surprise the Japanese:

> If these airplanes are first employed against targets other than against Japan, the surprise element will be lost; and the Japs will take the necessary actions to neutralize potential useable bases and secure additional bases in China that will prevent the operation of these airplanes against Japan, until the all-out attack is made.[9]

As mentioned in the previous chapter, President Roosevelt was as determined as Arnold to bomb Japan, expressing a revulsion at the Japanese behavior in China even before the attack on Pearl Harbor. Secretary of State Cordell Hull subsequently suggested that Tokyo be bombed from the Aleutian islands. In January 1943, at the Casablanca conference, the British and Americans discussed the bombing of Japan. Here General Marshall put forward the opinion that Japanese industry was "so vulnerable to the air that heavy attack would destroy her capacity to maintain her war effort."[10] Roosevelt certainly agreed, pointing out the positive effect on Chinese morale. At Casablanca, the president specifically suggested basing bombers in India and refueling them in China. Marshall emphasized the supply problem and the enormous expense involved. Roosevelt, however, insisted and informed Chiang Kai-shek that he would send General Arnold to Chungking to discuss the matter. In the China-Burma-India (CBI) theater, Stilwell and Chennault argued over whether to emphasize bombing Japan from Chinese bases, as Stilwell advocated, or to focus upon tactical air operations against Japanese forces in China, proposed by Chennault. The president supported Chennault, directing an increase in the airlift over "the Hump."

Although, as noted, the first objective of the Allies was the defeat of Nazi Germany, the U.S. and Britain pledged "to maintain and extend unremitting pressure against Japan."[11] At the QUADRANT conference at Quebec in August 1943, Arnold presented his "Air Plan for the Defeat of Japan," describing B-29 employment against Japan. The Superfortress would be used as a "potent softening up weapon" against the home islands. This plan (CCS 323) had been put together quickly to bring before the Combined Chiefs of Staff at Quebec. Theater commanders however, had not been consulted. The first production models of the B-29 Superfortress came off the Boeing lines in July 1943 and Arnold proposed deploying them to central China. With their 1500-mile operational range, they would be able to strike Japan's war industry. The B-29 plan projected that damage inflicted on Japan would lead to the Combined Chiefs objective of defeating the Japanese twelve months after Germany's capitulation.[12]

Gen. George C. Kenney, MacArthur's air commander in the Southwest Pacific theater, lobbied Arnold hard in 1943 to deploy the B-29s to northwestern Australia. He informed Arnold that he already had available all-weather runways in northern Australia to accommodate the B-29s. Kenney's operational concept called for targeting the Japanese oil production and refining capacity in the Netherlands East Indies. According to Kenney, oil was the single commodity that Japan "must have to carry on the war. She conquered the Netherlands East Indies to get it and without it she is through as a serious opponent in a few months."[13] Kenney apparently thought that he had a chance to succeed with Arnold on the deployment of the plane "with which we will win the war," but he was doomed to disappointment. Arnold never seriously considered deploying the B-29s to Australia. Kenney, nonetheless, was disappointed and skeptical of what deployment to China might accomplish strategically. "I hope there is a quick victory that way," he wrote Arnold on July 28, 1943, "but frankly I am worried about the thoroughness of study, investigation and planning prior to the decision to employ it in that theatre. There is a colossal amount of work still ahead of someone."[14]

Arnold's plan subsequently was revised, designated as "Matterhorn," and approved by Roosevelt. On November 10, 1943, prior to the Cairo conference, the president cabled Churchill:

> We have under development a project whereby we can strike a heavy blow at our enemy in the Pacific early next year with our new heavy bombers. Japanese military, naval and shipping strength is dependent upon the steel industry which is strained to the limit. Half of the coke for that steel can be reached and destroyed by long-range bombers operating from the Chengtu area of China. The bombers can supply themselves by air, from bases to be constructed near Calcutta, without disturbing present airlift commitments. ...
>
> In order to expedite this project, I ask you to arrange for the Government of India to render every possible assistance in the construction of these four air bases for long range bombers. ...
>
> This is a bold but entirely feasible project. Together by this operation, we can partially cripple the Japanese naval and military power and hasten the victory of our forces in Asia.[15]

This was in line with Roosevelt's thinking about air power: Produce more planes, especially heavy bombers, to smash the enemy. He was a major proponent of strategic bombing, advocating that long before the U.S. could land ground troops in the enemy's homeland, long-range bombers could strike Germany and Japan. Also on November 10, Roosevelt requested Chiang Kai-shek to build five bomber fields in the Chengtu area, to be ready by the end of March 1944. The president noted that "I am personally convinced we can deal the Jap a truly crippling blow, so close to our hearts, by this sudden, surprise attack." Roosevelt supported rapid production of B-29s, which he saw as having "a strong influence" on the course of the war. He wanted no effort spared. He chafed at the delays that Arnold was experiencing in getting the B-29s operational, in October 1943 noting to Marshall: "The last straw was the report from Arnold that he could not get the B-29s operating out of China until March or April next year. Everything seems to go wrong. But the worst thing is that we are falling down in our promises every single time. We have not fulfilled one of them yet."[16] During the rest of 1943 and until the B-29 became operational in the Pacific in the fall of 1944, Roosevelt kept bringing up the subject to Marshall and Arnold.

At the close of November 1943, at the Teheran conference, Roosevelt inquired of Stalin as to the possibility of basing hundreds of heavy bombers in the Soviet maritime provinces to attack Japan. He also asked Stalin to approve a physical survey of the territory, to be accomplished in secrecy. Months went by before Premier Stalin replied that he was prepared to grant Roosevelt's request to base B-29s in Kamchatka. However, the Soviets kept delaying the plan for one reason or another and it was never implemented.

Weeks before the Cairo conference of November 1943, President Roosevelt received the bad news from Arnold that the B-29 would not in fact be deployed to China by January 1944, a date that Arnold had given to General Marshall months before. Arnold informed the president on October 11, 1943, that he regretted "exceedingly" that difficulties with engine production meant that deployment of B-29s to China would be delayed to March or April 1944. At that time, he informed Roosevelt, 150 B-29s should be in China, one hundred of which could be employed against Japan.[17] Roosevelt was upset by this news and informed Marshall that everything seemed to be going wrong as far as American promises to the Chinese were concerned: "I am still pretty thoroughly disgusted with the India-China matters," FDR intoned. "I do not see why it is necessary to use B-29s. We have several other types of bombing planes."[18]

Arnold then emphasized to Roosevelt on October 18 that the B-29 was the only bomber that could reach Japan from available bases. The B-24s and B-17s did not have the necessary range. Moreover, "due to labor troubles which have held up engine production, the 'bugs' inherent in any new airplane and the logistical problems involved, the present plan for using B-29s against Japan proper is still being studied within the Air Staff."[19] Roosevelt's increasing frustration with the B-29 program triggered the immediate interest of Robert P. Patterson, Under Secretary of War, and Harry Hopkins. Patterson suggested that the president sign a memorandum to all officials involved in the program to expedite action.

Prompt production of B-29s, Patterson stated, "will have a strong influence on the course of the war. ... No effort should be spared."[20] Hopkins asked Adm. William D. Leahy, as the representative of the Joint Chiefs of Staff, to emphasize the importance of the program to those officials responsible for production. To Leahy, Hopkins noted on November 19, 1943, that "the B-29 business has been an awful headache."[21]

Arnold then determined to take action to make certain that at least 150 B-29s would be deployed to China by mid-April so that the bombing campaign against Japan could start by May 1944. In November, Arnold asked the Joint Chiefs to assign top priority to the B-29 production program. The Joint Aircraft Committee, to which the JCS referred the matter, concluded that the major B-29 problem was in the manufacturing process rather than a shortage of materials. Second, in late November, Arnold activated the XX Bomber Command under Brig. Gen. Kenneth B. Wolfe, at Smoky Hill Army Air Field, Salinas, Kansas, controlling two B-29 wings.

In late 1943, B-29 crew training was delayed because very few B-29 aircraft were available in Kansas. By the end of 1943, only sixty-seven pilots had completed checkout flights and only one B-29 had flown a long-range training mission. Things were so bad in Kansas that Arnold was forced to substitute B-17s and B-24s in the flight training program. Meanwhile, Wolfe sent advanced parties to India and China to determine the status of base construction. Arnold, pressing forward under great pressure from Roosevelt and Marshall, was not satisfied, and ordered Wolfe to India and China to see for himself and to accelerate base construction. Wolfe even flew to Burma to ask General Stilwell to loan him several Army construction battalions, which Stilwell agreed to do.

While desperately attempting to straighten out the B-29 program, in February 1944, Arnold dealt with the question of launching bombing operations against Japan from eastern Siberia. Preliminary planning called for three hundred bombers to be located on airfields in the Vladivostock and Tambousk-Khubarousk areas. On February 8, 1944, in a message to Brig. Gen. John R. Deane in Moscow, Arnold wanted to know whether there would also be airfields available for three hundred fighter aircraft.

He emphasized that ambassador Harriman could assure Premier Stalin that forthcoming discussions would not go beyond the president, Leahy, Marshall, King, and Arnold. Also, Spaatz was already making arrangements for discussions in Moscow with a view toward starting round-trip shuttle bombing operations from England and Italy to the Soviet Union.[22] In mid-1944, the Joint Chiefs followed up Arnold's entreaties by requesting Deane to determine the location of potential airfields as well as logistical capabilities to support AAF bombers and fighters. Specifically, the Joint Chiefs asked Deane for data on the location, condition, capacity, and probable availability of airfields; provisions for air defense; and logistics to include supply, maintenance, servicing, and housing.[23]

In the United States, the B-29 program continued to run into all sorts of difficulties. Of the ninety-seven aircraft that came out of the factories by mid-January 1944, only sixteen were flyable. Thus, XX Bomber command did not have even one B-29 combat-equipped. By early March, it became clear to Arnold that the AAF would not meet the scheduled delivery of 150 aircraft by the end of the month. Making a personal trip to Salinas with Maj. Gen. Bennett E. Meyers, Arnold found the production a shambles, "void of organization, management, and leadership." No one seemed to know where missing parts and equipment were. Arnold ordered Meyers to remain in Kansas to supervise a crash effort and he assigned the B-29 project the top AAF priority.[24]

What followed in March and April 1944 became known as "The Battle of Kansas," the effort to get 150 B-29s deployed to the China-Burma-India (CBI) theater by mid-April. Contractors and subcontractors were directed to stop everything else to get missing aircraft parts flowing immediately into the bases in Kansas. The "pell-mell" project was finally turned around under General Meyers and in late March the first B-29 was turned over to the XX Bomber Command and departed for India. The flight from Kansas to India was 11,530 miles, through Marrakech, Cairo, Karachi, and Calcutta. By April 15, some 150 planes had left for the CBI from the United States. In mid-1943, Arnold had organized the 58th Bombardment Wing, comprising thirty B-29s in each of four groups. In November, the 58th was integrated into the newly formed XX Bomber

Command, training in Kansas. By April 1944, with the help of more than 700,000 laborers, bereft of modern equipment, airfields had been carved out in India and China. Also by April, more than 20,000 AAF personnel had arrived in the theater. In early June, a year after the first B-29 had flown, the 58th Wing conducted its first operational mission over Bangkok, Thailand.[25] All of this amounted to a kind of mad dash through the training and logistical cycles; no expense was spared. It was as if Arnold had personally willed this dramatic compression of time.

An interesting sidelight to the B-29 flights to India was that the second aircraft to leave the United States stopped over in England prior to flying on to Marrakech. The plan was to get the Germans and Japanese to think that the B-29 was going to be used in the Allied invasion of Europe. While in England, this B-29 was inspected by Generals Eisenhower and Doolittle as well as key British officials, and was photographed by a German reconnaissance plane.[26]

The deployment to India in April 1944 was marked by a number of crashes including five near Karachi in a two-day period. It turned out that the culprit was the high temperatures in the Indian subcontinent, frequently reaching 115 degrees Fahrenheit, which caused engine failure. This problem was subsequently solved by engineering experts at Wright Field and the National Advisory Committee on Aeronautics. Meanwhile, Arnold looked forward to deploying additional B-29 groups, ultimately to the Marianas: "Although our air offensive is still only in its early phases, the citizen of Tokyo or Nagoya has already begun to have an inkling of the cost and destructiveness of modern war. In the not too distant future he will be impressed with its full meaning."[27] In retrospect, there was nothing inevitable about the success of the B-29 program. As Eric Larrabee emphasized: "The B-29 was conceived in self-confidence and purchased on faith."[28] Even some officers in the AAF—at the risk of their careers—in 1943 argued that the program should be terminated. The fact that the B-29 effort ultimately succeeded has been described as an "unprecedented event in the history of industrial America."[29] One can imagine what it would take today in politics and bureaucratic red tape, time, and machinations to get such a massive program through to completion. Hansell retrospectively emphasized that the "most courageous decision" Arnold made "was the acceptance of the B-29 before the damned thing had ever flown. He built factories to build these airplanes, and gave them top priority at a time when the airplane was still in a test stage. That was a tremendous gamble."[30]

In retrospect, Maj. Gen. Curtis E. LeMay, who would replace Hansell as commander of the B-29 force, emphasized that Arnold "had worked a miracle" in being able to procure the raw materials for the B-29 program. LeMay viewed it as a battle with the Army and the Navy, who wanted tanks and battleships, for the needed resources. LeMay however, thought that Arnold's greatest achievement was organizing the Twentieth Air Force under the Joint Chiefs with Arnold as executive agent.[31]

Operation Matterhorn, the B-29 operations out of China beginning in June 1944, logistically never made much sense. It was undertaken, as we have seen, under great pressure from Roosevelt, who insisted that the United States shore up Chinese morale and keep China in the war. In late 1943 and early 1944, thousands of workers were involved in building the B-29 bases in the Chengtu area of China. However, significant problems with the Matterhorn operation were apparent and pointed out to Roosevelt and Arnold in January 1944 by Maj. Gen. Claire L. Chennault, commander of the Fourteenth Air Force in China. Chennault argued for air attacks on "the Japanese flank," against shipping on Chinese inland waterways, on ports, and in sea lanes along the Chinese coast. As for the B-29s, Chennault wrote the president that success from long-range bombing "takes a long time to produce decisive results." According to Chennault, the Matterhorn project, as now planned, was "tactically dangerous." He believed the division of command unsound and that Matterhorn should be integrated into the Fourteenth Air Force.[32] To Arnold in Washington, Chennault also emphasized "certain serious defects in the plans as they now exist." Staging fields in eastern China would be required for the B-29s as they would have to fly at comparatively low altitude during the first few hours of flight to long-range targets. Although understanding the importance of bombing the Japanese home islands, Chennault remained pessimistic about Matterhorn:

> After making due allowances for the powerful armament of the B-29 and with a full knowledge of the impracticability of furnishing fighter escort, I am convinced that the cost of such an operation against Japan from bases in the Chengtu area will be prohibitive.[33]

Chennault recommended to Arnold that a unified air command combining all air forces and supporting services operating in China be placed under command of the Fourteenth Air Force.[34] Arnold however, remained true to his concept that B-29 operations would be conducted independently through the Commanding General, Army Air Forces, acting under directives of the Joint Chiefs of Staff.

In November 1943, Arnold had established XX Bomber Command to conduct B-29 training in the United States. By April 1944, eight airfields were available for the B-29s in India and China. Brigadier General Wolfe led the XX Bomber Command to India under Operation Matterhorn. Wolfe's first strike against the Japanese home islands occurred on June 15, 1944, but his operation suffered from maintenance and logistical difficulties. This was a start, but no more. The initial B-29 raid in June was not successful, but the Japanese now realized they could expect to be bombed. Sixty-eight B-29s got off, but only forty-seven made it to the Imperial Iron and Steel Works at Yawata in Kyushu. Only slight damage was inflicted and seven planes were lost, most from operational failures. Arnold was not satisfied. Despite the fact that XX Bomber Command's fuel supply was down to 5000 gallons, he wanted Wolfe's B-29s to step up their attacks including a 100-plane raid against Anshan. Wolfe did not think Arnold's assessment of his maintenance and logistics realistic. As a result, Arnold relieved Wolfe in favor of Maj. Gen. Curtis E. LeMay, who had pioneered bomber tactics with the 305th Bomb Group in England. "With all due respect to Wolfe," Arnold stated, "LeMay's operations make Wolfe's very amateurish."[35] LeMay improved XX Bomber Command's record, but the operation still suffered from supply difficulties. Supplies had to "fly the Hump," over the Himalayas, the world's highest mountain range. The distance from China to targets in Japan proved a major obstacle, too. Tokyo was more than 2,000 miles from the B-29 staging bases in China. That exceeded the range of the bombers.

Arnold never expected to deal Japan a crushing blow using bases in China. In October 1944, XXI Bomber Command (a second subunit of the Twentieth Air Force activated in August 1944) was setting up in the newly captured Mariana Islands, which lay 1,500 miles from Tokyo. Use of the Marianas not only put most of Japan within the B-29's striking range, but also made it possible to supply and sustain hundreds of B-29s at once. Iwo Jima was subsequently used as a search and rescue site. Arnold named Maj. Gen. Haywood S. Hansell, Jr., commander of XXI Bomber Command. On November 24, Hansell launched his first strike against the home islands.

Hansell has suggested that the issue of control of strategic air forces was "thornier" than solving the B-29's technical problems. Be that as it may, the B-29 strategic bombing campaign against the Japanese home islands raised the crucial question of operational control. Given the mission of long-range strategic strikes against Japan, with the objective of smashing her industrial and social fabric, who would control this force? The questions of how to organize, control, and employ air forces had occupied Arnold well before the war. Once the United States entered the conflict, these questions became critical and consumed his thinking. He was deeply discouraged by the command setup in the Pacific. Although from the beginning of U.S. entry into the war he strongly favored true unity of command in the Pacific, he was sufficiently realistic to know that it would not happen, especially after the Joint Chiefs of Staff hit the wall and decided to carve the Pacific into theaters with Nimitz and MacArthur commanding separate operational theaters, the Central Pacific and the Southwest Pacific, respectively. President Roosevelt was not about to step into this hornet's nest and decide between MacArthur and Nimitz.

The absence of unity of command became a kind of ghost that hovered over the entire Pacific.[36] In retrospect, MacArthur emphasized that the failure to establish unity of command was one of the costliest mistakes of the war. Arnold no doubt agreed with this assessment, both during and after the war noting that joint command was no substitute for real unity of command. At the time of Pearl Harbor he described the command situation as "a Yes and No Organization." Command was divided: "We were relying on a Joint Board with its joint plans-joint actions-joint agreements-joint tasks-joint missions-with no unity of action and no military commander capable of making a firm decision as to the use of combined forces. A joint agreement, yes; but wars are not won by agreements. Who was responsible for reconnaissance in the waters surrounding the Hawaiian islands? The Army? Yes and no. The Navy? Yes. Both Army and Navy? Yes and no."[37] In retrospect, Arnold raised the question of whether the U.S. ever had any unity of command in the Pacific. Again, he answered it with a yes and no. He explained that there was unity of command individually under MacArthur, under Halsey, and under Nimitz, but not in the entire Pacific except under the Joint Chiefs. Unity would only be gained in the Joint Chiefs "if two naval officers and two Army officers could agree."[38]

As the war against Japan progressed, various theater operations started to overlap. To complicate the issue of command even more, the B-29 then entered the equation. Arnold termed it "a real strategic weapon which carried its operations well beyond the sphere of influence of either MacArthur's or Nimitz's command." He was determined to employ this strategic weapon in accord with AAF strategic doctrine as opposed to relinquishing any control of the B-29 force to theater commanders. This meant concentrating the command of the B-29 very long-range force against the Japanese home islands.

In Europe, the Eighth Air Force and the RAF operated in consonance with the Casablanca directive of January 1943, which placed the Combined Bomber Offensive under control of the Combined Chiefs of Staff with Sir Charles Portal, Chief of Air Staff, as executive agent. Unity of command did not exist in Asia nor the Pacific and in addition none of the theater commanders—Nimitz, MacArthur, or Stilwell—were sympathetic or familiar with the objectives of the B-29 campaign.

Hansell, in his memoir, notes that the strategic campaign demanded unity of command for this sustained offensive. This meant that the B-29s

could not be diverted from their primary objectives by theater commanders. According to Hansell, these theater or "field" commanders—
Nimitz, MacArthur, Stillwell—were very powerful: "Each wanted to apply
the B-29s to his own strategic theater purposes, and each resented any
incursion into his area of control. Yet there was one area in which unity
of air command and continuity of effort was imperative. That was the
target area itself, Japan, which was under the control of none of them."[39]
Arnold, in his memoir of wartime global service, makes clear that he fought
hard to keep the B-29s from being diverted to tactical missions in the
various Pacific theaters. Such "diversions" would have violated basic air
power principles and resulted in "scattering our airplanes all over the
world." Arnold's concept, long articulated, featured massing the maximum number of B-29s to destroy Japan. He called it "the Battle of Japan."
Yet, according to Arnold, all during the war MacArthur, Nimitz, Stilwell,
and Mountbatten wanted the B-29s for their tactical operations. None
of these theater commanders, according to Arnold, understood the
B-29 mission and none were sympathetic to what the Strategic Air Force
was attempting to accomplish.

He reiterated this to Spaatz and Eaker on April 16, 1945, when he
was pressing the Joint Chiefs to establish the U.S. Strategic Air Forces in
the Pacific. Also, Arnold always claimed that Admirals King and Nimitz
approached him to reorganize the strategic air forces as part of the
Navy—placing the fleet and the long-range air forces under a single
entity. He emphasized that he was not about to place the Twentieth Air
Force under MacArthur or Nimitz because "we were operating beyond
the battle area controlled by either of them—far beyond. Without a single over-all commander in the Pacific, MacArthur and Nimitz each visu-
alized the operation of the Twentieth Air Force as being for the benefit of
his particular campaign plans." As he had from the earliest days of the war,
Arnold continued to favor unified command: "As there never was unified
command in the Pacific, I retained command of the Twentieth Air Force
until V-J Day."[40] Arnold had always thought that the War Department
dragged its feet over the question on unified command, not "wishing to
get the Navy mad at us." The Navy should therefore not be criticized,

but all the inefficiencies in overlapping command should be allowed to be continued.[41] This made Arnold exceedingly angry and frustrated.

The questions of how and why Arnold made the decision to create the Twentieth Air Force remain somewhat murky. Arnold himself stated in his memoir that he reached this decision reluctantly although this seems far less than compelling. Given the lack of unity of command in the Pacific, Arnold claimed that he had to retain command of the B-29s, that "there was nothing else I could do. I could not give them to MacArthur because then they would operate ahead of Nimitz' command; I could not give them to Nimitz since in that case they would operate in front of MacArthur's advance. So, in the end, while everybody wondered why I kept personal command of the Twentieth Air Force—the B-29s—there was nothing else I could do, with no unity of command in the Pacific. I could find no one out there who wanted unity of command, seemingly, unless he himself was made Supreme Commander." The official history of the AAF notes that Arnold had never held a wartime operational command and consequently the arrangement with the Twentieth Air Force gave him some satisfaction. True, Arnold always retained some regret about never commanding operational air forces in the field. In April 1945, after Eaker complained to Arnold about being posted back to AAF headquarters in Washington, Arnold blew up: "Who in hell ever did ask to go to Washington? Do you think I ever asked to go there and stay for ten years? Someone has to run the Army Air Forces. We can't all be in command of combat Air Forces all around the world!"[42] Yet, Arnold all along had big plans for the B-29 force, going back to the developmental days and "The Battle of Kansas." Although initially plans called for the Superfortress to be employed in Europe, the vast distances in the Pacific and the need to prosecute the strategic air war against Japan argued for deployment to the Pacific theater. Once America entered the conflict, Arnold was determined to show, according to AAF strategic air doctrine, that a sustained strategic bombing offensive could drive a modern, industrialized nation out of the war. The creation of the Twentieth Air Force fit nicely into his vision of a "global air fleet," directly under the Joint Chiefs, with executive direction by the Commanding General, Army Air Forces.

Consequently, in the autumn of 1943, he had decided that circumstances dictated that he would have to command the B-29 force, that he simply could not afford to have this force tied down to any one theater where they would be employed in ways not comporting with AAF doctrine. Until the Twentieth was established, numbered air units had been assigned to theater commanders, operating under directives from the Joint Chiefs of Staff or the Combined Chiefs. These air units were the so-called theater air forces, organized into fighter, bomber, and service commands. Staff officers of the Twentieth, serving in Washington, would be "dual-hatted," holding positions concurrently in AAF headquarters and Twentieth Air Force headquarters.

In September 1943, the Air Staff had outlined the requirement for "a cohesive overall control of strategic air operations, free of the direction (commanders) of local areas, and subject only to the Joint or Combined chiefs of Staff." A similar organization had been created in the European theater, the U.S. Strategic Air Forces in Europe (USSTAF), headed by Spaatz, and including Eighth Air Force operations from the United Kingdom and Fifteenth Air Force long-range bombing operations from bases in Italy. The Combined Chiefs exercised control over USSTAF through their executive agent, Air Chief Marshal Charles "Peter" Portal, RAF Chief of Air Staff. The British, who ultimately anticipated contributing a bomber force to the strategic campaign against Japan, recommended that—as was the case in Europe—the Twentieth Air Force come under the control of the Combined Chiefs. The U.S. Joint Chiefs however, emphasized that the strategic campaign against the home islands was an American responsibility.

Hansell's version of how the creation of the Twentieth was sold to Admiral King and the JCS goes back to March 1944 when the AAF presented its strategic concept to the Joint Chiefs. This outline of Pacific strategy emphasized that the primary B-29 force would be based in the Marianas. Additional groups would be located in Chengtu, China; the Philippines; and the Aleutians. All would participate in a concerted bombing campaign against Japan, coordinated under unified command.[43] With this as background, Hansell recalled that the way in which Admiral King agreed to accept formation of a Strategic Air Force seemed "almost triv-ial." Hansell had obtained Arnold's permission to discuss the subject with King and he proceeded to point out to King the similarity of the B-29 command problem to that faced by the U.S. fleet in the Pacific. King agreed and the concept was subsequently approved by the Joint Chiefs.[44] None-theless, this version of Hansell's seems curiously cavalier, since King was certainly no special friend of the Army Air Forces. According to the official history of the AAF, King favored what he termed a Joint Chiefs of Staff Air Force, headed by the Commanding General, Army Air Forces, as executive agent of the Joint Chiefs of Staff. Nonetheless, given King's and the Navy's view of strategic bombing, it remains difficult to fathom the admiral's acquiescence in the establishment of the Twentieth Air Force.

Thus, in early 1944, the complex question of command and control of the B-29 force evolved simultaneously with Arnold's determined fight to get the Superfortress operationally deployed to the Pacific. As noted, the crux of the problem was that operations of the Very Long Range (VLR) B-29 force would involve several theaters. This is perhaps best illustrated by command difficulties involving the U.S. Chiefs of Staff, the China-Burma-India theater, the British Chiefs of Staff, and Lord Louis Mountbatten, Supreme Allied Commander, Southeast Asia (SACSEA).

Mountbatten wanted the XX Bomber Command to use the B-29s for long-range reconnaissance and strike missions in Thailand. However, Lt. Gen. Joseph W. Stilwell, American commander in the CBI, issued a General Order in January 1944 stating that the XX Bomber Command, oper-ating under directives from the U.S. Joint Chiefs of Staff, would come under Stilwell's command and control. Unfortunately, in issuing his General Order, Stilwell had failed to coordinate with Mountbatten, who consequently brought the issue to the British Chiefs of Staff. Lord Mountabatten was not pleased, pointing out the infeasibility of giving Maj. Gen. George E. Stratemeyer, Stilwell's air advisor—subordinate to Mountbatten's air commander Air Marshal Peirse—command of B-29s based in China.

Mountbatten however, was quick to admit that the entire question of control of the B-29 force was difficult, involving missions that "are based on one theater, pass through a second and may be directed at targets in another theater." He wanted these bomber operations coordinated with the theater commander. The command and coordination problem, he noted, was new and he, as the theater commander, should have been consulted before Stilwell promulgated his General Order. Unless coordination included all theater commanders involved, a clash in priorities was likely between B-29 operations and theater missions.[45]

The British Chiefs agreed that "bombing of targets in the Inner Japanese Zone, once started, must be continued intensively and must have overriding priority over other offensive air operations."[46] Thus, although the British Chiefs insisted that they remained "anxious not to interfere in the strategic direction" of the B-29s, they emphasized that long-range bomber operations were intimately tied into the CBI theater and consequently the most "careful coordination of operational and administrative matters will be essential."[47] Arnold for the moment finessed the issue by assuring Air Chief Marshal Sir Charles Portal of the British Chiefs of Staff that the AAF would arrange for coordination.

To the British Chiefs, the U.S. Chiefs of Staff in April agreed that development of the "Strategic Army Air Force" raised "practical" problems that required coordination with the British Chiefs. These could be solved through the Combined Chiefs of Staff. Moreover, the Americans failed to foresee many problems in the near future. Also, for at least the next twelve months, well into 1945, "the responsibility for ... the logistic support and coordination of other units in the VLR program will devolve on U.S. agencies."[48] Looking to the future, as to participation of the RAF in the air offensive against Japan following the defeat of Germany, the U.S. Chiefs could not foresee any likelihood of British participation any earlier than mid-1945. Should a British VLR force become available at that time, this question might be re-examined. This, in effect, was a polite, albeit straightforward, brush-off. Apart from the CBI theater, the war in the Pacific was an American "show." Control of Twentieth Air Force units by the U.S. Chiefs would be necessary to secure proper coordination in Pacific operations. Accordingly, "the build-up and deployment of VLR units to insure the most effective employment of these forces require that the U.S. Strategic Air Force (VLR) operate directly under the U.S.

Chiefs of Staff."[49] Arnold would command the VLR force from Washington as executive agent of the U.S. Joint Chiefs of Staff. The British ultimately let the matter drop.

In April 1944, the Twentieth Air Force was activated, commanded by General Arnold in Washington, serving as executive agent of the Joint Chiefs. This was a unique arrangement and the precursor of the postwar Strategic Air Command as a "specified" command reporting directly to the Joint Chiefs of Staff. Arnold was authorized by the War Department "to implement and execute major decisions of the Joint Chiefs of Staff relative to deployment and missions, including objectives of the Twentieth Air Force." Logistics support for the Twentieth was assigned by the Joint Chiefs to the theater commander. As delineated by the JCS, the mission of the Twentieth Air Force was "to achieve the earliest possible progressive dislocation of the Japanese military, industrial, and economic systems and to undermine the morale of the Japanese people to a point where their capacity and will to wage war was decisively weakened."[50]

As his first Chief of Staff of the Twentieth, Arnold had appointed Hansell, who had significant experience as a bomber commander in Europe and as one of the pioneers of the high-altitude precision bombing doctrine. Hansell stepped down as Chief of Staff in order to take command of the XXI Bomber Command. On October 12, 1944, Hansell flew to the Marianas to assume his new position. To replace Hansell as Chief of Staff, Twentieth Air Force, Arnold selected an officer whom he had mentored since the American entry into the war. In 1942, he had brought Lt. Col. Lauris Norstad—then thirty-five years old—into his personal Advisory Council. Arnold then sent the young officer to England and subsequently to North Africa as assistant chief of staff for operations, Twelfth Air Force. In 1943, Brigadier General Norstad planned operations for the Northwest African Air Forces prior to moving to Italy to become director of operations for the Mediterranean Allied Air Forces. In mid-1944, Arnold went to Italy and informed Norstad that he would be returning to Washington as the Twentieth's Chief of Staff. Norstad was not pleased, having played a major role in the Italian campaign, but Arnold of course prevailed.

Shortly after assuming his post in August as the Twentieth's Chief of Staff, Norstad in September 1944 summarized the evolution of the Strategic Air Force in a presentation to the Joint Army-Navy Staff College, noting that deployment of the XX Bomber Command to China had been undertaken by operational necessity and despite enormous logistical problems. "B-29s can bomb Japan from various areas," Norstad pointed out, "from China, the Northern Philippines, from the Marianas, and from the Aleutians. Each of these areas lies within a different Theater of operations. The choice of initial deployment was ... largely determined by necessity. It was only from bases in China that bombs could be put on Japan. Tremendous logistical difficulties were accepted. ... "[51] Subsequently, bases in the Marianas had become available earlier than anticipated, posing questions of control and coordination. "Unity of command," Norstad emphasized, "is required at the target." For some time to come, only the B-29s would be able to keep "constant pressure" on the Japanese home islands. This pressure must be operationally coordinated. It was not sufficient "merely to bomb Japan. The targets selected, the timing, the weight must be chosen with surgical skill." The Twentieth was created to destroy Japan's "means of fighting by destroying those economic and industrial establishments upon which her military strength depends."[52]

Norstad's description of the mission of the Twentieth Air Force was especially revealing. The mission was not only the destruction of Japan's industry and economy, but also undermining "the morale of the Japanese people to the extent that their capacity for war is decisively weakened." He then confronted the question of whether air power could drive Japan out of the war: "Whether or not air bombardment alone can defeat a power like Japan is no concern of ours."[53] Norstad added, however, that the time required to completely destroy Japan's steel-making industry might be more than it takes "to effect an invasion of Japan itself."

Meanwhile, on October 4, 1944, Arnold felt the need to inform General MacArthur about the Twentieth's mission and future operations: "I think it well to write to you directly on this matter," concerning "some of the problems involved in the deployment of the B-29s of the Twentieth Air Force and the future relations of the force with your Theater."

The XX Bomber Command operated against strategic objectives in compliance with directives from the Joint Chiefs of Staff. About half of the unit's operations would be in support of Pacific operations along with important photographic reconnaissance. MacArthur's recent successful operations opened up the possibility of bases in the Visayas from which B-29s could operate against targets in the Pacific and "the Japanese Inner Zone." Operations from the Chengtu area of China had been severely restricted by logistical limitations. "It is my desire," Arnold wrote, "to move this force as early as possible to bases from which it can operate with full effectiveness."[54] According to Arnold, the time factor was critical. If bases in the Visayas could be made available, he would do everything he could to assist MacArthur.[55] Informing MacArthur was important to Arnold as MacArthur was the Southwest Pacific theater commander and Arnold wanted to enlist his support, keep the lines of communication open, and continue to have good relations with the sometimes mercurial MacArthur.

The fact that Arnold in organizational terms was "executive agent" of the Joint Chiefs did not mean that the chiefs hovered over his every decision on, for example, suggested targeting or tonnages. Quite the contrary. Arnold and his staff pretty much enjoyed *carte blanche* in running the Twentieth from Washington. The B-29 campaign against the Japanese home islands fit into the JCS strategic direction that intensified bombardment should impact the enemy's war-making ability. Certainly, Marshall was not about to intrude into Arnold's operational decision making. He maintained trust and confidence in his air chief, both Arnold and Marshall following Roosevelt's—and then Truman's—charge to do everything to end the war in the Pacific as soon as possible with the least loss of American lives.

In September 1944, Lt. Gen. Barney M. Giles, Chief of the Air Staff, wrote to General Marshall to clarify administration of the Twentieth Air Force as it pertained to Army regulations and War Department directives. Describing the Twentieth as the VLR bomber force, or the Strategic Air Force, Giles stressed its uniqueness as a force operating in more than one theater. The question of the relationship of the Twentieth to the theater commander naturally flowed from those operations.[56] Consequently, the Joint Chiefs directed that in a strategical or tactical emergency a theater commander could take and employ the VLR bomber force for purposes other than their primary mission as long as the JCS were immediately informed of such action. Theater commanders were responsible for providing bases for the VLR force, for the defense of these bases, and for logistical support of the Twentieth. Giles recommended to Marshall that administrative authority should be delegated by the War Department directly to the Commanding General, Twentieth Air Force, who would thus have the same authority as a theater commander. As such, the commander of the Twentieth should be considered as a theater commander "for the purpose of applying the various Army Regulations which deal with administration."[57]

Arnold had won his point that the long-range B-29 force would not be tied down to any theater of operations nor any theater commander. In effect, this meant that the AAF could "go over the heads" of the Pacific commanders: Nimitz, MacArthur, and Stilwell. Thus, the essential fact remained that during the entire Pacific war, as D. Clayton James emphasizes, the Joint Chiefs of Staff functioned fairly effectively as the corporate supreme Pacific command despite almost constant disagreements. Although, as noted, Arnold had managed to establish the Twentieth Air Force in June 1944 without a major battle with the naval leadership, the Navy by late 1944 and 1945 was upset at having Arnold controlling the Twentieth as executive agent of the Joint Chiefs, since the B-29 bases were located within Nimitz's theater. Major General LeMay, commanding the B-29s of the XXI Bomber Command, described the situation this way: "Arnold did this so we would have a command in the Pacific where we were free to fly over anybody's theater, to do an overall job. Naturally, Admirial Nimitz wanted everything he could get his hands on; General MacArthur wanted everything he could get his hands on; and General Stilwell wasn't behind-hand in wanting everything as well. And we were flying over all three of their theaters. We simply had to have central coordination on this deal."[58] Perhaps Eric Larrabee put it best: The B-29s "made up the first aggregate of air power that was truly global ... in principle they could operate anywhere ... they were a war-winning weapon or they were nothing."[59]

Thus, the organizational setup was unique in that the Twentieth was the only major U.S. operational field force that was being run from a headquarters in Washington. Nor was this organization basically a paper arrangement. Arnold held the reins tightly. As he informed Hansell and then LeMay, he was watching them closely, almost on a daily basis. Although certainly Norstad and Kuter played extremely significant roles, Arnold signed the letters and cables to his operational field commanders.[60] He asked questions related to sorties, tonnage, and targets. He not only hectored Hansell and LeMay, but also constantly badgered Norstad and Kuter. Arnold followed targeting sequences closely. He was the boss, and that is exactly the way Marshall and Roosevelt wanted it.

This unprecedented command organization placed the Army Air Forces on an equal basis with the Army and Navy in the Pacific. The Twentieth had now become an independent entity reporting through Arnold directly to the highest American strategic policy-making group: the Joint Chiefs of Staff. Hansell called creation of the Twentieth "one of the most important events in the history of the United States Air Force." The new organization reflected the AAF's long-held doctrine: The great range of the air arm made it possible to strike the enemy's industrial and economic fabric, thereby crippling his war-making capacity. Arnold wanted to demonstrate the independent power of the air arm and he emphasized to his operational commanders that the Joint Chiefs were giving them the opportunity to do just that. The U.S. press understood the unique character of the Twentieth Air Force. The *Cleveland Plain-Dealer* noted editorially that "the United States has today what amounts to an independent air service. It is the 20th Air Force, which was organized to conduct operations of the B-29 Superfortresses ... This situation is a natural result of the evolution of the long-range bomber. The great range of the B-29s enables them to fly beyond the limits of normal operations in any theater of war and to strike heavy blows at the heart of enemy territory."[61]

However, the formation of the Twentieth and its subsequent initiation of long-range operations raised expectations in Arnold's mind and, consequently, put enormous pressure on the operational commander of the XXI Bomber Command in the Marianas. Arnold, whose defining characteristic was impatience, would not be satisfied with anything less than immediate results in the bombing campaign against the Japanese home islands.

4

Arnold Places LeMay in Command

In July 1944, Brigadier General Hansell, then the Chief of Staff, Twentieth Air Force, wrote to the Joint Staff Planners: "Sustained B-29 operations against the aircraft industry of Japan from bases in the Marianas will commence on or about 1 November 1944. Within three months thereafter, the effects of these attacks will begin to be felt." As it turned out, in a great irony, Hansell in effect had written his own epitaph as commander of the XXI Bomber Command.

As noted, the XX Bomber Command's B-29 Matterhorn operation led by Wolfe and then LeMay, established under great pressure from Roosevelt, suffered from major logistical difficulties. Similarly, operations in the Marianas under Hansell got off to a slow start. Arnold, already seemingly anticipating a race in the summer of 1945 to force Japan to surrender without an invasion, had been quite clear in his marching orders to Hansell. The AAF commander termed the effort to knock Japan out of the war with the B-29 campaign as the "The Battle of Japan." He reminded Hansell that he was "watching you from day to day with the greatest anticipation." Arnold reminded Hansell that "we have a big obligation to meet ...

we must in fact destroy our targets and then we must show the results so the public can judge for itself as to the effectiveness of our operations."[1] This was vintage Arnold: get the job done quickly and then we shall show the results to the American people. Arnold had an extraordinarily sensitive ear to the citizenry.

No other U.S. commander who was also a member of the Joint Chiefs sustained such oversight on his operational commanders in the field. It almost seemed that Arnold was attempting to will success in the B-29 offensive, in the same fashion that he had hectored Eaker in Europe and then sent him reluctantly packing to command in the Mediterranean. In LeMay, he found a commander who understood clearly the pressure that Arnold was under in Washington. This was no mean feat on LeMay's part. Early on, in India commanding the XX Bomber Command, LeMay wrote to Arnold on October 19, 1944, that "I shall continue to expend all my efforts to give you the results you desire and expect." Moreover, in the Pacific war, LeMay from the start never hesitated to spell out operational problems, but always made it a point to emphasize to Arnold what was being done to solve them. LeMay made clear to Arnold that he was not satisfied with the weight of bomb loads, something uppermost in Arnold's mind. The B-29's capacity suffered from insufficient power in the R-3350 engines. Bomb load was limited by gross take-off load: "The take-off is a very serious problem with the B-29 and is the high point of any flight."[2] Thus, LeMay had the ability to keep Arnold up to date on his problem-solving moves.

There were additional difficulties, LeMay emphasized. Combat crews lacked experience in the theater: "their experience with the B-29 prior to arrival in this Theater was sadly lacking. Many crews had never dropped a bomb from the B-29 and very few had flown it in formation."[3] Prior to October 1944, thirty-five percent of LeMay's total B-29 flying time occurred in cargo operations to the Chengtu area. LeMay, however, instituted a training program to correct the situation. Runways in China, made of limestone, tended to be dusty or muddy, and were slow for take-offs. However, these difficulties, which affected bomb capacity, were being corrected. Nonetheless, the single, most critical element remained engine improvement. LeMay put it starkly: "The B-29 airplane is capable of a considerable higher performance than the R-3350 engine ... will permit, as the maximum gross operating weight is limited by the power available for take-off and climb. Until more power is available, we cannot fully capitalize on the capabilities of the airplane." Overall, LeMay summarized:

> The principal factors which have adversely affected our range and bomb capacity are being corrected. It is reasonable to assume that we are now in a position to capitalize on past experience. This, together with the advent of cooler weather and the contemplated future changes in engine cooling, should permit a substantial increase in bomb loads over those carried on the initial operations of the Command.[4]

Arnold not only prodded his field generals, but consistently stoked competition between his commanders. On November 17, 1944, he wrote to LeMay, noting the significant improvement in B-29 operations, especially when it came to carrying a large weight of bombs. "The progress you have been making," Arnold cabled LeMay, "in adding to your bomb load is most gratifying. You will recall that when you first took command of the XX, one of my greatest concerns was the fact that the B-29 had not yet demonstrated its ability to carry a reasonably large weight of bombs. We haven't completely whipped this to my satisfaction yet, but I am pleased with the improvement."[5] The comparison to Hansell's operations was obvious. The work being done by LeMay's XX Bomber Command, Arnold stated, was setting a standard for all B-29 units: "We are passing to Hansell everything of interest from the XX Bomber Command, and he, in a recent letter, noted that he would have to push his people pretty hard to stay in the same league with your command."[6]

In early December 1944, Arnold reminded LeMay that prior to his going to India he had emphasized to him the enormous importance of the B-29 campaign. Moreover, the success of the B-29 project was absolutely "vital to the future of the Army Air Forces." Arnold impressed upon LeMay that, although there would always be problems, none were insurmountable, and they should not be used as "an excuse" for doing anything other than the best job possible under the circumstances. Arnold thought that the B-29 was the best bomber aircraft that the world had ever seen and he admonished LeMay that "I expect you to be the one to prove this." Arnold was thus convinced that LeMay had the "right attitude" and was the man to drive the B-29 campaign to the finish. This proved to be a harbinger for Hansell and his command of B-29 operations in the Marianas. Back in Washington, Norstad was already noting Arnold's frustration with Hansell's early operations. Patience was not one of Arnold's long suits and he was most anxious to show Roosevelt, Marshall, and the American public that the Twentieth Air Force could make a decisive contribution to the war against Japan. This was in fact his great obsession and he would not let it go until the war ended.

Arnold's relief of Hansell in January 1945 reflected the same frustrations that had hounded him when he sent Eaker from England to command the Mediterranean Allied Air Forces. In both instances, Arnold wrote to his operational commanders that "from the President on down," people were entitled to know what is being accomplished by strategic bombing. Arnold was not satisfied. It was not just a matter of mounting sorties and dropping bombs. The function of bombardment was to destroy enemy facilities and industry that supported his war-making capability. Bombardment must be applied where "the return is worth the cost."[7] Consequently, target selection must always be based upon thorough analysis. The strategic striking force will always be "relatively limited." It must be employed, Arnold emphasized, "with precision" against the most vital objectives.[8]

Arnold was asking, specifically: What was destroyed? Was the enemy's ability to wage war affected? What facilities or industries supporting his war effort were destroyed? How much damage was done, and to what? Instinctively impatient to show results, Arnold in Washington found that he was in a difficult position when it came to answering these questions. He needed to show Marshall and Roosevelt that the Army Air Forces were making a large contribution to beating down the enemy. Initially to Eaker, and now to Hansell, he emphasized that the answers to such questions would greatly help "in defending your operations." And in January 1945, Arnold gave Roosevelt an update on the incendiary attack on Nagoya, inferring to the President that more and better bombing results were in the offing.

As he viewed it, in putting great pressure on Hansell, Arnold was guided by the frustrating experience of the European bombing offensive. Arnold remembered that prior to Pearl Harbor, in August 1941, the Air War Plans Division promulgated AWPD-1 at President Roosevelt's request. AWPD-1 outlined a sustained air campaign against Germany and if necessary, an invasion of the continent. Target systems included electric power, transportation, aircraft production, petroleum, and synthetic oil. Further, it noted that "if the morale of the people is already low ... then heavy and sustained bombing of cities may crush that morale entirely." In Europe, Arnold firmly believed (Spaatz and Eaker concurred) that German morale could be broken with the result that Allied troops would have a comparatively easy time applying the final touch. After Germany fell, Japan could be knocked out without great difficulty. Air leaders figured that early, simultaneous air campaigns against Germany and Japan would not be possible. These assumptions formed the basis of AWPD-42 (September 1942) which envisioned a combined bomber offensive over Europe, the AAF conducting daylight operations and the RAF bombing at night.

On January 21, 1943, the Combined Chiefs of Staff issued the Casablanca Directive for the joint bomber offensive, which described the primary objective as "the progressive destruction and dislocation of the German military, industrial and economic system, and the undermining of the morale of the German people to a point where their capacity for armed resistance is fatally weakened." This directive established the major target systems as submarine yards and bases, aircraft industry, transportation, oil, and other important industries. "We shall not only destroy industrial objectives," Arnold observed, "but the moral fibre of the people to resist."[9] This was in line with Arnold's call for "continuous application of massed air power against critical objectives."

In late 1943, Arnold relieved Eaker from his Eighth Air Force command (effective December 22, 1943) sending him to the Mediterranean as Air Commander-in-Chief of the newly formed Mediterranean Allied Air Forces. In Washington, Arnold had been under considerable pressure to show results. In a retrospective written in 1974, Hansell defended

Eaker's approach to command of the Eighth Air Force. Higher head-quarters, noted Hansell,

> If it is thousands of miles away in a different environment, one can hardly be expected to understand fully the perils and vicissitudes of daily operations ... Blistering criticisms and imperious demands from Washington came crackling over the air ... I do not suggest that incompetence should be shielded or tolerated, but competence itself can be shattered by unreasonable attitudes and demands from above.[10]

Here Hansell obviously inferred a defense of his own operations and a harsh criticism of his superiors in Washington at Twentieth Air Force headquarters (read Arnold and Norstad) who were hounding him and breaking his spirit. As Eaker himself put it: Arnold "had the faculty of leading all subordinates to their highest possible effort; he picked many subordinates for prominent positions when I well knew that he did not particularly care for them, but he judged that they had the ability to do the job required." In this big switch, the major reorganization of top air commanders during the war, it seems that Arnold and Spaatz agreed that Eaker should be transferred to the Mediterranean Allied Air Command.

Eaker realized that he was under enormous pressure to get out more bomber sorties:

> If we had kept this up day after day we would have had no bombers left. I said to General Arnold that it was going to be my policy to conduct our operations at such a rate that we will always be growing and therefore a more menacing force. I will never operate at such a rate that I will be a diminishing and vanishing force ... this argument was conducted over a period of several months ... quite intense, quite bitter.[11]

The official explanation of this reorganization posits that Spaatz was senior to Eaker, had worked well with Eisenhower, and was long thought to be Arnold's choice to lead the final phase of the European campaign. Also, Eaker's experience working with the British made him an excellent fit to work with an integrated air command under a British theater commander in the Mediterranean. *The Army Air Forces in World War II* noted that

"Eaker's long experience in England and Doolittle's experience in Northwest Africa and the Mediterranean naturally suggested a reversal of the proposed assignments for the two men."[12]

Arnold had mentioned the switch to Eisenhower, who had agreed with it, although he informed Marshall that Eaker would also be acceptable.[13] The fact is that Arnold, with characteristic impatience and wanting instant results, desired that Eaker be transferred. Eaker was understandably disheartened, knowing that Eisenhower would have been content to have him remain in England. According to Eaker himself, Arnold thought that the Eighth Air Force's campaign was lagging and had constantly hectored Eaker to get out more missions.[14]

With the relief of Eaker as background, in retrospect, there seems little doubt that Hansell was doomed to failure from the start. Although an experienced bomber commander in the strategic air war over Europe, a distinguished strategic bombing planner and conceptualist, and the first chief of staff of the Twentieth Air Force, his doctrinal rigidity prevented him from making key adjustments to save his flagging bombing campaign against Japan. Although at the start Arnold and Norstad, Chief of Staff of the Twentieth and Arnold's right hand, professed confidence in his ability and program, there were telltale signs early on that Hansell was in trouble.

Arnold was risking everything on what he called "The Battle of Japan." He had personally driven the B-29 through production and "busted the China shop" to get the VLR force deployed to the Pacific. Arnold and Norstad made it clear to Hansell that expectations were extraordinarily high. In Arnold's mind, the performance of the B-29s in the Pacific was linked directly to the future creation of an independent air force. Arnold stated it baldly to Hansell: "You realize as well as anyone the important part that you and the XXI Bomber Command will play in the Twentieth Air Force program, and consequently, in the program of the entire Army Air Forces."[15] Implicit here was Arnold's belief that the record yet to be made by the Twentieth would prove to be a landmark in the evolution of the concept of an American independent Air Force. Establishment after the war of an independent United States Air Force was ever-present in

Arnold's mind. With his extraordinary foresight, he had taken the step in 1943 of forming a postwar planning division in Army Air Forces headquarters in Washington.

Moreover, Arnold informed Hansell that he was counting on his first few missions to establish the high standards for future operations. For the first major missions, "I know that you are doing everything within your power to make them highly successful. I am confident that because of your effort they will be successful."[16] However, Twentieth Air Force headquarters in Washington was keeping Hansell on a tight leash. Norstad, as the Twentieth's Chief of Staff, directly under Arnold, issued general targeting guidelines to Hansell, trusting that circumstances "will permit us to give you considerable latitude" in selecting targets and dates. Coordinated missions involving the XX and XXI Bomber Commands would be the major exception. "It is our aim," Norstad informed Hansell, "to give you a priority list of objectives and then to permit you to take them in your stride." Norstad then added that this may well prove to be "a vain hope."[17]

The capture of the Marianas in the summer of 1944 provided Arnold and the Twentieth with the opportunity to strike Japan's industrial centers from 1500 miles out. Attacks by Hansell's forces against the aircraft industry proved difficult due to heavy clouds obscuring the target areas. Even on days with decent visibility, strong winds at high altitude compromised the bombing effort. Also, when operations began in November 1944, only 119 aircraft were available, and by March 1945, fewer than four hundred. Poor maintenance and airfield facilities resulted in only 3.3 sorties per month per aircraft in November 1944. Under LeMay in July 1945, a rate of 7.1 was accomplished. The weather delays that Hansell suffered early on, postponing his initial bombing attack from the Marianas, although allegedly understandable to the Washington headquarters, only stoked Arnold's impatience. Hansell's failure to produce results quickly resulted in great frustration for Arnold. It also placed Norstad, as the Twentieth's Chief of Staff, in an uncomfortable position. Norstad recounted that "it was a difference of opinion as to whether we were to decide in Washington the local conditions in the Marianas."[18]

Hansell was well aware that he faced a critical time limit from Washington. Norstad on December 7, 1944, felt the need to "jack up" Hansell's confidence level. Indicating that he realized Hansell was "worried about the Chief's feelings," Norstad emphasized that Arnold's impatience was not directed at Hansell, but at "the circumstances": "You were not 'on the pan' at the time," Norstad recounted. Nonetheless, Norstad warned Hansell that although "the Boss" wanted to receive informative letters, he did not want long letters detailing "minor troubles or problems." Arnold desired a letter or charts every two weeks that indicated progress, not problems: "If there are really serious major problems which you feel absolutely must be brought to his attention," Norstad emphasized, "don't hesitate to do so, but I think the normal run of difficulties will only be an annoyance to him and can be better handled by me anyway." Unfortunately for Hansell, he had plenty of problems, some of them "major."[19]

Norstad offered Hansell a suggestion aimed to keep him out of "hot water." Should Hansell really feel strongly about something, and want to yell about it, he could send a personal letter to Norstad and the Twentieth's Chief of Staff would keep the communication out of official channels, in other words, away from Arnold, whose health was chancy at best, having suffered several heart attacks. Meanwhile, Hansell should not forget that he had "been given a mission by General Arnold." He had been given some latitude to select targets and the size of force, but progress would be closely checked by Norstad and Arnold. Interestingly, Norstad found it necessary to comment that Maj. Gen. Laurence Kuter, Director of Plans, was a loyal supporter that Hansell could count on and personally trust. Hansell, it seems, had received back-channel information, and had some good reason to believe that Kuter had been undermining him back in Washington.[20] Norstad indicated that he would visit Hansell during the first week in January. As it turned out, the visit was for the purpose of relieving Hansell from command in favor of Curtis LeMay.

Unfortunately for Hansell, his summation of his first month's operations struck Arnold and Norstad the wrong way, as overly negative. The results, although encouraging, Hansell noted, were "far from the standards we are seeking." As noted, Norstad and Arnold had made it clear that they expected Hansell's first missions to immediately set a high standard. His airmen were having difficulty putting bombs on targets: "The primary target is always a rather small section of enemy territory and it looks particularly small when seen from an altitude of something over five miles. Frequently you cannot see it because of clouds or overcast and must depend upon your instruments. We have not put all our bombs exactly where we wanted to put them and therefore we are not by any means satisfied with what we have done so far. We are still in our early, experimental stages. We have much to learn and many operational and other technical problems to solve."[21]

The fact was that even when good weather prevailed over the target area, severe fronts hobbled the B-29s on the long flight from the Marianas. Formations fell apart, navigation errors were difficult to correct, and aircraft frequently returned early or bombed a target of opportunity. The wind velocity at high altitudes was impossible to overcome, resulting in strain on both men and equipment. Note also that the ballistics of incendiary clusters made them inaccurate when dropped from high altitudes in the face of strong winds.

The major problem for Hansell was his insistence on running high-altitude daylight precision operations. Norstad, dedicated to an incendiary campaign, and Kuter of Arnold's staff continued to remind Hansell of the need to conduct incendiary attacks against Japanese urban areas as recommended by Arnold's Committee of Operations Analysts (COA). This committee, formed in December 1942 by Arnold, comprising military and civilian specialists, concentrated its efforts on target selection. Originally, it supported the European bomber offensive. In the spring of 1943, the COA began an intensive study of potential Japanese targets in support of the coming B-29 offensive. A report by the committee of September 4, 1944, convinced Arnold's headquarters, which had pressured Hansell to conduct incendiary raids, that area incendiary attacks stood the best chance of knocking Japan out. War industry pock-marked Japanese cities. These decentralized industrial targets could not be destroyed by high-altitude precision bombing in any timely fashion. The precision concept was dead. The COA estimated the probable effect on Japanese war production of concentrated area incendiary bombing assumed to destroy seventy percent of housing in Tokyo, Kawasaki, Yokohama, Osaka, Kobe, and Nagoya. These cities possessed a combined population of almost

fifteen million (as of July 1944), about twenty percent of Japan's total population. They harbored more than one-third of the workers in Japanese
manufacturing and almost one-half of all workers in priority industries.[22]

These six cities amounted to a much more concentrated target area
than comparable German industrial areas. "No other industrial nation,"
the COA emphasized, "is dependent upon so small an area for so substantial a portion of its manufactured products." All twenty-five major German
urban targets of the RAF in 1943 did not amount to as high a percentage
of industry as these six Japanese cities. Moreover, highly flammable wood
characterized much of Japan's urban construction. The committee estimated that as a result of incendiary attacks, almost 3,500,000 people in
the six cities would need to be evacuated; approximately 7,750,000 de-
housed; more than 500,000 fatalities could be expected; and almost forty
percent of priority industrial plants would be seriously damaged. As a consequence, an estimated 7,600,000 man-months of labor would be lost,
an average of ten weeks lost for each of the 3,200,000 industrial laborers
in the six cities.[23] Also an October 12, 1944, scientific report forwarded to
the Army Air Forces through Vannever Bush, made the following remark-
able prediction:

> Advance estimates of force required and the damage to Japanese war
> potential expected from incendiary bombing of Japanese cities indicate
> that this mode of attack may be the golden opportunity of strategic
> bombardment in this war—and possibly one of the outstanding oppor-
> tunities in all history to do the greatest damage to the enemy for a min-
> imum of effort. Estimates of economic damage expected indicate that
> incendiary attack of Japanese cities may be at least five times as effec-
> tive, ton for ton, as precision bombing of selected strategic targets as
> practiced in the European theater. However, the dry economic statis-
> tics, impressive as they may be, still do not take account of the fur-
> ther and unpredictable effect on the Japanese war effort of a national
> catastrophe of such magnitude—entirely unprecedented in history.[24]

In retrospect, Hansell always remained uncertain specifically as to who
was behind the change to incendiary bombing over Japan. He thought

the switch in thinking evolved after he left his post as the Twentieth's Chief of Staff to take over the XXI Bomber Command in the Marianas. However, the drive for an incendiary campaign goes far back to deliberations in 1943 of the COA and various reports from top scientists, some who, like Bush, held that incendiary bombing might be the best opportunity of strategic bombardment in this war. And of course the potentially explosive flammability of Japan's cities was well known for decades. "I do not know," Hansell speculated, "whether this change was brought about by Norstad or by General Arnold. At any rate, General Arnold had to be in agreement with it. When General Arnold was in disagreement with anything pertaining to the Army Air Forces it was not difficult to find that out."[25] When the COA, knowledgeable scientific thought, and Norstad concluded that an incendiary campaign was dictated, Arnold's obvious reaction would have been "whatever it takes!" Hansell was obviously on the right track here: Norstad, who was calling the shots from Washington, and Kuter continued to promote the incendiary campaign; Hansell's campaign was flagging; and moreover, Hansell remained rigid in his commitment to high-altitude "precision" bombing. Arnold did not really need to be convinced by Norstad and Kuter; he had already made up his mind. There was no way Hansell could save himself.

However, Hansell remained reluctant to undertake an incendiary campaign, unshakable in his commitment to precision bombing of industrial targets. One veteran of B-29 operations described Hansell's commitment as a desire to conduct a "civilized" bombing campaign against enemy industry without excessive civilian casualties.[26] To be sure, Hansell encountered severe maintenance and weather problems that affected his fledgling force, and he emphasized these to Arnold. The AAF commander—and Norstad and Kuter—was not interested in Hansell's problems.

Hansell's unyielding commitment to high-altitude precision daylight bombing did him in. In a lengthy letter to Arnold on January 14, 1945, following his relief, Hansell noted that the weather and strong winds over Japan were too much to overcome and he failed to persuade Brig. Gen. Rosie O'Donnell's 73rd Wing that high-altitude daylight bombing was preferable to radar bombing at night. After his relief, Hansell admitted that he "was seriously considering relieving one or more of the (73rd's) group commanders" who opposed high-altitude daylight bombing. Maj. Ralph H. Nutter, who was a navigator for both Hansell and LeMay in Europe and in the Pacific, wrote that Hansell's problems with O'Donnell had impaired his judgment and turned him "lonely and withdrawn."[27]

Not only had Hansell's campaign suffered from poor bombing results —he termed the lack of accuracy "deplorable"—but he was beset by major maintenance problems that caused high abort and aircraft ditching rates. The poor bombing accuracy reflected Hansell's insistence on bombing from 30,000 feet where jet stream winds made it impossible to hit targets with any degree of accuracy. By his own admission, he was forced "to take drastic action" requiring the 73rd Wing's lead crews to bomb from 30,000 feet over the bombing ranges every day if possible and not less than once every third day. Additional drastic action, Hansell wrote Arnold, was needed to bring down the abort and ditching rates, which were running extraordinarily high. "We came to this theatre," he recounted, "with new airplanes. We operated from an incomplete air base lacking in maintenance facilities and completely lacking in depot support." Nutter wrote that Hansell was "overwhelmed" by maintenance problems on Saipan. In summary, Hansell informed Arnold that the Twentieth Air Force was now "nearing the end of the pioneering phase." However, Arnold, who was always fixated on sortie numbers, was frustrated by the number of aborted mission flights that continued to plague Hansell.

Hansell had always chafed at the comparison of his operation to LeMay's, frequently brought up by Arnold and his staff. Now, in his swan song to Arnold, Hansell went into his own detailed, mission by mission comparison. He concluded that the accomplishments of the 73rd Wing, as compared to LeMay's 58th Wing, didn't "look too bad." After a long explanation of his problems with getting the 73rd Wing to believe in daylight precision bombing, to improve bombing accuracy, reduce the abort rate, and reduce aircraft ditching, Hansell closed his farewell letter with a barely veiled slap at Norstad. On reflection, Hansell thought that Norstad had sandbagged him with his suggestion that Hansell not bother Arnold with any of his problems since they would only annoy the "Chief" and could be better handled by Norstad himself. Hansell now informed Arnold that he had "erred" in not providing Arnold with his problems in detail:

"I have felt that my first consideration should be to solve my problems as best I possibly could, rather than to send complaints to you. Perhaps I have overdone this conception." [29]

The fact of the matter, however, was that Arnold and his Washington headquarters lost faith in Hansell's championing of high-altitude precision daylight bombardment. The string had run out on this concept that Hansell had pioneered prior to the war and over the skies of western Europe. In the spring of 1945, Arnold, Norstad, and Kuter, under the pressure of time constraints, knew that they had to deliver immediate results or the last chance for a knockout blow would be lost. Hansell failed to have a realistic assessment of the situation in Washington.

Hansell argued that the change to urban area attacks over Japan was made hastily and without proper regard for national policy and alternate strategies. The same arguments, he emphasized, were posited in the European theater "and our determination to persevere in the selected target method was later shown to be the wise decision." Hansell admitted that the jet stream and cloud cover made visual bombing exceedingly difficult while radar precision bombing had yet to prove reliable. Moreover, Japanese cities were more vulnerable to incendiaries than any other urban areas in the world. Hansell wanted more time to prove that selective bombing—especially of the electric power grid and transportation—could succeed. The XXI Bomber Command had only been operating for three months: "The force was small, it was ill-trained, and it had much to learn and improve." Its accomplishments, he admitted, had been disappointing. Hansell made the analogy with the European theater: "If a similar decision had had to be made after three months of operations of the Eighth Air Force—by mid-November 1942—and if the decision had been based upon accomplishments to date in terms of selected targets destroyed, then it is quite likely that the American strategic air concept would have been abandoned in Europe also.[30]

Time however, was a commodity that Arnold did not possess. He was under enormous pressure in Washington where the Joint Chiefs were solidifying the objective of invading the Japanese homeland. The American people and their political leadership wanted an end to the war as quickly as possible. Still, the problem for Arnold remained that Marshall and MacArthur viewed invasion as the *quickest* way to force Japan to surrender. The rationale for this strategy—as opposed to bombardment and blockade—has never been adequately explained. Conrad Crane, in *Bombs, Cities, and Civilians,* emphasized: "with the air resources available, the fire raids seemed to be the easiest and the quickest method for destroying the ability of Japan to wage war."[31] Surely it was clear to the Joint Chiefs of Staff in the summer of 1945 that Japan had been defeated militarily and that the strategy of bombardment and blockade (and the mining campaign) had the Japanese on the ropes. LeMay put it this way: "We knew that the war was won, but how much longer would it go on?"[32] Lt. Gen. Ira C. Eaker, who had been recalled to AAF Headquarters in Washington by Arnold in May 1945, emphasized that Arnold and the AAF leadership were absolutely convinced that an invasion was not required to knock Japan out of the war. Japan had become isolated, her strategic materials dried up, her war-making capacity all but spent, and the morale of Japanese citizens was plummeting under incessant bombing attacks. LeMay's planned offensive against Japan's transportation network, primarily railways, promised to trigger widespread food shortages in the Japanese homeland.

The difficulty was time. Although based on LeMay's estimate Arnold maintained that the Japanese could not hold out past October, Marshall remained unconvinced. The pressure on Truman and the Joint Chiefs was enormous. The Soviets were about to enter the conflict and the American public was tiring of a war approaching four years in duration. In retrospect, Hansell faulted the invasion strategy:

> Invasion should not have been regarded as the sine qua non of victory. There was an intense concern with "time," caused by the arbitrary selection of a November 1945 invasion date. Still, there should have been no limitation on strategic operations dictated by the shortage of time. Time was on our side. With every day that passed, the combination of sea blockade, aerial mining, and strategic bombing, was bringing Japan nearer to inevitable disaster.[33]

Hansell further noted that invasion was not a requirement, but one of several alternatives. The U.S. had no territorial designs on Japan, and the

objectives were to return territories conquered by the Japanese and to prevent Japan from repeating the carnage of military aggression. This could
be accomplished by selective bombardment and blockade. He also emphasized that the unconditional surrender policy was not absolutely vital to
U.S. war aims. Hansell defended the "precision" bombing of selected targets, making the point that—*given sufficient time*—it would have forced
a surrender. Incendiary bombing with its destruction of urban areas was
"in no sense an objective of the United States Government or of the strategic air offensive." The goal was capitulation of the Japanese.

Hansell juxtaposed the invasion dilemma this way: "The air issue was
strongly influenced by the invasion issue because the proponents of invasion
held the balance of power and they seemed to believe that urban destruction would contribute more directly to weakening of Japanese defenses
and would both hasten the date of invasion and weaken the resistance on
the beaches. Time became the dominant feature in surface strategy." Yet,
backing up in his own mind again, Hansell remained unclear as to why the
Army strategists, led by Marshall and MacArthur, thought that urban area
attacks would favor the invasion. He really instinctively came to the conclusion that it was the dramatic "measurable effects" that drove JCS and
presidential policy on urban attacks. And hinting at the views of Arnold,
Norstad, and Kuter, General Hansell stated that "there were elements of
the Army Air Forces who shared this view."[34] Here it is relevant to observe
that Arnold and the leadership of the Army Air Forces have frequently
been charged with being rigid and dogmatic in their doctrine and strategy.
There is truth to this, but at the same time it should be noted that in the
Pacific the U.S. Army leadership was no less rigid in promoting its strategy of invading Japan as the *quickest* way to force a surrender. Marshall
and MacArthur were unyielding, insisting that an invasion remained necessary even after the atomic bomb on Hiroshima.

As an architect of the high-altitude precision bombing doctrine and
the commander of the XXI Bomber Command, Hansell's retrospective
views on the strategic bombing offensive and the use of atomic bombs
are exceptionally relevant. He believed, like his boss, Gen. Hap Arnold,
that the atomic bomb was a political weapon, needed to shock the Jap-

anese into surrender. The bomb gave the emperor a way out. Hansell, however, posits an additional rationale concerning invasion and the U.S. Army: "The atomic bomb was needed both to convince the Japanese that further resistance was futile, and to convince the American army that invasion was unnecessary. The result would be a tremendous saving in Japanese and American lives. The 'bomb' may not have been needed to bring defeat to Japan, but it was needed to convince the Japanese military that the game was up and to save the U.S. Army from its obsession with a costly invasion. And the bomb's demonstrated power would be required after the war to deter Russian domination of Europe."[35]

With an invasion of Japan being planned, time was running out for Arnold and his Air Force to show that a modern, industrialized nation could be forced to surrender without its necessity. He kept pounding Hansell to increase bomb tonnage and sorties. When Hansell failed to produce, Arnold turned to LeMay. In retrospect, Hansell wrote that Arnold failed to understand what the XXI Bomber command had achieved. According to Hansell, his command's performance was quite good, but this was not apparent until after the war. It should be noted that Hansell himself recognized the strong case for incendiary bombing of Japan. He noted that appropriate target materials on Japan were not available and that results from his daylight precision campaign had been disappointing. Incendiary attacks could be run free from severe weather problems. Moreover, Japanese precision industrial targets were located in vast urban areas that could best be destroyed by area bombing, Japanese cities being exceedingly vulnerable to incendiary strikes. The truth of the matter was that Hansell had been placed in a most difficult position, circumstances from weather to logistics to the 73rd Wing's problems, all arrayed against him. And on top of this, the Washington headquarters demanded instant results, despite Norstad's disclaimers. Hansell's insistence that he did not have the proper intelligence and target materials only highlighted his reluctance to turn away from high-altitude precision bombing. In retrospect, he noted that LeMay had the proper experience in bombing at night. Also, Hansell thought that if perhaps he had "those extra few months" (January–March) that LeMay had, he may have come to the same conclusion.[36] Hansell thought that given the pressure of the time and the on-going planning for an invasion, area incendiary bombing was the appropriate tactic.[37] In retrospect, Hansell emphasized that "there is no doubt that the incendiary strategy was decisively effective."[38]

Thus, having bet everything on the B-29 campaign, Arnold in January relieved Hansell and called on the one man who had consistently demonstrated leadership and imagination in the strategic bombing business: Curtis E. LeMay. The relief of Hansell in favor of LeMay was one of the crucial decisions of the Pacific war. As Norstad tells it, Arnold was becoming increasingly frustrated with Hansell's operations, but was reluctant to make a change in command. Upon Norstad's and Kuter's prodding, Arnold came clean and indicated that he wanted LeMay. According to Norstad, when he suggested to Arnold that he personally fly to the Pacific and break the news to his commander, Arnold refused and directed Norstad to do it.[39]

Arnold's health remained a serious issue throughout the war. During 1943–1945, he had a number of heart attacks that put him out of action for various periods of time. Then while preparing to meet with Churchill and Stalin at Yalta, on January 17, 1945, Arnold suffered a massive heart attack that required him to convalesce in Miami until late March. Yet, characteristically, he always bounced back, frequently sooner than he should have, giving his doctors—and also General Marshall—fits. Even after the January 1945 attack, requiring extended convalescence, Arnold in June flew to the Pacific and subsequently attended the Potsdam conference in July 1945. At any rate, Norstad flew to Guam and had LeMay come in from India and Norstad gave Hansell a personal letter from Arnold and informed the two commanders of the change as directed by Arnold. According to Norstad: "I had to decide to take action before we lost the god-damned war ... because the Old Man really had come to a point where he was torn between his great fondness for Hansell—very warm personal feeling—and what had developed. And surely there were more circumstances in which Hansell had no control over those which he did have control ... an irreversible lack of competence."[40] LeMay himself later commented that Hansell "was a real disappointed man because he had worked a long time for this. He did a lot of things his contemporaries didn't think of, trying to get set up for this command ... they didn't think he was no good. He just didn't get this job done very well, or not fast enough."[41]

Since Arnold had suffered a heart attack, Norstad later claimed that as the Twentieth's Chief of Staff, at this point he got "practically no interference" from Arnold. Norstad recalled that he received "some cryptic notes" from Arnold, but generally he left him alone: "He was really terrific with me at this stage. There was always this pattern which compelled him to put out a blast to everybody once in awhile to keep them on their toes. But, he left me alone. I was careful to do everything in the name of the Old Man."[42] Hansell claimed twenty-two years after the war that Arnold had grave doubts about success with the B-29, although Arnold never wavered in his confidence in the bombers. As to his relief, Hansell noted that "this is what a top commander must do. I have a good deal of quarrel with his manner of doing it."[43]

Hansell took it as best he could, but he was a sensitive man and it was difficult for him. Basically though, Hansell understood the situation. In Arnold's mind, LeMay was the best combat commander in the air forces. Also, LeMay had proved in the CBI that he knew how to solve operational problems with the B-29. Brig. Gen. Roger Ramey took over command of the XX Bomber Command, which would be phased out. The XX and the XXI would be consolidated under LeMay in the Marianas. LeMay stated that he knew that "Arnold and Norstad were dissatisfied" with Hansell's operations.[44] Norstad reiterated to LeMay on January 19, 1945, following Hansell's relief, what was uppermost in General Arnold's mind concerning the B-29 campaign. Arnold wanted bombs on target, a larger force sent out, and thus a greater weight of effort. "We are surely interested," Norstad emphasized, "in seeing the largest practicable force operated at the highest reasonable frequency since this naturally leads to the greatest amount of destruction. ... What General Arnold wants is the greatest possible number of bombs dropped on our priority targets in any given periods of time." To LeMay, Norstad added, "I am sure you fully appreciate this ... you have the unqualified confidence of this Headquarters."[45]

LeMay emphasized that Arnold had done "a great job" building up the B-29 force and gaining command directly under the Joint Chiefs.

And although dependent on the theater commander (Nimitz) for logistics and supplies, LeMay set up a C-54 logistics operation from California that flew 120 hours per month. Taking over from Hansell, LeMay realized in January and February 1945 that the weather remained a huge obstacle to bombing over Japan: "During the best month, we had maybe seven days of bombing and only three days on the worst month. This was bad for high altitude bombing."[46] At 30,000 feet, jet stream winds were almost two hundred miles per hour.

According to LeMay, he "came to" in late February 1945, six weeks after succeeding Hansell. He knew that his radar operators were poorly trained: "we were not getting much accomplished." The experience in India, LeMay emphasized, indicated operational failures at high altitude. Moreover, the B-29s could carry heavier payloads at low altitude. Also, he was convinced that the Japanese did not have a low-altitude defense. LeMay had to answer this question: "Did actually very much in the way of low-altitude flak exist up there in Japan? I just couldn't find it."[47] Consequently, the weight of operational experience pointed to the incendiary attacks at night at low level, and some of his staff agreed, arguing "that it would be o.k. to revolutionize our whole process and go over Japanese targets at low altitudes." Nonetheless, others thought it would be "a slaughter."[48] In January, shortly after returning to Twentieth Air Force headquarters in Washington, Norstad wrote LeMay to clarify Arnold's thoughts on maintenance and the ditching problem that had so bedeviled Hansell. Although desirous of having LeMay get out the largest practicable force as frequently as possible, Norstad emphasized that aircraft not up to appropriate maintenance standards should not be forced into operation at the risk of ditching them. Arnold wanted priority targets destroyed and thus was concentrating more on damage reports. Noting that LeMay would soon have "the biggest and best air striking force in the world," Norstad stated flatly that he knew of no one better qualified to command this force and that there was no doubt that LeMay would "fully justify General Arnold's confidence in your judgement and ability."[49]

LeMay was well aware of Arnold's determination and impatience: "General Arnold, fully committed to the B-29 program all along, had crawled out on a dozen limbs about a thousand times, in order to achieve physical resources and sufficient funds to build those airplanes and get them into combat. ... So he finds they're not doing too well. He has to keep juggling missions and plans and people until the B-29s do well. General Arnold was absolutely determined to get results out of this weapons system."[50]

It was clear that, prior to his death, Roosevelt increasingly came to emphasize an intensive bombing campaign against Japan. In February 1945, he had mentioned to Soviet Premier Stalin, the need to destroy Japan and its army in order to save lives. The record indicates that neither president was swayed by considerations of morality. Also, any administration would want to justify to the public the enormous costs of the B-29 and atomic bomb programs.

LeMay had been warned by Norstad that if he did not succeed in the bombing campaign, an invasion would be required. LeMay knew that potentially he could well suffer the same fate as Hansell. In mid-February 1945, carrier planes struck Japan for the first time, causing severe damage to the Musashino aircraft plant in the Tokyo area. This attack by Navy planes prompted a frustrated Arnold to write to his deputy, Lt. Gen. Barney Giles: "I know that there are one thousand other reasons for not getting two, three or four hundred B-29s over Japan on every possible occasion. This cannot be done if we accept excuses and do not face the issue. ... From my viewpoint .... I would not be surprised any day to see the control of the 20th Air Force pass either to Nimitz or MacArthur."[51]

This concern and rivalry with the Navy was not only true at the highest levels of command; for example, even a professional operator like LeMay found himself in hot water over a remark he had made to a reporter on November 19, 1944, in India, when he was commanding the XX Bomber Command. LeMay's remark, published in *Skyways Magazine,* denigrating carrier-based operations, found its way up the command chain to General Marshall. Admiral King had brought it to Marshall's attention and Norstad subsequently issued a statement praising carrier-based operations. "I can assure you," Marshall informed King on March 13, 1945, "that no one is more embarrassed over the publication of this statement than is General LeMay himself."[52]

LeMay emphasized: "General Arnold needed results. Larry Norstad had made that very plain. In effect he had said: "You go ahead and get results with the B-29. If you don't get results, you'll be fired. If you don't get results, also, there'll never be an Strategic Air Forces of the Pacific. ... If you don't get results, it will mean eventually a mass amphibious invasion of Japan, to cost probably half a million more American lives."[53] After talking to Norstad, his bomb wing commanders, and his staff, a number of whom were opposed to a change in tactics, LeMay made the decision in March that turned the bombing campaign around. The B-29s would go in at low level, between 5,000-9,000 feet. Norstad had given LeMay the impression that, as far as tactics were concerned, Arnold was for anything that would hasten the end of the war. Thus, LeMay decided not to inform Arnold in advance:

> Why should I? He's on the hook in order to get some results out of the B-29's. But if I set up this deal, and Arnold O.K.s it beforehand, then he would have to assume some of responsibility. And if I don't tell him, and it's all a failure, and I don't produce any results, then he can fire me. And he can put another commander in here, and still have a chance to make something out of the 29's. This is sound, this is practical, this is the way I'll do it; not say one word to General Arnold.[54]

LeMay however, in retrospect made it clear that he never got any "direction" from Norstad. He knew that Norstad was "honchoing" the campaign, "buttoning the thing all up." But LeMay commented that "Norstad would never go out on a limb for anybody in his life. ... I didn't ask him any concurrence with what I was going to do."[55]

LeMay's idea was first of all to extend the bomb run: "We didn't know where half the bombs fell. After figuring out the probabilities of getting hit by flak, I decided to extend the bomb run. Extending the bomb run is the main reason that U.S. bombers got their bombs on the targets."[56] Secondly, LeMay needed to get under the weather:

> The B-29 was in a development status, there were "bugs" in it and operating at high altitude aggravated our mechanical problems. The

weather was very bad in Japan; only three to seven days per month were suitable for visual bombing. .... We had to come down under the weather, right down on deck if necessary, to get the job done. I made the decision. If it failed, Arnold could have chosen someone else for my job. The use of fire bombs coincided with the initiation of the low altitude attacks.[57]

On March 9–10, 1945, the low-level incendiary attack on Tokyo resulted in a conflagration—the most destructive bombing raid of the entire war—signaling the start of the sustained burning-out of Japan's major urban areas. The March attack on Tokyo by 334 B-29s was the single greatest disaster suffered by any nation in the history of war. High winds fed the fires, water even boiling in the rivers and canals. The B-29s destroyed sixteen square miles of Tokyo, demolishing one-fourth of all its structures. More people were killed and injured than in the atomic bombings of Hiroshima or Nagasaki. More than one million people were left homeless.

Two weeks after the great Tokyo attack—followed by four more urban area incendiary raids—Norstad convened a press conference in Washington to extol LeMay "as a courageous commander [who] has employed a presumably high-altitude bomber for low-level incendiary attack with outstanding effect, and as a result we have a new tactical punch in a very versatile airplane." The great irony here was that due to Arnold's convalescence, it fell to Norstad to conduct the press conference that in effect signaled to the American public that the corner had been turned in the strategic bombing campaign over Japan. One can imagine the thoughts of the man who had risked his reputation and career on driving the B-29 to production and operational status: General Hap Arnold. Norstad explained that in the first Tokyo raid, LeMay solved the difficult operational problem of dropping a heavy incendiary tonnage on a target area within a very short time. During March, in LeMay's attacks on Tokyo, Nagoya, Osaka, and Kobe, "it is very doubtful that such a high cost has ever previously been inflicted upon any people." In a comparison with Hansell's operation, Norstad made the point that although the rate of B-29 operations had been significantly increased, the loss rate had dropped sharply. And as to specifically what phase LeMay's operation was now in, Norstad preferred to describe it as "initial" as opposed to Hansell's terming it "experimental."[58]

Norstad was questioned by the press as to the change from explosives to incendiary bombing. He replied that incendiaries were an "economical method" of destroying small, decentralized industries. The number of home industries in Tokyo was estimated at 45,000. It is impossible, Norstad stressed, to pinpoint small targets scattered over a large area. Bombing with incendiaries was the most effective way to hit these targets. The Army Air Forces possessed little information on the Japanese industrial web, as opposed to the detailed target data on German industry. In urban areas, Japan's industries frequently were complemented by residences that housed work benches and machine tools. After the end of the war, scientist Karl T. Compton noted this fact to President Truman:

> Standing in the ashes of a substantial portion of the burned homes
> are various types of machine tools like lathes, drill presses, etc. Here
> family groups were manufacturing repetitive parts like nuts, bolts,
> or coils which were delivered to the manufacturing centers for use in
> the assembly of military weapons. In the area we examined, approximately one fifth of the homes showed evidence of such activities.[59]

Destroying Japan's home industries, Norstad stressed, would severely curtail her war production. Conflagrations in urban areas might spread to specific, priority targets, thus precluding separate precision raids. Low altitude attacks—between 5000 and 8000 feet—increased bomb loads. A B-29 at high altitude carried only thirty-five percent of the load of planes attacking at low altitude. Norstad denied that this amounted to a switch in tactics: "The mission of the Air Force is the reduction of the Japanese ability to produce war goods. That is accomplished by ... every means at the disposal of the attacking force."[60] Norstad emphasized the strategic objective rather than replying to the obvious question about what was clearly a major change in tactics, from bombing with explosives from high level to employing incendiaries at low level. Here Norstad dissembled, for the change to massive incendiary bombing amounted to a major departure. Moreover, from the time that Norstad succeeded Hansell as the

Twentieth's Chief of Staff, he all along argued that the Twentieth's targeting concept was aimed primarily against the destruction of Japan's economic and industrial complexes as opposed to the morale of the Japanese people. Norstad had stated in September 1944 that destroying morale was "of no great concern." The major point was destruction of their economic and industrial capacity.[61] From March 1945 on, the question of whether incendiary attacks were directed against the population or industry became a false one. It was now not an either/or proposition. Twentieth Air Force Headquarters in Washington considered the incendiary raids as targeting *both* population—the labor force—and industry.

This brings up the question of who was running the Twentieth Air Force from its headquarters in Washington during Arnold's absence due to his heart attack. This has occupied the attention of historians for decades. After his attack in mid-January 1945, Arnold was immediately sent by his attending physician to Miami Beach to get him out of Washington and the Pentagon maelstrom. During late January, February, and into March, Arnold maintained daily teletype communications with his deputy Lt. Gen. Barney Giles and with Norstad. During this period, Norstad attended high-level staff meetings with Marshall, as well as briefings, and communicated with LeMay in Guam. In this way, Norstad certainly sat in for Arnold, but it is also clear that Norstad knew exactly what Arnold wanted and in no way was he about to issue any directive or guidance that he knew to be counter to Arnold's views.[62]

With the dramatic turn of events in March, Arnold subsequently held a press conference on March 29 in Washington where he outlined what the B-29s were about to do to Japan. "The Twentieth Air Force," he noted, "has not yet grown up—it's just a young lad. But it will be fully grown before the end of summer." By the end of the summer, Arnold emphasized, one thousand plane attacks were possible: "We are going to use every airplane we can effectively against Japan, even if it means using every airplane we are now using in Europe."[63] Arnold noted that more than three quarters of the industrial "target sector" in Tokyo had been burned out, along with one third of the industrial area of Kobe, half of Nagoya, and more than two thirds of Osaka.[64]

As the noted columnist David Lawrence commented: "At last all branches of armed services are coming to have an appreciation of air power which puts it in proper perspective as not necessarily the decisive but perhaps the indispensable weapon of this war." Lawrence then emphasized: "It would not be surprising if it is in the Pacific war that air power demonstrates its real capacity for over-all damage on the enemy." Commenting in March 1945 on Arnold's precarious health, the columnist wrote that the AAF commander had recently spent time in the hospital: "This is the moment when he would have liked to have been more active but his countrymen know that the preparation and plans he laid down are bearing fruit and that the organization he has built up is carrying on splendidly. Air power is demonstrating itself as the absolute prerequisite of modern war and it is being fitted into the over-all strategy by the United States Joint Chiefs of Staff in such an effective and harmonious way that this development is worthy of more notice than it is getting."[64]

Moreover, Hap Arnold during the war never lost sight of the importance of the independent strategic bombing campaign to the future of the air forces: namely, the drive for an independent United States Air Force. He had long believed that such a strategic campaign could drive a modern, industrialized nation out of the war without the need for a land invasion. The conflict with Japan in the Pacific presented such an opportunity for Arnold and the Army Air Forces. Arnold, sensing in June 1945 that Japan might be on the ropes, had flown out to the Pacific to get LeMay's personal assessment. LeMay informed him that, due to the bombing and the naval blockade, the Japanese could not hold out any longer than October. In fact, Arnold was aware that LeMay's estimate had been emphasized by a preliminary report of the U.S. Strategic Bombing Survey, based on the effects of strategic bombing of Germany, that an invasion of Japan would not be required. However, Marshall and Gen. Douglas MacArthur, Southwest Pacific theater commander, supported the planned invasion.

Aware that Truman was about to ask for an all-important meeting with the Joint Chiefs to consider planning for an invasion, Arnold, as mentioned, had flown to the Pacific for an on-the-spot assessment of the bombing campaign. Arnold's strategy was to have the AAF go along with the planned Kyushu invasion while simultaneously attempting to knock the Japanese out with the bombing campaign. Arnold was also cognizant of the view of the Joint Chiefs that intensive air bombardment of the home islands was a prelude to invasion. Consequently, Truman's decision on June 18, 1945, to go ahead with planning for invasion of Kyushu in November 1945 led to a formal JCS decision to intensify air bombardment and blockade, along with the assault on Kyushu, in order to set the stage for the decisive invasion of the industrial heart of Japan through the Tokyo Plain.

The concept framed by the Joint Chiefs was to create the proper conditions through bombardment and blockade to make the ultimate invasion of the Tokyo Plain "acceptable and feasible." By November, the Japanese situation was expected to be "critical." Although Truman had approved the Kyushu assault by November 1 and the invasion of the Tokyo Plain by March 1, 1946, the JCS left open the possibility that the bombardment and blockade might in fact induce Japan to surrender. They noted that between November and March more bomb tonnage would be dropped on Japan than had been delivered against Germany during the entire European war. All of this planning was of course done prior to the dropping of the atomic bombs in August 1945. As it was, the B-29s dropped 147,000 of the 160,800 tons of bombs—more than ninety percent of the total—dropped by all aircraft on the Japanese home islands. Ninety percent of the total U.S. bomb tonnage fell on Japan during the last five months of the war.

LeMay's incendiary attack on Tokyo turned not only the B-29 campaign around, but marked a decisive turning point in the Pacific war. It was, Arnold informed his bomber commander, "brilliantly planned and executed." Norstad described LeMay's operations in March as "nothing short of wonderful … the most impressive that I have seen in the field of bombardment." Arnold let LeMay know that the March 10 raid on Tokyo was most impressive "even to old hands at bombardment operations."[65]

This is what Arnold was waiting for; it had been a long road from 1942–1943, when strategic operations in Europe were sputtering and the B-29s had yet to appear in the Pacific. Now, with the Nazis all but out of the war, Arnold thought that Japan was going through a critical period that would only become worse after Germany's surrender. "This fact," Arnold wrote LeMay, "imposes a great responsibility on the Army Air Forces, since we alone are able to make the Japanese homeland constantly aware of the price she will pay in this futile struggle." By July, Arnold emphasized, LeMay would have almost one thousand B-29s, giving him the capability to destroy "whole industrial cities."[66]

Like Arnold and Norstad, Lt. Gen. Barney Giles, Arnold's Deputy Commander, thought that the March turnaround by LeMay's force opened the way for the XXI Bomber Command to make "a major contribution" to ending the Pacific war. Giles reflected Arnold's view when he wrote to LeMay on April 20, 1945, that sorties and bomb load capacity in March "exceeded even our most optimistic plans up to six months ago." The "peculiar setup of the Japanese industrial targets and urban areas" made them especially vulnerable to B-29 incendiary attacks.[67]

LeMay himself was feeling optimistic about what his command was accomplishing, so much so that he voiced his opinion that "the destruction of Japan's industry by air blows alone is possible." This brought a mild rebuke from Norstad in Washington, who noted that while he had no argument with LeMay's statement, War Department policy prohibited predictions or speculation by general officers. Predictions were looked upon with "a very jaundiced eye." The AAF cause, Norstad emphasized, would best be served by keeping "entirely clear of predictions of any nature for some time to come." The situation was so sensitive, according to Norstad "now that the denouement in Europe has begun, and a particularly strong check-rein is exerted right now lest someone be inspired to predict the end of the war again, or be the innocent cause of some controversy over the congressional plan for consolidation of the military and naval establishments."[68] This slap on the wrist reflected Arnold's sensitivity to public relations and his daily monitoring of the activities of LeMay and his command. It also showed Norstad's and Arnold's great interest in the on-going movement in Congress to reorganize the defense establishment once the war ended. The role played by the Twentieth Air Force—an independent strategic bombing force under the direction of the Joint Chiefs—in the coming defeat of

Japan would have a major impact upon the shape of postwar negotiations for defense reorganization and an independent Air Force.

After the success of the incendiary attacks in March, both Arnold and Norstad concluded that an acceleration of these raids over the next few months stood a good chance of driving Japan out of the war. "With a greater respect we now have for our fire-making ability and the greater weight that we are able to lay down," Norstad observed, Japan's war-making ability will be seriously affected and the enemy might well "lose their taste for more war." Norstad pointed out that targets selected in March amounted to a compromise between industry and a "susceptibility to fire." Targets in April more nearly represented key industrial areas. Norstad went so far as to predict—rightly as it turned out—that Japan might capitulate about three months after Germany's surrender. This period would be "Japan's hour of decision." LeMay's XXI Bomber Command, "more than any other service or weapon, is in a position to do something decisive." It was about to become, Norstad emphasized, "the biggest and best air striking force in the world today." LeMay was about to "fully justify" Arnold's confidence in his ability and judgment.[69]

And LeMay was ready for the test. In April, he informed Norstad and Arnold: "I am influenced by the conviction that the present stage of development of the air war against Japan presents the AAF for the first time with the opportunity of proving the power of the strategic air arm. I consider that for the first time strategic air bombardment faces a situation in which *its strength is proportionate to the magnitude of its task.* I feel that the destruction of Japan's ability to wage war lies within the capability of this command, provided its maximum capacity is exerted unstintingly during the next six months, which is considered to be the critical period. Though naturally reluctant to drive my force at an exorbitant rate, I believe that the opportunity now at hand warrants extraordinary measures on the part of all sharing it."[70]

The sudden, dramatic turn-around in the fortunes of the B-29 campaign was not lost upon the American press. "The people of Japan," *The New York Times* intoned, are now hearing "the high-away sound of hostile motors" on a daily basis. "The real air war against Japan has just begun," the paper noted: "The question is going to be asked of the Japanese people by our planes, however, as to just how long they can hold out against massed air attack. They have not had to answer up to now." *The New York Times* concluded: "If the air attacks are devastating enough to force the Japanese to unconditional surrender, then it will be the least costly victory a nation ever won. If they do not achieve that aim, they nevertheless will have served as a softening-up operation."[71] It was clear that both Twentieth headquarters in Washington and XXI Bomber Command headquarters in Guam thought that with LeMay's successful operations in March–May 1945 a signal opportunity had arrived to drive Japan out of the war. Thus, the Twentieth's staff in Washington began to plan a follow-up cataclysmic incendiary offensive against Japanese cities.

Norstad's staff felt that the time was ripe; intensified incendiary attacks could now have far-reaching effects on the Japanese: "The effect on the morale of the Japanese people of the burning of the major cities with the destruction wrought therein and casualties caused cannot be evaluated statistically but the possibility exists that this alone might break the will of the people to continue to fight. This may be the thing that will bring home the futility of continuing the war to the Japanese people as well as to the leaders of Japan."[72] Lying behind this thinking in the spring of 1945 was the imminent collapse of Nazi Germany, which the Twentieth's staff figured might provide Japan a face-saving opportunity to end the war with a negotiated peace. The idea was to take advantage of the defeat of Germany "and the effect the collapse of Germany will have on the morale of the Japanese people." Norstad's staff saw the primary objective as "affecting directly the largest number of Japanese people possible in the shortest period of time. The secondary purpose would be to further the program of destroying the Japanese industrial system as a whole." This was the clearest exposition to date of the connection between morale bombing and the destruction of urban area cottage industries. Publicly however, at least in March, Norstad hewed to the line that the switch to incendiary bombing posited no change in the overall objective of crushing Japan's war industry. The plan for incendiary offensives that culminated in the attacks on Tokyo in May featured the selection of urban targets based upon their flammability. Targeting focused on "burnable areas" in Tokyo, Yokohama,

Kawasaki, Nagoya, and Osaka. Planning called for 300 and 400-plane raids concentrated in the shortest possible period. Publicly however, the Twentieth's policy would be "to maintain that some is precision rather than area bombing. It is precise to the extent that it is directed against specific target sections of highly industrial concentration, not area liquidation of an entire city."

Thus, the distinction between bombing industry and morale had become false. In retrospect, according to Japanese author Hoito Edoin:

> By the end of 1944, Japan was truly fully mobilized, and in the normal sense there were no more civilians in Japan. The government considered the civilian population to be just as much an element in the prosecution of the war as the soldiers at the front. There was no way by 1944 that civilians could be separated from the military in Japan.[74]

To Twentieth Air Force headquarters and to LeMay, targeting policy could not separate cottage industries from the civilian workforce population.

Also, LeMay's operations and the planning for a new bombing offensive pointed to capitalizing on this success in the arena of public relations, an area long emphasized and promoted by Arnold. Here, Norstad's staff pointed to the evolution of the Twentieth Air Force as the "world's first global air force." An announcement by the Joint Chiefs in early April described three Pacific commands: land, sea, and the Twentieth Air Force. This assumed existence of the Twentieth as an independent Air Force in the Pacific on equal footing with the land and sea forces. Twentieth Air Force headquarters in Washington took the position that "We let the Joint Chiefs announcement speak for itself, and our attitude reflects our appreciation of this recognition of our role in the Pacific war." The Twentieth's staff in Washington took the view that the B-29 campaign "has passed the experimental and initial phases of its history and is currently embarked upon an adult effort based on experience." However, the staff took pains to note that "under no circumstances shall anyone comment that air power might defeat Japan single-handedly or that such a prospect looks favorable."[75]

Historians continue to ask why FDR did not question the bombing campaign with its large loss of civilians. Strategic bombing is what Roosevelt wanted. He failed to intervene in its execution because of the fact that he not only strongly supported it, but he actually implored Marshall and Arnold to prosecute the bombing campaign with everything they had. Of this, there is no doubt. And as to the charge that LeMay did not receive direction from Washington, he in fact got plenty of advice from Washington, in the person of Norstad. Norstad made it clear to LeMay that Arnold and the Twentieth's planners wanted an incendiary campaign. LeMay was well aware that Arnold wanted results and he didn't much care how his operational commander got them. LeMay was on the chopping block, under enormous pressure from Washington. He was not operating in a vacuum out of Guam.[76] The idea that had LeMay reported to MacArthur or Nimitz, his incendiary bombing of cities would have been constrained fails to take into consideration that Arnold reported directly to the Joint Chiefs and that Nimitz and MacArthur were of course focused on their own tactical operations.

By the middle of July, Twentieth headquarters was satisfied with the progress of the B-29 campaign, but continued to reassess the results, especially on Tokyo, Kawasaki, Yokohama, Nagoya, Osaka, and Kobe. Over one hundred square miles of the urban industrial area of these cities had been burned out. This was a total war attack concept "in which the importance of the individual plant tends to be somewhat decreased while the aggregate importance of many plants, and in fact all economic resources, including the labor force, tends to be increased. This is particularly true in Japan because of the relative immaturity of her industry and her transportation system." According to Norstad's staff: "We are fortunate that Japan's urban industrial areas are burnable."[77] Thus, with the incendiary campaign and the blockade having an increasingly deleterious effect on Japanese morale and war production, the Joint Chiefs of Staff in Washington turned their attention to two major issues: the planning for an invasion of Japan and the thorny question of command arrangements.

5

June 1945: A Meeting at the White House

The spring of 1945 witnessed an intensive review of strategy and command by the Joint Chiefs. MacArthur continued to put himself forward as the potential supreme commander in the Pacific, the one to lead the ultimate invasion of Japan. Realizing that King and the Navy leadership would never accept it, MacArthur at the close of 1944 looked forward to the ultimate assault on Japan which would end the war. He wrote to Marshall: "I do not recommend a single unified command for the Pacific. I am of the firm opinion that the Naval forces should serve under Naval Command and that the Army should serve under Army Command. Neither service willingly fights on a major scale under the command of the other. ... The Navy, with almost complete Naval Command in the Pacific, has attained a degree of flexibility in the employment of resources with consequent efficiency that has far surpassed the Army. It is essential that the Navy be given complete command of all its units and that the Army be accorded similar treatment. Only in this way will there be attained that complete flexibility and efficient employment of forces that is essential to victory."[1]

Prior to the decision on final command arrangements, the Joint Chiefs weighed command problems in the Pacific for several months, once again laying bare long-simmering issues. Arnold was not a major part of these deliberations. The Twentieth Air Force strategy and tactics were devised at XXI Bomber Command in Guam and Twentieth Air Force Headquarters in Washington, without input from the Joint Chiefs, who were primarily concerned with overall strategy, administration, and command in the Pacific (as it might affect the mission of the Twentieth).

While in the spring of 1945, the JCS gave the green light to the November 1 Kyushu invasion, in their continuing discussions over the details of blockade and invasion, not once did they discuss the Twentieth Air Force's *detailed* targeting plans for an intensified incendiary campaign and the specific attack on the Japanese transportation system or how these planned attacks might mean that an invasion would not be required. There were several reasons for this. Arnold was out of Washington part of the time, and in ill health. Moreover, as noted, he notoriously held his cards close to his vest, not wanting to cross Marshall, nor willing to go out on a limb and predict flatly that the Twentieth could decimate the enemy out of the war, having nothing to gain by such a ploy. Too, although the Twentieth took administrative direction from the JCS, Arnold, Norstad, and the Washington staff ran the strategic air war independently.

Marshall and the War Department General Staff, buttressed by MacArthur's admonitions from the Southwest Pacific, jousted with King (and also Leahy) within the confines of the Joint Chiefs and their committees. Marshall and the Army were not about to allow the Navy to command the invasion landing forces that would force the surrender of Japan. Actually, this issue had surfaced in September 1944 over the question of whether Luzon or Formosa should be captured first. At that time, Marshall recommended that all Army forces in the Pacific should be placed under a single commander. King objected to giving the Army command of the potential Formosa operation, which he saw as part of the Navy's responsibility for control of the sea lanes off the China coast. The problem was solved when the JCS directed MacArthur to take Luzon and Nimitz to move into the Bonins and Ryukyus.

In December 1944, as the Leyte operation was ending, MacArthur sent his views to Marshall on "a matter of the most immediate and gravest urgency," related to command in the Pacific. Large-scale land operations were on the horizon, MacArthur intoned, and "we are so handicapped by the artificial area boundaries and command that the ultimate success of the war against Japan is in gravest jeopardy." His solution was simple, to the core: All naval forces should be placed under a single commander and all Army forces under a single commander under direction of the Joint Chiefs. A commander required for any specific operation would be separately appointed under the dictum of "paramount interest." MacArthur reiterated that "disaster is certain under the present nebulous and faulty command structure." The problem of command was "perhaps the gravest issue in the Pacific."[2]

King objected and basically the problem was tabled for the time. Admiral Nimitz, meanwhile, recommended that the Pacific Ocean Areas, exclusive of Japan, should be a single theater under unified command. Nimitz proposed, in effect, that for the invasion, "when land operations involving large armies are undertaken in Japan, the land area of Japan should constitute a new theater," with the new theater commander responsible to the Joint Chiefs. Nimitz as CINCPOA would command the amphibious operations. Prior to the April decision, Marshall laid out the Army's position that all Army forces in the Pacific theater be placed under a single Army commander and all naval forces under a single Navy commander, all under JCS direction.

Interestingly, the official history of the JCS in World War II noted a recommendation in the spring from Lt. Gen. Barney McK. Giles, Chief of the Air Staff, writing for Arnold, emphasizing appointment of a Supreme Commander for the war against Japan "and which places under his complete and direct control, on a coordinate and coequal basis, the land, sea, and air forces involved in that war."[3] In any event, Giles proposed that of course the Twentieth Air Force continue to operate under the Joint Chiefs of Staff.

In April and May 1945, with the bloody battle for Okinawa as backdrop—almost 7000 U.S. killed and 36,000 wounded—the Joint Chiefs of

Staff conducted an intensive review of Pacific strategy including the critical question of whether or not an invasion of the Japanese home islands would be necessary. This followed a decision in April by the Joint Chiefs on command arrangements for the final phase of the war. General MacArthur was named to command all Army forces in the Pacific. Admiral Nimitz was assigned command of all naval forces. General Arnold, commanding the Twentieth Air Force, would continue to operate the long-range strategic bombing campaign as executive agent of the Joint Chiefs. Though the Navy had argued in favor of the existing arrangement in which Nimitz would control the assault on Japan, Marshall refused to yield, and it appears that just prior to his death, on April 12, 1945, Roosevelt weighed in for the Army. Nimitz was directed to complete operations in the Ryukyus and to "maintain control of sea communications to and in the western Pacific as are required for the accomplishment of the overall objective." MacArthur was charged with completing "the occupation of Luzon and conducting such additional operations in the Philippines as required for the accomplishment of the over-all objective in the war against Japan." The JCS reiterated that Arnold would continue to command the Twentieth Air Force and to cooperate with both theater commanders in preparation for the invasion.[4]

In early April, Marshall informed MacArthur of the review of strategy by the Joint Chiefs and requested his input. Marshall emphasized that major issues to be considered were "the potential high casualties that might be incurred with an invasion of the home islands; the necessity to beat down Japanese air power; preventing reinforcements from reaching Japan from the Asian mainland"; and finally, the possibility of forcing a surrender without an invasion of Japan. Marshall also noted that "Russia's entry into the war would be a prerequisite to a landing in the Japanese homeland in December 1945." Overall, the Army Chief of Staff noted that one school of thought questioned the need for an invasion while another argued that an invasion was "the quickest and cheapest way to assure the end of the war." Here Marshall laid out the divergence in strategy between Leahy, King, and Arnold on the one hand and Marshall and the Army's view on the other.[5]

In late April, MacArthur replied with a lengthy analysis. Rejecting a strategy of "bombing Japan into submission without effecting landings in the homeland," he advocated an invasion of southern Kyushu leading to the subsequent "decisive assault" on Honshu.[6] MacArthur's rejection of relying solely on the bombardment and blockade strategy of course mirrored not only his own fixed view, but Marshall's and the Army's long-held opinion. Although bombardment and blockade would result in fewer casualties, MacArthur reemphasized that it would prolong the war indefinitely. "It assumes the success of air power alone," he stated, "to conquer a people in spite of its demonstrated failure in Europe, where Germany was subjected to more intensive bombardment than can be brought to bear against Japan."[7] In Europe, he noted, the United States, Britain, and Russia were forced to mobilize all available ground troops to force the Germans out of the war. This was a view that Marshall and the War Department staff held throughout the war.

In his recommendation for an attack on Kyushu, MacArthur allowed that it would present an opportunity to apply the full power of ground, naval, and air resources, placing the Allies in a favorable position for the assault on Honshu. Moreover, such a strategy "would continue the offensive methods which have proven so successful in the Pacific campaigns."[8] MacArthur was convinced that an invasion of the Japanese homeland might well force the enemy to capitulate on Kyushu "earlier than anticipated," thus presaging the assault on the Tokyo Plain in March 1946 (CORONET). However, he noted potential circumstances that might militate against this strategy, including insufficient air power to support the operation. In general, should this occur, a different course of action should be pursued "to maintain unrelenting pressure upon the enemy."[9]

In summary, MacArthur thought that sufficient resources were available to carry out his proposed operations. The Japanese fleet had been decimated and the enemy's air forces had been reduced to suicidal strikes, its ability to sustain action rapidly diminishing. Admiral Nimitz also supported the Kyushu invasion, recommending the November 1 target date. Thus, MacArthur and Nimitz supported Marshall and the Army planners who believed that an invasion of the home islands was the best strategy to force unconditional surrender at the earliest date. Nonetheless, the official JCS History noted that there remained uncertainty as to the ultimate necessity and desirability of invading Japan. This again underlined the point that Arnold and King continued to hold their cards closely. They did not openly and with vigor oppose invasion planning at the high table of JCS planning.

Also, in April 1945, the Joint Chiefs concluded that military cooperation with the Soviet Union, to establish air bases in Siberia and a supply route through the Kuriles, was no longer vital to the Pacific strategy. The Joint Chiefs cancelled outright the Siberian air base project. The Chiefs basically came to the conclusion that an invasion of the Japanese homeland could be mounted without Soviet entry into the war. And while a surrender potentially might be forced by bombardment and blockade, according to the Joint Chiefs it would probably involve an unacceptable delay.[10] This again, reflected the long-held Army view.

It remained uncertain however, that an unconditional surrender could be forced by any means. The Joint Chiefs noted that unconditional surrender was "foreign to the Japanese nature." It was possible that Japan might be defeated militarily without an unconditional surrender, in April 1945 a situation similar to that prevailing in the war against Nazi Germany. Continued bombardment and blockade might only bring about the possibility of a negotiated peace. On the other hand, if Japan were convinced of the inevitability of defeat, it might be possible to define unconditional surrender in a way that a Japanese government could accept. At any rate, the Joint Chiefs considered that continued land-based bombardment of the home islands would create by December 1 a situation "necessary for invasion insofar as the Japanese reserve materiel position is concerned and her capability for moving what remains to her in reserve materiel."[11]

On May 25, 1945, the Joint Chiefs of Staff issued the Kyushu invasion directive to MacArthur, Nimitz, and Arnold, setting a target date of November 1, 1945. The evolution of specific command arrangements for the OLYMPIC directive however, resulted in protracted disagreement between King and Marshall. King argued that the amphibious part of OLYMPIC had to be headed by an admiral while Marshall insisted that

the ground force commander have responsibility for the overall invasion campaign. In late May, the issue was resolved when King agreed that
MacArthur would have "primary responsibility ... including control, in
case of exigencies, of the actual amphibious assault through the appropriate naval commander." Nimitz had responsibility for the naval and amphibious phases but would "correlate his plans" with MacArthur's. Moreover,
the invasion directive specified that the land campaign and its requirements were primary and this would "be taken into account in the preparation, coordination, and execution of plans." Arnold, commanding the
Twentieth Air Force, was directed to cooperate in the plans, preparation
and execution of OLYMPIC "and in the continuance of the campaign in
Japan." At times, as determined by the Joint Chiefs, the Twentieth would
come under the direction "of the appropriate commander" for support of
OLYMPIC operations.[12] Consequently, there was no dispute over these
arrangements for the Twentieth, with MacArthur controlling all land-
based air operations.

It should be noted however, that while OLYMPIC planning proceeded in the spring and summer of 1945—and the incendiary bombing
went on unabated and with even greater ferocity—there was constantly
present the possibility that everything, including the invasion planning
itself, was subject not only to review, but ultimately even to postpone-
ment. Although Marshall and MacArthur continued their heavy support
of the invasion as the quickest way to force a surrender, Leahy, King, and
Arnold had not been convinced, but in their own minds, for perhaps
different reasons, thought OLYMPIC would not be necessary.

Several weeks later, the Joint War Plans Committee issued a memo
aimed as background for President Truman's June 18 meeting with the
Joint Chiefs as well as for possible use by Truman in July at the upcoming
tripartite conference with Britain and the Soviet Union in Berlin. This
memo noted that "the only sure way, and certainly the quickest way to
force the surrender of Japan is to defeat her armies on the main Japanese
islands." The stated overall objective was to force Japan's unconditional
surrender by "Lowering Japanese ability and will to resist by establishing sea and air blockades, conducting intensive air bombardment and

destroying Japanese air and naval strength; and invading and seizing objectives in the industrial heart of Japan."[13]

The planning memo by the Joint War Plans Committee emphasized the assault on Kyushu as a prelude to the invasion of "the industrial heart of Japan through the Tokyo Plain."[14] By November 1945, the Japanese "situation" was predicted to be critical, their home fleet no longer a factor and their air arm expected to continue to concentrate on suicide attacks. Japan's ability to move ground forces from Asia to the home islands was much reduced. Although in June 1945 planning went forward for an invasion of the Tokyo Plain, the Joint Chiefs had yet to direct execution of any operation after the assault on southern Kyushu, as part of the overall plan for the invasion of Japan, code-named DOWNFALL. That decision awaited "further developments." Thus, the Joint Chiefs hedged their bet. Before an invasion of the Tokyo Plain, "every effort" would be made to intensify the blockade and bombardment. Between June and November, "more bombs will be dropped on Japan than were delivered against Germany during the entire European war." Should the bombardment of the home islands fail to produce a surrender and should invasion of the Tokyo Plain subsequently be judged not feasible by the planned date of March 1946, then "a course of action to extend bombardment and blockade is open to us." At the same time, the Joint Chiefs concluded that Japan could be defeated in the home islands whether the Soviets entered the conflict or not. The Chiefs emphasized that "the best policy is not to press the Russians for any commitment."[15]

Following Roosevelt's death in April and the surrender of Nazi Germany in early May 1945, President Truman had little time to gain understanding and command of the situation in the Pacific prior to making critical decisions in the war against Japan. Although greatly weakened, the Japanese still had millions of men under arms and controlled vast territory. President Roosevelt's death not only shocked the nation and catapulted Harry S. Truman into the presidency, but it represented a severe blow to Arnold, who had forged an important relationship with FDR during the war years. As noted, Roosevelt prior to the war had initiated a vast buildup of air power and Arnold remained most grateful to the president:

> Franklin Roosevelt was not only a personal friend, but one of the best friends the Air Force ever had. He had supported me in the development of the Air Force in its global options to an extent that I little dreamed of a few years before, when I was in the doghouse. Many times he seemed more like a fellow airman than he did the Commander in Chief of all our Armed Forces, and I, one of his subalterns, in charge of aviation. I knew that we would miss him tremendously.[16]

At the same time, Arnold had "high hopes" that Truman would support the air arm in the future.[17]

As to command and control in the Pacific, the Joint Chiefs had informed Truman that command, control, and direction of the war in the Pacific remained the responsibility of the United States absent as much as possible of British intrusion on the combined level. Any efforts to bring direction of the conflict "under the laborious, argumentative, and time-consuming system of combined control should be vigorously opposed."[18] Also, Admiral Leahy requested that the Joint Chiefs draft a memorandum on the campaign against Japan for Truman's June 18 meeting. This was accomplished by the Joint War Plans Committee, Leahy emphasizing that President Truman wanted details in the campaign against Japan and to be "thoroughly informed of our intentions and prospects" to prepare for his discussions with Stalin and Churchill at Potsdam. Truman wanted an estimate, Leahy noted, "of the time required and the losses in killed and wounded that would result from an invasion of Japan." Alternatively, Truman desired an estimate of time and casualties that could be expected from the attempt to defeat Japan "by isolation, blockade, and bombardment by sea and air forces." It was Truman's intention, Leahy informed the Joint Chiefs, to make decisions so as to economize "to the maximum extent possible in the loss of American lives. Economy in the use of time and in money cost is comparatively unimportant."[19]

The memo by the Joint Chiefs for Truman began by noting that the overall objective was to bring about at the earliest possible date the unconditional surrender of Japan. "We believe," the Joint Chiefs stated, "that the only sure way, and certainly the quickest way to force the surrender of Japan is to defeat her armies on the main Japanese islands." The unconditional surrender of Japan would be forced by, first, lowering the Japanese ability and will to resist by establishing sea and air blockades, conducting intensive air bombardment and destroying Japanese air and naval strength; and, second, invading and seizing objectives in the heart of Japan. The Joint Chiefs made the point that unconditional surrender was "foreign to the Japanese nature." Consequently, the Chiefs were concerned that the Japanese military—spread over various areas in Asia—would not necessarily recognize a formal surrender by their government. If this were the case, the enemy armies would have to be defeated everywhere.[20]

Although the JCS in late May had directed the invasion of southern Kyushu (OLYMPIC), no subsequent operations had yet been directed. Additional decisions "would better await further developments." However, planning for the invasion of the Tokyo Plain on or about March 1, 1946, continued to move ahead. Meanwhile, emphasizing that invasion planning and blockade and bombardment were not mutually exclusive, the Joint Chiefs stressed that prior to CORONET, every effort would be made to intensify and capitalize on the blockade and bombardment: "If the blockade and bombardment concept is capable of achieving decisive results, these will, in all probability, be brought about by this scale of effort prior to the planned date for the invasion of the Tokyo Plain. However, in the event this invasion is not considered feasible and acceptable on the planned date, a course of action to extend bombardment and blockade is open to us."[21] Thus, the American planners certainly considered that the invasion of Kyushu, along with bombardment and blockade, could conceivably bring about "decisive results" prior to the scheduled invasion of the Tokyo Plain. Moreover, should CORONET not be considered feasible, they contemplated even heavier bombardment and blockade.

Like Truman, the Joint Chiefs kept the question of potential American casualties uppermost in mind. The number of casualties depended upon the length of the land campaign and the scale of opposition. An "educated guess" by the Joint Chiefs for OLYMPIC and CORONET resulted in a total figure of 193,500 casualties as follows: 40,000 killed, 150,000 wounded, and 3500 missing in action. The planners thought that the Japanese could be defeated in the area of the Tokyo Plain by mid-1946; but should other operations be required prior to CORONET, then the war might not be over until the end of 1946.[22]

In line with the view of General Marshall that the quickest way to defeat Japan and force a capitulation was by invasion, the Chiefs stated that they were unable to predict an end to the war by bombardment and blockade. They concluded that this strategy would result in "a long war, which would have an adverse effect upon the U.S. position vis-a-vis other nations who will, in the meantime, be rebuilding their peacetime economy." In view of the planners' concern about potential casualties should an invasion be mounted, it seems curious that their view about bombardment and blockade was stated with such certainty, especially in light of the stunning results achieved by the bombing campaign in March–May 1945. But again, it should be noted that Marshall (and MacArthur) felt strongly that strategic bombing did not drive Germany out of the war and he was certain that the same would hold true about Japan.[23]

As to the potential role of the Soviet Union in the campaign against Japan, the U.S. joint planners made clear that in their view the major Soviet objective should be the defeat of the Japanese Kwantung Army in north China. The Soviets should also conduct air operations against Japan, collaborating with U.S. air forces, and interdicting Japanese sea traffic between Japan and the Asian mainland. However, the Joint Chiefs emphasized that the United States could defeat the Japanese in their home islands whether or not the Soviet Union entered the war. In fact, in June 1945 the prevailing view in the topmost American military and political circles was that the U.S. could force Japan to surrender without Soviet entry into the conflict.[24]

On June 14, the same day that Admiral Leahy informed the Joint Chiefs of the meeting with Truman, the Chiefs requested that MacArthur and Nimitz prepare for a sudden Japanese surrender. Although noting that there was no evidence that such an event was likely, the Joint Chiefs directed that plans be made to take immediate advantage of favorable circumstances, such as sudden collapse or surrender. This guidance to the Pacific commanders indicated that the Joint Chiefs thought that Japan's situation was militarily hopeless and wanted to be ready for any conceivable eventuality.

The June 18 meeting was attended by Truman, Leahy, Marshall, King, Lt. Gen. Ira C. Eaker (representing Arnold, who was in the Pacific), Stimson, Forrestal, and Assistant Secretary of War John J. McCloy. The president, who trusted Marshall's judgment more than anyone else's, asked first for the Army Chief of Staff's opinion. As an expression of his own view, Marshall read a digest of a memorandum prepared by the Joint Chiefs for Truman: "Our air and sea power has already greatly reduced movement on Jap shipping south of Korea and should in the next few months cut it to a trickle if not choke it off entirely. Hence, there is no need for seizing further positions in order to block Japanese communications south of Korea." Marshall stressed that the status of operations against Japan "was practically identical with the situation which had existed in connection with the operations proposed after Normandy." Estimates were that by November 1 the B-29 campaign "will have smashed practically every industrial target worth hitting in Japan as well as destroying huge areas in the Jap cities."[25]

Pointing to the weather as a major factor in the November 1 target date for OLYMPIC, Marshall stated that MacArthur and Nimitz agreed with this date. Waiting much after November would delay the invasion by up to six months. Marshall noted that an invasion of Kyushu was essential to a strategy of "strangulation," appearing to be the "least costly" operation after Okinawa. Expressing the basic Army view, Marshall emphasized that a "lodgement in Kyushu is essential both to tightening our stranglehold of blockade and bombardment on Japan, and to forcing capitulation by invasion of the Tokyo Plain." Japan might eventually capitulate if prospects seemed hopeless, brought on by air bombardment and sea blockade, a landing on Japan, and "perhaps coupled with the entry or threat of entry of Russia in the war."[26] It was important to note, Marshall added, that air power alone could not defeat the Germans and it would not be sufficient to knock Japan out of the war. This was a view that Marshall had made a number of times within JCS discussions, and he now reiterated that not only Ira Eaker, Arnold's representative, but also General Eisenhower agreed with it. Thus, Marshall insisted to Truman that invasion remained the quickest, most certain way to force a Japanese surrender.[27]

However, Marshall thought that the first thirty days in Kyushu "should not exceed the price" of the Luzon action. While noting the increase in casualties in Luzon, Iwo Jima, and Okinawa, Marshall stated that experience in the Pacific was so diverse that it was wrong to advance an estimate as to potential casualties in an invasion of Japan: "It is a grim fact that there is not an easy, bloodless way to victory in war and it is the thankless task of the leaders to maintain their firm outward front which holds the resolution of their subordinates."[28] Marshall added that after a landing in Japan, Russian entry into the war might well be the decisive action forcing a capitulation. Marshall also took this opportunity to remind the president of the dangers of combined command: "the obvious inefficiencies of combined command may directly result in increased cost in resources and human lives."[29]

General Marshall also pointed to a telegram he had received from MacArthur in which the Southwest Pacific commander noted that the Kyushu operation "presents less hazards of excessive loss than any other that has been suggested and that its decisive effect will eventually save lives by eliminating wasteful operations of non-decisive character. I regard the operation as the most economical one in effort and lives that is possible."[30] Admiral King also agreed with Marshall's assessment, pointing out that within three months the effects of Okinawa-based air power would be felt in Japan.

As to casualty estimates, Admiral Leahy stressed that a thirty-five percent rate had been suffered in the Okinawa campaign. He also pointed out that insisting on unconditional surrender would result in a desperate stand by the Japanese, thus increasing American casualties in a potential invasion. Leahy did not think "that this was at all necessary." King thought that a potential Kyushu casualty rate would fall somewhere between the Okinawa and Luzon rates. Marshall noted that the total number of troops expected to mount an assault in Kyushu was put at 766,700. When Truman asked what opposing numbers they might expect, Marshall replied eight Japanese divisions or approximately 350,000 troops. As to reinforcements, Marshall stated that it was becoming "increasingly difficult and painful."[31] This troop estimate by Marshall and the possibility of reinforcements proved to be wrong, as it subsequently became clear that the Japanese had reinforced their Kyushu forces in a big way. Although King certainly believed—long before this meeting with Truman—that an invasion would not be required to defeat Japan, he went along with the invasion option. King was also aware that Admiral Nimitz in the Pacific, disturbed by the heavy casualties in the Okinawa campaign, now thought that "the long-range interests of the U.S. will be better served if we continue to isolate Japan and to destroy Jap forces and resources by naval and air attack." King also believed that Soviet entry into the war was not indispensable and that the U.S. need not "beg them to come in."[32]

Secretary of War Stimson, although agreeing that the Kyushu operation appeared to be necessary, emphasized that there existed in Japan "a large submerged class" that did not support the war but would fight tenaciously if the homeland were invaded. Admiral Leahy again pointed out that the unconditional surrender policy only made the Japanese more determined to fight and prolong the war, thus increasing U.S. casualties. President Truman replied that he had "left the door open for Congress to take appropriate action," but that he could not make any move at this time to influence public opinion on unconditional surrender. Although he approved the Joint Chiefs continuing to plan for the Kyushu invasion, he hoped to avoid "an Okinawa from one end of Japan to the other," and if necessary decide as to final action later on.[33]

Lt. Gen. Ira Eaker represented Arnold at this meeting as, it will be recalled, Arnold was in the Pacific being briefed by LeMay, who had told him that the Japanese couldn't stay in the war past October 1945. Moreover, Arnold had been so impressed by LeMay's professional judgment on the status of the B-29 campaign, that he ordered LeMay to fly at once to Washington to brief the Joint Chiefs. Also, Arnold had received a cable from Marshall informing him that there was to be a meeting of Truman and the JCS to discuss the question: "Can we win the war by bombing?"[34] Marshall's describing the upcoming meeting in these terms is certainly curious since he obviously felt that the answer to this question was resoundingly in the negative. Arnold, on Guam, aware that air forces were being transferred from Europe to the Pacific, had received a preliminary report from the United States Strategic Bombing Survey on the significant impact of the strategic bombing on Germany.

Earlier in June, Arnold had requested Franklin D'Olier, chairman of the U.S. Strategic Bombing Survey, to have a number of USSBS representatives present a preliminary report of its findings of the effects of strategic bombing on Germany. This was accomplished, D'Olier noted, with a view that this information "might possibly serve in the war against Japan as contemplated in the directives from the president and the Secretary of War to the Survey."[35] Although in June the Strategic Bombing Survey had not finished its investigations, D'Olier stressed that it was in fact well-documented, represented interrogations of most of the personnel in German war production, examined production records, and inspected German industrial facilities.

This interim report of the Survey emphasized that "the strategic air offensive, as developed and employed in the latter part of 1944, effectively paralyzed the German war economy and thereby contributed in decisive measure to the early and complete victory which followed." The USSBS concluded that the Germans were primarily worried about air attacks on their basic industries such as oil, steel, power, and transportation: "The attacks on oil and transport were the decisive ones." According to the Survey, sustained destructive attacks were most important. No indispensable industry was put out of commission permanently by just a single strike: "Attacks had to be repeated before recuperation was made impossible. To destroy an important target system and keep it destroyed required extremely heavy and sustained attack. This emphasizes the importance, within the limits allowed by tactical considerations, of concentrating energies upon a minimum number of target systems." The targeting philosophy of attacking all links in a chain has not proved successful, the Survey emphasized. It is far better to destroy single links in critical chains; this has proved far more productive and long-lasting. The preliminary D'Olier report noted that the Japanese war industry appeared more vulnerable to air attack than Germany's. Moreover, unlike Germany, Japan was powerless to stop the U.S. air attacks. "It is apparent," the report concluded, "that Japan's position as a strong military and industrial power is already terminated."[36] The report recommended continued raids on urban industrial concentrations by area attacks, which it considered a more "efficient method" than precision attack. Importantly also, it strongly proposed that a campaign against the Japanese transportation system be given a top priority. This would include an intensified blockade of the Japanese home islands as well as a concentrated attack on the rail network and coastal shipping.

With the information provided by the D'Olier interim report, the Joint Target Group recommended that the first targeting priority go to an "overwhelming" attack on Japanese rail transportation and coastal shipping "to disintegrate the Japanese home islands industrially; as an economic entity; and as a final defense zone."[37] The Target Group believed that heavy incendiary attacks would accelerate a Japanese collapse that would finally materialize through the invasion by land forces.

In a memorandum based on the Survey's interim report, chairman Franklin D'Olier wrote to Stimson that "the general view is that the fullest possible employment of strategic bombardment against Japan can contribute in a most important way toward achieving a decision with the minimum cost of American lives."[38] However, such results could only be expected when the most careful choice of targets and bombs was made and only if sufficient time was given to attain an adequate scale of effort. This report of the Strategic Bombing Survey, along with LeMay's estimate, gave Arnold a jolt of optimism and he noted, "If we could win the war by bombing, it would be unnecessary for the ground troops to make a landing on the shores of Japan. Personally, I was convinced it could be done. I did not believe Japan could stand the punishment from the air that Germany had taken."[39] Thus, at least in his own mind, Arnold addressed Marshall's point that strategic bombing had failed to drive Germany out of the war. Japan, with its highly flammable cities, was not Germany.

Maj. Gen. John W. Huston, who edited Arnold's World War II diaries, speculates that Arnold's problematic health was a major factor why Arnold himself did not hurry back to Washington from Guam—a grueling 8000-mile trip—to brief Truman and the Joint Chiefs. As it turned out, LeMay was somewhat delayed en route to Washington but briefed the Joint Chiefs on June 19, one day after Truman made his decision at the meeting on the eighteenth, to go ahead with the two-step invasion of Japan on November 1, 1945, and March 1946. LeMay recalled his meeting with the JCS, stating the Joint Chiefs paid absolutely no attention and that Marshall "dozed" throughout and that "the Joint Chiefs were not at all interested in what a two-star general had to say."[40] In retrospect, LeMay thought that as a two-star field commander, he was in effect being dismissed to go back to the Pacific to run his bombing campaign while the Joint Chiefs handled business at the top level in Washington. Returning to Guam, LeMay noted that "the whole general staff believed they had to invade Japan as they had invaded Europe." When Arnold sent LeMay hurrying to Washington it remains unclear whether he wanted LeMay to make the case to the president for strategic bombing on the eighteenth. More likely, and as it turned out, Marshall relied on Eaker, a three-star with seniority and a great deal of experience dealing with high-level military and political leaders, such as Prime Minister Churchill, for example.

On the eighteenth, Eaker had been requested by President Truman to present the airman's view on the potential Kyushu invasion. Eaker replied with the *official* AAF view, i.e., he agreed with the opinion expressed by General Marshall. Moreover, he had just received a cable from Arnold in which the AAF commander again expressed his "complete agreement" with Marshall. A blockade of Honshu, Eaker emphasized, rested on having air bases available on Kyushu. The air plan projected employing forty groups of heavy bombers from Kyushu. Further, according to Eaker, those who pressed for the use of air power alone against Japan "overlooked the very impressive fact that air casualties are always much heavier when the air faces the enemy alone and that these casualties never fail to drop as soon as the ground forces come in."[41] Eaker's somewhat quixotic position, termed "deferential" by Huston, remains troubling. It is, however, emblematic of Arnold's view that he should refrain from opposing Marshall and Truman head-on in regard to the invasion. There is no doubt that Eaker in his own mind knew full well that Arnold thought an invasion unnecessary.[42] From the sequence of events in the Pacific and in Washington, it seems obvious that Eaker presented the official AAF line to Truman on the eighteenth—Kyushu was required as a bomber base—without raising the real possibility that an invasion would not be necessary. Arnold, in the Pacific with LeMay, certainly had come to the conclusion that Japan could be forced by blockade and bombardment to surrender. In retrospect, Eaker reflected that in the summer of 1945 no one in the top AAF leadership thought that an invasion would be required.[43]

What is also obvious is that neither Arnold nor Eaker was about to cross Marshall in front of President Truman on the eighteenth. The Army Air Forces owed a great deal to Marshall, going back to the late 1930s when Marshall began to understand what the airmen needed to build up an American air force. Once the United States entered the war, Marshall had followed through, supporting Arnold in building the air forces and ramming through the crucial 1942 War Department reorganization that made the AAF coequal with the ground forces and the service forces. Thus, in early 1942 the airmen had gained autonomy, providing them the authority and flexibility to employ global air power. This is something that Arnold never forgot and it fueled his discretion in dealing with Marshall. Consequently, the over-arching reality remained that Arnold would not oppose the great man who had seated him at the Allied high policy table, had given him almost unlimited resources, had allowed him to run the air forces as he saw fit, and now was giving him the green light to pound Japan, albeit—as Marshall saw it—as a prelude to a massive invasion. Also, of course, Arnold as commander of the Twentieth Air Force reported directly to the Joint Chiefs while prosecuting the B-29 campaign against Japan. There is no question that Arnold and Marshall enjoyed a uniquely complementary relationship during the war. Marshall summed it up by emphasizing that Arnold "was always loyal."[44] Marshall, spare in countenance and in communicating, contrasted with his subordinate, the impetuous airman. To Arnold, the most important facet of their relationship was Marshall's steadfast support of Army air power. Although not always in agreement with Arnold, the Army's Chief of Staff generally supported him in the critical issues of aircraft production and allocation and the strategic bombing campaigns in Europe and the Pacific. Marshall however, never deviated in his view that ground invasions were absolutely necessary to force Germany and Japan to surrender.

However, in June Arnold had clearly made up his mind to operate on two tracks: he would officially back the War Department now on OLYMPIC and CORONET while at the same time drive LeMay to intensify his urban area attacks, which he thought might well force Japan to capitulate prior to November 1945. Also, Arnold wasted no time in making use of the interim USSBS report, forwarding a memorandum to the Joint Chiefs in late June prior to his leaving in July for the Berlin conference at Potsdam. To the Joint Chiefs, Arnold pointed to the report's conclusion that by late 1944 the strategic air offensive had paralyzed the German war economy. Consequently, the report recommended "the fullest possible employment" of strategic air attack against Japan.

Here, Arnold again in the summer of 1945 struggled with the dilemma of supporting an invasion while in his own mind thinking that bombardment and blockade could force Japan out: "I consider that our concept of operations against Japan should be to place initially complete emphasis on a strategic air offensive complemented by a naval and air blockade. While the presently planned scale of air bombardment is expected to create conditions favorable to an invasion of the Japanese homeland on 1 November, it is believed that an acceleration and augmentation of the strategic air program culminating in a land campaign will bring about the defeat of Japan with the minimum loss in American lives."[45] Thus, Arnold backed Marshall in the sense that bombardment and invasion were not considered mutually exclusive. Arnold noted a report of the Joint Target Group that indicated that the military and economic capacity of Japan could be destroyed by dropping 1,620,000 tons of bombs on Japan. It was thought that this amount of tonnage would disrupt industry, paralyze transportation, and seriously affect production and distribution of food." Arnold thus proposed that the bombing campaign, along with the naval and air blockade, might well force a surrender by Japan. If this should prove not be the case, it would nonetheless pave the way for a ground assault. The Joint Target Group called for tightening the air-sea blockade and "that at a reasonably early date" all communication with the mainland and all coastal shipping would be interdicted. The Joint Target Group had concluded that "The completion of the suggested program will prevent recuperation of Japan as a nation for many years and will leave the Home Islands unable to support their pre-war population until and unless a complete new industrial system can be rebuilt. Whether a formal capitulation is ever obtained by these means still remains within the choice of the Japanese government."[46] To those who posit that Arnold failed on June 18, and again at the Potsdam conference, to lay out a plan for how and when Japan could be forced to capitulate, it is well to point out that he was not about to tie himself and the AAF to "how and when." He certainly had a general strategic plan, and following LeMay's briefing on Guam, a target date for Japan's denouement. He had absolutely nothing to gain by attempting to formally present a plan to the JCS with a specific date for Japan's capitulation.

Thus, when it came to the question of whether or not an invasion was necessary, the Navy and Army Air Forces were in agreement. King, Leahy, and Arnold believed that blockades and bombardment could force Japan to capitulate without an invasion. They did not, however, openly argue this case to President Truman at the July 18 meeting, but rather acquiesced in the planning for OLYMPIC on the basis of gaining more naval and air bases to prosecute the blockade and bombing. If ultimately an invasion was required, the continued blockade and bombardment would lessen the anticipated casualties. Marshall and MacArthur argued that there remained no certainty that bombardment and blockade could end the war within the foreseeable future and that consequently an invasion would be necessary.

In July, the Joint Chiefs reiterated their overall objective of forcing the unconditional surrender of Japan by sea and air blockades and intensive air bombardment leading up to an invasion. The assault on southern Kyushu would be a prelude to "the decisive invasion of the industrial heart of Japan through the Tokyo Plain." Air and naval bases were being developed on Okinawa with the expectation that by November 1 some 2700 land-based aircraft would be operating from this area. Consequently, by November the Japanese situation was expected to be "critical." Home fleet units "have already been so reduced as to no longer constitute a controlling strategic factor. Their air arm is already committing training planes to combat and will probably continue to devote much of their remaining air power to suicide tactics."[47] The JCS considered this part of the plan inviolable.

Following the Kyushu invasion, the assault on the Tokyo Plain was planned for March 1, 1946; however, the Joint Chiefs hedged their bet by noting that, prior to this date, the bombardment and blockade would be intensified and in the event the invasion was not considered "feasible and acceptable," an even greater extension of bombardment and blockade would be considered. It also remained possible that a Japanese capitulation could evolve following the assault on southern Kyushu. The question of potential casualties was ever-present. "Our casualty experience in the Pacific war," the Chiefs noted, "has been so diverse as to throw serious doubt on the validity of any quantitative estimate" of casualties in the future. Recent campaigns resulted in the following U.S. casualties (killed, wounded, or missing): Leyte, 17,000; Luzon, 31,000; Iwo Jima, 20,000; and Okinawa, 46,700.[48]

Also, the Combined Intelligence Committee issued its estimate of the campaign against Japan. The Japanese Navy had been reduced to a shell, its Air Force concentrating on suicide missions. The Japanese Army, consisting of about four and a half million men, retained little mobility and was constricted by supply shortages. Nonetheless, there remained little chance of a surrender until the Army acknowledged defeat in the field. The Japanese military concentrated on defense of the home islands, specifically Kyushu and Honshu, with a total force of over two million men.

They also aimed to build up their forces in Manchuria, Korea, and north China against a potential move by the Soviet Union. This force could total approximately a million and a half men. The committee thought the Japanese unlikely to employ a strong air effort to defend Manchuria at the expense of defense of the home islands.

In July 1945, according to U.S. intelligence, the Japanese were making desperate efforts to avoid utter defeat or unconditional surrender. Foremost was the attempt to convince her enemies that an assault on the home islands would prove enormously costly in casualties and time. Concomitantly, according to intelligence sources, Japan continued to make every effort to persuade the Soviet Union to remain neutral. Should the situation deteriorate even further during the summer, Japan might even make an attempt to engage the Soviets as a mediator in order to end the conflict. The ruling Japanese government aimed to fight as long as possible to avoid a shattering defeat and to gain a better position in any negotiated peace.

According to the Intelligence Committee, the sea blockade and strategic bombing had had a devastating effect on civilian morale. The bombing had made millions homeless and destroyed large urban areas of Japan's most important cities. The potential entry of the Soviet Union into the war might convince the Japanese "of the inevitability of complete defeat." Although the Japanese people historically believed in sacrifice for the nation, "they would probably prefer national survival, even through surrender, to virtual extinction."[49]

Nonetheless, prior to Potsdam, there were no indications that the Japanese were prepared to accept unconditional surrender. Key issues remained in the person of the emperor and the position of the Army: "The Army leaders must, with a sufficient degree of unanimity acknowledge defeat before Japan can be induced to surrender. This might be brought about either by the defeat of the main Japanese armies in the Inner Zone or through a desire on the part of the army leaders to salvage something from the wreck with a view to maintaining military tradition."[50]

Meantime, Arnold had some unfinished organizational business to accomplish. While in the Pacific, after hearing LeMay's report on the

status of the B-29 campaign against Japan, he immediately concluded
that a U.S. Strategic Air Forces in the Pacific needed to be formed at
once "and all dillydallying about it stopped. Strategic bombing must be
unhampered in its organization, administration, logistics and operations.
It must have a free hand so as to drop the maximum bombs in the minimum time; that means Navy and Army must keep hands off."[51] In the prosecution of the war against Japan, Arnold stressed that the U. S., in cooperation
with the Allies, could bring about the defeat of Japan by "lowering the
Japanese ability and will to resist by application of direct pressure upon
the Japanese economy by means of maximum strategic bombing complemented by naval and air blockade and intensified and culminated by
ground invasion with concurrent tactical air operations."[52] This statement
presented the rationale for establishing the U.S. Army Strategic Air Forces
in the Pacific. Here Arnold was going back to his concept of unfettered
command of strategic operations, which in June 1944 had led to formation
of the Twentieth Air Force. Thus, in the summer of 1945, planning for
OLYMPIC accelerated, and Arnold and his staff geared up for a massive
incendiary onslaught against the home islands. Concomitantly, within the
Joint Chiefs of Staff, as we have seen, tensions among the services continued to manifest themselves. Although there were plenty of issues between
Arnold and King, both believed that Japan could be brought down by blockade and bombardment. Marshall and MacArthur disagreed, strongly advocating a land invasion of Japan.

These cross-currents brought into relief the complex relationship between Arnold and MacArthur, two officers who had crossed paths over
their long careers, going back well before the war. MacArthur had long
been identified with the Philippines. In the context of World War II however, his relationship with Arnold focused on issues in the Southwest
Pacific, where Kenney performed as MacArthur's air commander, and
also in the realm of the Joint Chiefs, where MacArthur's input weighed
heavily with Marshall. Arnold and MacArthur worked and sparred cau-
tiously with each other. This was at least partly due to the fact that each in
an important way was in debt to the other: MacArthur, because Arnold
had sent him the brilliant George Kenney and, Arnold because he greatly

appreciated the use that MacArthur was making of Kenney's air forces. Moreover, in the sometimes brutal fight for theater resources, MacArthur and Kenney relied on Arnold's largesse to build up their Far East Air Forces. In this regard, Arnold frequently had to be cajoled and even hectored, especially during late 1942 and 1943 when resources were at a premium. On occasion, when in Washington, Kenney went over Arnold's head and brought his case for more planes directly to Roosevelt, who was usually sympathetic to the airman.

From time to time in 1944 and 1945, Arnold informed MacArthur of his plans for what he termed the Strategic Air Force. Here, as noted, the issue of control was paramount, and became increasingly so in the spring and summer of 1945. In June, it will be recalled, Arnold went to the Pacific to assess LeMay's B-29 campaign, and more generally, the entire Pacific situation. He visited with, among others, Stilwell and Kenney, with whom he discussed "the unnecessarily hard way we went about fighting a war, with two commanders and two supply systems in the same theater." He also had a "quite spirited conversation," with MacArthur in his Manila headquarters. Despite the fact that Arnold and his staff in Washington had cabled MacArthur about the formation and the mission of the Twentieth, here in the summer of 1945 Arnold concluded that MacArthur neither had an understanding of the Twentieth's relationship with the JCS nor comprehended the urban area bombing campaign.[53]

Arnold recalled in his memoir that MacArthur even went so far as to favor an independent Air Force including ground support air units and added that he was willing to have an independent air arm in the Pacific in the summer of 1945 with either Arnold or Kenney as commanding general. And although after the war MacArthur stated that lack of unity of command was one of the great costly mistakes of the war, he made clear to Arnold that he opposed a supreme commander; in Arnold's words, he "accordingly was willing to sacrifice unity of command." MacArthur remained convinced that the Navy would never give up any of its control and that, in Arnold's recollection, MacArthur "would have to give up everything necessary to achieve unity—hence, he had everything to lose and nothing to gain." He also thought that the Navy was already building up facilities for its postwar configuration.[54]

Arnold and MacArthur discussed the progress of the B-29 campaign and, apparently with no surprise to Arnold, MacArthur failed to "entirely" understand what the urban and incendiary campaign expected to achieve. MacArthur viewed the bombing as playing a complementary role, feeling that there was no substitute for a massive invasion. Arnold described MacArthur as believing "that bombing can do a lot to end the war but in the final analysis doughboys will have to march into Tokyo." Arnold did not think that MacArthur's apparent reluctance to bomb cities was rooted in high-minded morality, but had a great deal more to do with service parochialism and the always contentious issues of roles and missions. No matter what the technology, MacArthur thought ground forces ultimately would have to fight for and take territory.[55] Like MacArthur however, Arnold was perturbed about the possibility that the Navy in the Okinawa area would determine to give their own permanent construction first priority. This was not his idea of unity of command. In addition, Nimitz objected to Kenney's plan for operating the Far East Air Forces ten miles offshore in future operations. In Arnold's view, this "was one hell of a way to run a war—to have the power but not be able to use it because you were interfering with someone else's prerogatives!" Arnold added in retrospect that it was fortunate that the war ended "much sooner than any of us expected, so these problems never reached a point where they caused an open break between the Army and the Navy."[56]

Thus in 1945, with the number of B-29s in the Pacific approaching eight hundred, Arnold concluded that the time had arrived to transfer command and control of the B-29 force and additional bomber groups to be transferred from Europe from Washington to the Pacific, establishing overall command of the strategic bombing force. Arnold recommended formation of the U.S. Army Strategic Air Forces (USASTAF) in the Pacific with the Twentieth Air Force as its nucleus. Arnold not only had in mind an organization similar to the Strategic Air Forces in Europe, but he wanted Gen. Carl Spaatz to move from Europe to lead the strategic forces in the Pacific. Arnold needed a senior air officer in the Pacific with the rank and stature to deal with Nimitz and MacArthur. General Spaatz, in whom he had great confidence, would be the obvious candidate for the job.

Establishment of the USASTAF elicited some discussion, primarily an objection by MacArthur who argued that within the proposed organization operating in the Pacific area there would be the Strategic Air Force, the Far East Air Forces, and Navy land-based and carrier-based air forces. MacArthur proposed that all land-based planes be coordinated under the control of a single commander, namely himself. King however, stated that since theater planning for the invasion was based upon the existing organization of the Twentieth Air Force, that all current directives be retained and the Twentieth be transferred from Washington to the theater. In effect, there would be no change; consequently, on his return from the Pacific on July 2, Arnold received JCS approval for creation of the USASTAF in the form that he originally requested.[57]

The USASTAF organization included combat and service elements not only of the Twentieth Air Force, but also of the Eighth Air Force and additional units as agreed upon by theater commanders or the Joint Chiefs. In mid-July, Arnold directed that Spaatz take command of the Strategic Air Forces in the Pacific with headquarters on Guam. Lt. Gen. Barney Giles was appointed to be Spaatz's deputy with LeMay as Chief of Staff. Under Spaatz would be Lt. Gen. Nathan Twining commanding the Twentieth Air Force in the Marianas and Lt. Gen. Jimmy Doolittle commanding the Eighth Air Force on Okinawa. Arnold would continue to command the Strategic Air Forces from Washington as executive agent of the Joint Chiefs of Staff. Arnold, however, had failed to inform LeMay that he was being replaced and it fell to Twining when he arrived on Guam to explain the new command set up to LeMay. Spaatz, upon arriving on Guam, was impressed with LeMay's operation and looked forward to the arrival of bomber units from Europe. LeMay however, had doubts as to whether these forces would be required. He told Spaatz that "this all came a little bit late. I don't think that they'll get fields built for these people before the war is over."[58]

The USASTAF commander was "charged with the primary responsibility for the conduct of land-based strategic air operations against Japan with the object of accomplishing the progressive destruction and dislocation of Japan's military, industrial and economic systems to a point where her capacity for armed resistance is fatally weakened." The Commanding

General, USASTAF, would "continue operations to support the accomplishment of the over-all objective to defeat Japan and will cooperate with CINCAFPAC and CINCPAC in the preparation and execution of plans for the invasion of Japan." He would cooperate with the other Pacific commands and they would meet his logistic needs, "subject to the over-all availability of resources." The Joint Chiefs, through Arnold, would forward directions to USASTAF.[59]

The positioning of Spaatz at strategic headquarters on Guam, commanding all strategic bombers—B-29s and B-17s—came close to provoking a major confrontation with the Navy. Arnold had received word from Marshall that the Navy wanted only the Twentieth Air Force Headquarters on Guam. Arnold had planned to base the B-29s on Tinian, Saipan, and Guam with the B-17s on Okinawa. "The Navy's attitude," Arnold emphasized, "of telling us what to do with our strategic bombing headquarters was, to me, intolerable. They certainly would not countenance the War Department's telling them where to locate the headquarters of their fleet units, and surely they had no strategic bombing experience."[60] With bombing forces moving from Europe to the Pacific, Arnold's goal was to inaugurate "the maximum mass bombing of Japan in the minimum of time." He suggested that Marshall inform the Navy that "we would definitely put our strategic bombing headquarters at Guam and it would be there with the other B-29 units, period!"[61]

Arnold's view that the Navy was poking into AAF issues "that were really none of their business" was assuaged by a visit with Admiral Nimitz. Actually, Arnold had always gotten along well with Nimitz, who stressed that he would welcome AAF officers on his staff. Moreover, he would be willing to have a representative of Spaatz's headquarters work with the Navy staff to determine shipping priorities, always a sensitive issue between the AAF and the Navy. Arnold concluded that Spaatz would have no difficulty in working things out with Nimitz. Not for the first time, he realized that "people down along the line were making mountains out of mole hills."[62] Still, problems would remain until the end of the war, for example between the Far East Air Forces and the Navy in coordinating strike missions from the Japanese Inland Sea.

Interestingly, a dissent to the mission of the Twentieth Air Force and the USASTAF was registered at AAF Headquarters by Brig. Gen. John A. Samford, Deputy Assistant Chief of Air Staff for Intelligence (Targets). In a memo to the Chief of the Air Staff, Samford claimed that the mission was "alienating rather than impressive." The wording—"progressive destruction and dislocation of the Japanese military, industrial, and economic systems to a point where Japan's capacity for war is decisively weakened"— struck Samford as placing strategic bombardment "on a pedestal as not being a means to an end but the end itself." This, according to Samford, handicapped "our relations both with other arms and with realistic civilians because of the inference that the strategic bombardment purpose is that of winning the war preferably unaided." Samford's voice though, was clearly drowned out in the summer of 1945 by the cacophony of B-29 attacks on the Japanese homeland.[63] Here Arnold was now satisfied that with Spaatz heading the B-29 forces in the Pacific, he had in place the proper organization to prosecute the final campaign that would bring Japan down.

General Arnold, making an address, placed great emphasis upon public relations during the entire war. He put great pressure on his operational commanders to get results and insisted during the war that they send him photos and data, corroborating their operations. Courtesy Air Force Historical Studies Office

Arnold inspects the Boeing plant at Wichita with Brig. Gen. Ray G. Harris, Midwestern Procurement District Supervisor (left), and J. E. Schaefer, Vice President and General Manager of Wichita Division. Arnold cut engineering and production corners to get the B-29 operational in the campaign to bomb the Japanese home islands. COURTESY AIR FORCE HISTORICAL STUDIES OFFICE

Secretary of War Henry L. Stimson played an important role in the early B-29 program and in the air power buildup prior to the war. He also played an important part in the Potsdam Conference, July–August 1945. COURTESY NATIONAL ARCHIVES

Harry L. Hopkins, a senior adviser to President Roosevelt, evolved into a conduit between FDR and Arnold. Hopkins argued for a major buildup of U.S. air power prior to World War II. COURTESY AIR FORCE HISTORICAL STUDIES OFFICE

Kenneth B. Wolfe, as a brigadier general, had been sent by General Arnold to command the XX Bomber Command in the China-Burma-India theater. Earlier, a key figure in the B-29 production program, Wolfe was replaced as commander of the XX Bomber Command by Curtis E. LeMay, a hard driver. COURTESY NATIONAL AIR AND SPACE MUSEUM

At the Quebec Conference, Arnold, back row, far left, presented the Air Plan for the Defeat of Japan. Seated in front, Canadian Prime Minister Mackenzie King, President Roosevelt, and British Prime Minister Winston Churchill. COURTESY AIR FORCE HISTORICAL STUDIES OFFICE

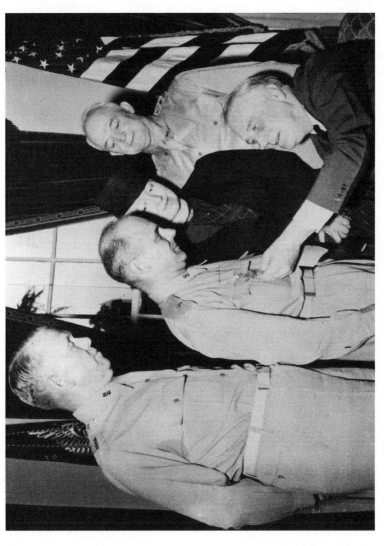

President Roosevelt presents the Medal of Honor to Lt. Col. James H. Doolittle for his leadership in the raid on Tokyo on April 18, 1942. From left, Gen. Marshall; Doolittle; Jo, Doolittle's wife; General Arnold; and seated, President Roosevelt. COURTESY NATIONAL AIR AND SPACE MUSEUM

General of the Army Douglas MacArthur, Commander of the Southwest Pacific theater, lobbied Arnold for air resources. In the summer of 1942, Arnold sent Maj. Gen. George C. Kenney to MacArthur. Kenney turned out to be one of the great operational airmen of the war. COURTESY AIR FORCE HISTORICAL STUDIES OFFICE

Attendees in January 1943 at the Casablanca Conference, where Roosevelt for the first time attempted to define "unconditional surrender." Left to right, front: Marshall, Roosevelt, King. Back: Hopkins, Arnold, Somervell, Harriman. Courtesy Air Force Historical Studies Office

President Franklin D. Roosevelt in November 1938 called for a major buildup of the air forces. General Arnold hailed FDR's clarion call as a "Magna Carta" for the nation's air arm, the first time that the Army Air Corps actually had a program. With Roosevelt's death in April 1945, Arnold said that the AAF "had lost the best friend it ever had."

Brig. Gen. Haywood S. Hansell, Jr., key air planner and advocate of high altitude precision bombing, who arrived in the Marianas in October 1944 to command the XXI Bomber Command. COURTESY AIR FORCE HISTORICAL STUDIES OFFICE

Adm. Chester W. Nimitz, Commander-in-Chief of U.S. forces in the Central Pacific, pictured here in August 1944, worked well with General Arnold, from time to time smoothing out disagreements between the Navy and the Army Air Forces. COURTESY U.S. NAVAL HISTORICAL CENTER

Home for the B-29s: Dispersed B-29s at North Field, Guam, in the Mariana Islands. In the forefront are planes of the 29th Bomb Group, 314th Wing. Background, B-29s of the 19th Bomb Group. Admiral Nimitz's Central Pacific command had taken the Marianas in August 1944. Subsequently, five airfields were built on Saipan, Tinian, and Guam. COURTESY AIR FORCE HISTORICAL STUDIES OFFICE

President Harry S. Truman presents Gen. Hap Arnold with the Distinguished Service Medal. COURTESY AIR FORCE HISTORICAL STUDIES OFFICE

Maj. Gen. Curtis E. LeMay, Commander of XXI Bomber Command of the Twentieth Air Force. In the spring and summer of 1945, LeMay's B-29s scourged Japan's major cities with incendiary attacks. COURTESY AIR FORCE HISTORICAL STUDIES OFFICE

President Harry S. Truman was gravely concerned about potential U.S. casualties in an invasion of Japan. While at the Potsdam Conference in July 1945, he was informed of the successful atomic test at Alamogordo, New Mexico, and subsequently gave approval to drop the atomic bomb.

Col. Paul W. Tibbets, Jr., pilot of the B-29 Enola Gay—*named after his mother—which dropped the atomic bomb on Hiroshima on August 6, 1945, a major event in Japan's capitulation, ushering in the atomic age.* COURTESY AIR FORCE HISTORICAL STUDIES OFFICE

With his drive and determination, Gen. Henry H. "Hap" Arnold, Commanding General, Army Air Forces, led the B-29 program to operational status. He commanded the Twentieth Air Force, reporting directly to the Joint Chiefs of Staff. COURTESY AIR FORCE HISTORICAL STUDIES OFFICE

General Arnold and General George C. Marshall, Army Chief of Staff, worked well together prior to and during the war. Marshall supported the buildup of the air forces and gave Arnold great flexibility in commanding the Army's air elements.

B-29s flying in formation during familiarization flights over the Marianas. COURTESY NATIONAL AIR AND SPACE MUSEUM

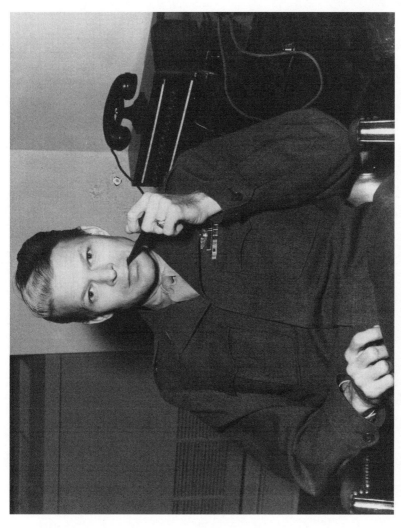

Brig. Gen. Lauris Norstad was Arnold's Chief of Staff of the Twentieth Air Force and a major force in the shift to incendiary bombing. COURTESY AIR FORCE HISTORICAL STUDIES OFFICE

The Potsdam Conference near Berlin in July 1945 was the last major wartime conclave. Norstad, Arnold, and Marshall, left to right, discussed atomic matters including potential targets for the A-bomb. COURTESY AIR FORCE HISTORICAL STUDIES OFFICE

B-29s of the 500th Bomb Group, 73rd Bomb Wing dropping incendiaries on installations at Yokohama, Japan, on May 29, 1945. COURTESY AIR FORCE HISTORICAL STUDIES OFFICE

B-29s of the 500th Bomb Group, 881st Squadron. COURTESY AIR FORCE HISTORICAL STUDIES OFFICE

On August 6, 1945, an atomic bomb was dropped from the B-29, Enola Gay, on the Japanese city of Hiroshima. Three days later, an atomic bomb was dropped on Nagasaki from the B-29, Bockscar. These atomic attacks prompted Emperor Hirohito to emphasize to his cabinet that the allies possessed "a cruel new weapon." COURTESY USAF COLLECTION

6

Arnold, Potsdam, and the Atomic Bomb

Arnold had only two weeks in Washington between his return from the Pacific and the TERMINAL conference in July at Potsdam with Truman, Churchill, Stalin, and the Combined Chiefs of Staff. This turned out to be the last major wartime conference, coming three months after Germany's surrender, and featuring Harry Truman, the new American president. Truman, who had been sworn in as president on April 12, 1945, and who for several years in the Senate had been Chairman of the Special Committee to Investigate the National Defense Program, had not known about the Manhattan Project to develop the atomic bomb. Stimson had been entrusted by Roosevelt with supervision of the atomic project while Maj. Gen. Leslie R. Groves managed it. On April 25, Stimson briefed Truman on the "highly secret matter," informing him that "within four months we shall in all probability have completed the most terrible weapon ever known in human history, one bomb of which could destroy a whole city."[1] After Germany's surrender in May, the Joint Chiefs had expressed concern that the American public would become weary of the war. Admiral King noted that pressure on the home front might "force a negotiated peace, before the Japs are really licked." Marshall was worried about "the possibility of a general letdown" after V-E Day, not only among the citizenry, but also within the American military.[2]

Yet, even in July, prior to Potsdam, when Japan's major urban areas had been decimated, Arnold continued to nettle his operational commanders in the field. Thus, he queried LeMay on the Japanese potential to develop jet interceptors, similar to the German Me-163 and Me-262. "We know he is working energetically along these lines," Arnold wrote, "in a desperate attempt to stave off defeat from the air."[3] Arnold implored LeMay to maintain heightened reconnaissance and intelligence in order to track any potential signs of Japanese activity in the jet field. "We have the Nip where we want him," Arnold noted, "and constant vigilance will prevent his having a chance to exploit anything he may have learned from the Hun."[4]

LeMay's reply pointed out that Japanese interest in jet aircraft had been intense and sustained over a long period. He tied the Japanese effort to the B-29 offensive: "It would be logical to assume that the Japs have concentrated experimental effort upon jet aircraft, especially during the past year, in an effort to develop an aircraft with high altitude performance, speed and fire power sufficient to cope with the B-29."[5] LeMay, however, felt confident that the Japanese effort was not about to produce an operational jet aircraft. The Japanese were now concentrating on the expected invasion of the homeland and their production now emphasized established models and replacement parts and engines. Conversion of production facilities to jet-propulsion was considered unlikely.

On June 29, prior to the Berlin Conference at Potsdam, the Joint Chiefs of Staff promulgated a memorandum detailing the "development of operations in the Pacific." In consonance with the overall objective of bringing about the unconditional surrender of Japan, the Joint Chiefs first emphasized the goal of intensifying the blockade and air bombardment of Japan in order to prepare the way for an invasion of Kyushu to be followed by "the decisive invasion of the industrial heart of Japan through the Tokyo Plain."[6] The Joint Chiefs decided to defer their thrust into the Ryukyus in favor of gearing up for the Kyushu assault on November 1, 1945, with a target date of March 1, 1946, for the invasion of the Tokyo Plain. In consonance with the DOWNFALL plan for the defeat of Japan, this planning for the two-pronged assault was predicated on the concept that "defeat of the enemy's armed forces in the Japanese homeland is a prerequisite to unconditional surrender."[7]

In addition, the Combined Chiefs of Staff in early July reassessed the status of the war against Japan, concluding that the Japanese were militarily defeated and in dire condition. Japan's last shot was to convince her enemies that continuance of the war would prove enormously costly and drawn out, "weakening the determination of the United Nations to fight to the bitter end." Thus, the Japanese were desperately attempting to keep the Soviet Union neutral, buying time for some kind of negotiated settlement with the Allies to end the war. According to the Combined Chiefs, the Japanese ruling groups found the unconditional surrender policy unacceptable. The majority of the Japanese population, however, considered "absolute military defeat to be probable." The blockade and bombing were taking a terrible toll. The B-29 campaign had made millions homeless and destroyed large areas of Japan's cities. Nonetheless, the Japanese were not ready to accept unconditional surrender.[8]

Just prior to the Potsdam conference, the Joint Chiefs, in a memorandum for President Truman, set forth revised details of the campaign against Japan. Again, the Chiefs pointed to an invasion as "the only sure way, and certainly the quickest way, to force the surrender of Japan."[9] The overall objective remained forcing Japan's unconditional surrender by maintaining sea and air blockades, conducting intensive air bombardment, destroying Japanese air and naval strength, and finally, invading the home islands. Planning called for an "assault" on Kyushu (OLYMPIC) to destroy enemy forces and gain bases to intensify the blockade and air bombardment. This plan was designed to put intense pressure on the Japanese so that at some point "they will admit defeat in order to avoid further destruction."[10]

The Japanese navy, according to the Joint Chiefs, was no longer viable. The air arm, committing training aircraft to combat, continued to devote major units to suicide operations. Thus, with Japanese forces in a critical state, after the Kyushu assault and prior to the planned invasion of the Tokyo Plain (CORONET), the Joint Chiefs planned a major effort to exploit the blockade and bombardment of Japan. With the addition of air bases on Kyushu, to accommodate about forty groups, the Joint Chiefs again pointed out that "more bombs will be dropped on Japan than were delivered against Germany during the entire European war." If, for some reason however, the invasion of the Tokyo plain should not be considered feasible on the anticipated date, "a course of action to extend bombardment and blockade is open to us."[11]

This then, was how the Joint Chiefs assessed the strategic situation in the summer of 1945, prior to Potsdam, and as it subsequently turned out, before the dropping of atomic bombs and the surrender of Japan. This raises two relevant questions for the historian: Were the Joint Chiefs correct in their insistence—actually going back earlier in the war—that an invasion of Japan would be necessary at the quickest way to end the war? And secondly, was the Allied insistence on unconditional surrender the correct policy? I believe that the answer to both questions is in the affirmative. Given the attack on Pearl Harbor, the character of the Pacific war—stunning, early victories by the Japanese, and the atrocities—the JCS would have been clearly negligent had they not consistently planned to ultimately invade Japan as the coup de grace. Certainly, the Chiefs in 1943 onward could not count on the bombing and blockade to end the war, although in retrospect that is the way it came out. As to the unconditional surrender policy, it had been cut by Roosevelt and Churchill from the very fabric of total war. Certainly the Japanese—early on thinking that the Americans would somehow accept a negotiated settlement of the conflict—retained no idea of the rage they had stoked in the U.S. body politic. Eric Larrabee, in his fine work on Roosevelt as Commander-in-Chief, has described the deeply felt character of the unconditional surrender policy:

> This was the route to which the President gave his powerful assent. The choice of it led a long way, longer perhaps than any other choice the Allies made. Their political objectives were implicit in the way they chose to fight, and could not be readjusted retroactively as the fighting drew to a close. That is, the total defeat of their enemies came first, and determined the strategies employed to that end.[12]

Unconditional surrender was the correct and indeed the inevitable policy, given the deep, implacable feelings aroused by the total war unleashed by Imperial Japan.[13] In early May 1945, when announcing the end of the war in Europe, President Truman made forcefully clear his agreement with the unconditional surrender policy:

> The Japanese people have felt the weight of our land, air, and naval attacks. So long as their leaders and the armed forces continue the war the striking power and intensity of our blows will steadily increase and will bring utter destruction to Japan's industrial war production, to its shipping, and to everything that supports its military activity.
>
> The longer the war lasts, the greater will be the suffering and hardships which the people of Japan will undergo—all in vain. Our blows will not cease until the Japanese military and naval forces lay down their arms in *unconditional surrender*.[14]

Truman and his advisers prepared for the Potsdam meeting. Acting Secretary of State Joseph C. Grew was convinced that the Japanese could be persuaded to capitulate provided that the Allies crafted a declaration that left the institution of the emperor intact. After Roosevelt died, Truman held his first cabinet meeting: Stimson tarried after the meeting, telling Truman he needed to speak to him about an urgent matter. According to Truman, Stimson informed him about "a project looking to the development of a new explosive of almost unbelievable destructive power." Truman noted that the information Stimson imparted "left me puzzled." It was the first information that he had received about the atomic bomb. Truman commented that it was "a miracle" that such a vast project could be kept secret from members of Congress.[15] On July 16, at Potsdam, Truman was informed of the successful atomic test at Alamogordo. It "not only met the most optimistic expectations of the scientists," he stated, "but that the United States had in its possession an explosive force of unparalleled power."[16]

The atom bomb project in the United States had its origin in a letter of August 2, 1939, from physicist Dr. Albert Einstein to President Roosevelt. Einstein noted the possibility of building a bomb of enormous power from uranium. Consequently, he stated that "certain aspects of the situation which has arisen seem to call for watchfulness and, if necessary, quick action on the part of the Administration."[17] Einstein pointed out to Roosevelt that the possibility of building a bomb was real: "This new phenomenon would also lead to the construction of bombs, and it is conceivable—though much less certain—that extremely powerful bombs of a new type may thus be constructed. A single bomb of this type, carried by boat and exploded in a port, might very well destroy the whole port together with some of the surrounding territory. However, such bombs might very well prove to be too heavy for transportation by air."[18] Subsequently, the Los Alamos laboratory, under Dr. J. R. Oppenheimer, was tasked with the project to develop an aerial bomb. Leslie R. Groves was promoted to major general and placed in charge of the Manhattan Engineer District, its objective to develop an atomic bomb.

This is the bare outline of how Einstein's letter got to Roosevelt. The details of this extraordinary event are far more interesting and complicated. The possibility of setting up a nuclear chain reaction in a large mass of uranium was suggested to Einstein by Leo Szilard, a Hungarian physicist and old friend.[19] The problem remained of how to deliver the letter to the president. Szilard, amazingly enough, suggested that Charles Lindbergh deliver it, unaware that the celebrity aviator was apparently sympathetic to Nazi Germany and had been decorated by Hermann Goering with Germany's medal of honor.[20]

Financier Bernard Baruch and MIT President Karl Compton were also considered. Szilard and Einstein finally settled on Alexander Sachs, an economist at the investment and banking house of Lehman Brothers and a friend of Roosevelt's. However, it took Sachs almost two months to deliver the letter to Roosevelt. On October 11, 1939, Sachs saw the president, and actually read a summation of the letter to him. According to Walter Isaacson, Einstein's biographer, Roosevelt replied: "Alex, What you are after is to see that the Nazis don't blow us up." President Roosevelt then indicated to his personal assistant that "this requires action."[21] Still, as it turned out, it took months to get the Manhattan Project rolling formally. In June 1942, the atomic bomb project was assigned to the U.S. Army Corps of Engineers. The Manhattan Engineer District was created to direct nuclear weapons development. Subsequently, Leslie R. Groves (then a colonel) was named to direct the Manhattan Project. Not only had the Germans been working on an atomic bomb, but the Japanese had also started work on it. The Japanese had established two atomic bomb research programs, one under the Army and another under the Navy. Neither program could be compared to the Manhattan Project. The Army's atomic research laboratory in Tokyo was in fact destroyed by a B-29 attack in April 1945.[22]

Although Arnold in the summer of 1943 had been informed of the Manhattan Project, in the spring of 1944 Maj. Gen. Leslie Groves gave him a detailed briefing on the status of atomic bomb development and an estimate of when the bomb might be ready for use. Groves wanted to employ the B-29 as the carrier, but was not certain that it would work out. And he thus suggested that the British Lancaster bomber might also be considered. Characteristically, Arnold, displeased, assured him that the AAF could do the job and that he would have a B-29 ready to accomplish the mission. Arnold and Groves plotted three major tasks for the air arm: providing modified B-29s able to carry the bomb, organizing and training the tactical unit to accomplish the mission, and finally, delivering the bomb on target. Additionally, Groves needed Arnold's help in testing the bomb's ballistics and transportation for equipment and materials.[23]

Groves recalls that in early 1945 the time had arrived to request the help of General Marshall's Operations Division (OPD) in planning for the actual operation. According to Groves, Marshall, especially sensitive to security requirements, reacted: "I don't like to bring too many people into this matter. Is there any reason why you can't take this over and do it yourself?"[24] Groves was surprised that Marshall wanted to keep the atomic operation completely out of OPD's hands, but Groves got together with Arnold and planned how to resolve the targeting issue. Ultimately, a special targeting committee was set up with inputs from the Military Policy Committee, scientists at Los Alamos, and operations analysts from Arnold's headquarters. Groves recounted that among the guidelines in target selection were the following: places chosen should greatly affect the ability of the Japanese people to continue the war, targets should have military significance, and targets should not have been attacked previously, thus enabling an accurate assessment of the bomb's effectiveness.[25]

The target committee initially selected Kokura, Hiroshima, Kyoto, and Niigata. The inclusion of Kyoto, a large city and a military target, was rejected by Secretary of War Stimson on the grounds that it had been the ancient capital of Japan with great religious significance to the Japanese people. Arnold and Groves had favored Kyoto on the target list, but Stimson remained adamant. When Groves informed Stimson that he would prefer checking with General Marshall, Stimson replied: "This is a question I am settling myself. Marshall is not making that decision."[26] Subsequently, Nagasaki was added to the list. In retrospect, Groves applauded Stimson's decision, noting that he was happy to have been overruled, and that "through Mr. Stimson's wisdom, the number of Japanese casualties had been greatly reduced."[27]

Arnold directed Maj. Gen. Oliver Echols, the AAF's air material chief, to take charge of the modification project, conducting ballistics, and organizing the B-29 combat unit. In turn, Echols chose Col. Roscoe C. Wilson as his special project officer with priority over all AAF projects. Wilson was directed to refer all major difficulties from any agency directly to Arnold. Modifications of B-29s, with a goal of fifteen aircraft, got underway early in 1944. During the summer, the organization of a special combat unit began; the 393rd Bombardment Squadron formed the basis for the 509th Composite Wing, Arnold selecting Col. Paul W. Tibbets, Jr. to command the new unit. Tibbets had flown heavy as well as medium bombers, flying heavies in North Africa and Europe, and also had experience as a test pilot with the B-29. General LeMay, commanding the XXI Bomber Command in the Marianas, learned about the atomic bomb and the building of a special unit to deliver it in March 1945. By July, the 509th Group was in place on Tinian island in the Marianas.[28] The successful test of the new bomb on July 16 in the New Mexico desert opened the way for President Truman at Potsdam to confer with Stimson, Marshall, and Arnold regarding the timing and targeting of the weapon.

The two major issues to be discussed at Potsdam were the employment of the atomic bomb and the entry of the Soviet Union into the war against Japan. At Potsdam on July 16, the first meeting of the Combined Chiefs described the situation for Japan as basically hopeless. The enemy could not counter Allied sea and air offensives, its capabilities reduced to suicide operations. Noteworthy, the Combined Chiefs made the point that the incendiary bombing attack on Japan's cities was having "profound" psychological and economic effects. War production centers had been shattered, resulting also in a loss of communications and control. A subsequent all-out campaign against transportation could result in a cataclysmic collapse within the Japanese nation. The Combined Chiefs, however, figured that there was little prospect of surrender until the Japanese military acknowledged defeat. The Potsdam conference, July 17 to August 2, saw Truman and Churchill approve the Combined Chiefs of Staff report on July 24 for the conduct of the war against Japan: "In cooperation with other Allies to bring about at the earliest possible date the defeat of Japan by: lowering Japanese ability and will to resist by establishing sea and air blockades, conducting intensive air bombardment, and destroying Japanese air and naval strength; invading and seizing objectives in the Japanese home islands as the main effort. ... " Further, the plan for the defeat of Japan (DOWNFALL), with the overall objective of unconditional surrender, aimed at invasions of Kyushu and Honshu as well as even intensifying the blockade and air bombardment. The Combined Chiefs emphasized that defeat of the enemy in the home islands was a "prerequisite" to unconditional surrender. The Combined Chiefs also noted that Soviet entry into the war against Japan should be encouraged and they further recommended that for planning purposes the date for the end of "organized resistance" by Japan should be November 15, 1946, and that this date should be adjusted periodically as circumstances dictated.[29]

Truman, in his memoir, insisted that at Potsdam the military had agreed with employment of the atomic bomb against Japan.[30] Arnold however, stated his position at Potsdam that—although not opposed to using the atomic bomb—employment of the bomb was not necessary to defeat Japan.[31] Margaret Truman, in her book on her father, states that Arnold alone of the Joint Chiefs thought that Japan could be bombed into capitulation by the conventional B-29 campaign.[32] The official U.S. Army history emphasized that Arnold at Potsdam read into the record a statement "representing the most optimistic point of view" of when the Japanese might be forced to surrender, namely by the end of October 1945: According to Arnold, "In the employment of these forces in the Ryukyus supplementing the present forces in the Marianas, we expect to achieve the disruption of the Japanese military, industrial and economic systems. ... We estimate that this can be done with our forces available in the month prior to the invasion of Japan. *Japan, in fact, will become a nation without cities, with her transportation disrupted and will have tremendous difficulty in holding her people together for continued resistance to our terms of unconditional surrender.*"[33] Moreover, as we have seen, Arnold was not present at the June 18, 1945, meeting at the White House, but was in the Marianas where he had met with LeMay. Apparently at General Marshall's direction, Gen. Ira Eaker sat in for Arnold at the meeting with Truman and the Joint Chiefs. Although Eaker stated his agreement—based, he said, on a cable he had received from Arnold—with the need to invade the home islands, Arnold had in his own mind decided that it would not be required, based on the briefing he had received from LeMay on Guam. For his part, Truman was well aware of the impact that blockade and bombardment were having on the Japanese home islands.

Secretary of War Stimson had drafted a declaration on July 2 along the lines that Ambassador Joseph Grew proposed. The final version of the Potsdam Declaration however, promulgated on July 26, made no reference to the future status of the emperor, as recommended by Stimson. In Stimson's memorandum to President Truman outlining his "Proposed Program for Japan," which became the basis for the Potsdam Declaration of July 26, he noted that plans were authorized and proceeding for the assault on Kyushu. Stimson was gravely concerned that the invasion would provoke "fanatical resistance" by the Japanese, similar to what the Americans faced on Okinawa and Iwo Jima. He noted his familiarity with the terrain, which impressed him as being conducive to "a last ditch defense."[34] Stimson was looking for an alternative to a potentially enormously expensive invasion. He thought that if the emperor were allowed to stay, and this could be communicated to the Japanese, it might make a difference and influence Japanese leaders toward a surrender. Stimson's thrust however, was opposed by Secretary of State James Byrnes.

An invasion, Stimson noted, would be an "even more bitter finish fight than in Germany." Consequently, he suggested as an alternative that the Japanese be given a warning, providing an opportunity to capitulate. According to Stimson, such a warning calling on Japan to surrender would be issued in plenty of time for a national reaction to occur. Stimson pointed to a number of favorable factors that the allies had in play as opposed to the situation against Germany. These included the tight blockade and the impact of the powerful strategic bombing campaign against the home islands to which Japan was exceedingly vulnerable.[35]

Stimson was convinced that the timing was appropriate, that Japan was now susceptible to such a thrust, more so than generally believed. Japan, he emphasized, "is not a nation composed wholly of mad fanatics of an entirely different mentality from ours." Prior to the takeover by the military in 1931, he noted, Japan had adhered to the norms of international life and discourse. Japan presently had the capacity to recognize the folly of a fight to the finish and to accept an unconditional surrender. Conversely, Stimson thought that an invasion and a horrific fight, with its impact on the civilian population, which would be enlisted in the fight, would be enormously debilitating, with no analogy with the case of Germany. Thus, he concluded that a carefully timed warning be issued to Japan by the allies calling for a surrender "to insure its complete demilitarization for the sake of future peace."[36] This warning would make clear the overwhelming force that was about to be unleashed with its attendant massive destruction and removal of influence and authority of those who embarked Japan upon conquest. Japanese sovereignty would be restricted to the main home islands. The Allied occupiers would withdraw from the Japanese homeland when there had been established a government inclined towards peace, of a character representing the Japanese people.[37]

A number of Stimson's points found their way into the Potsdam Proclamation Defining Terms for Japanese Surrender (usually called just the Potsdam Declaration), most having to do with rebuilding industry and maintaining international trade relations. However, his major point about keeping the institution of the emperor was not included.[38] Meantime, on July 16, at Alamogordo, New Mexico, the atomic bomb was successfully exploded. Reports of the test arrived at Potsdam where Stimson informed Truman and Churchill. On July 24, Stalin was told about the existence of the bomb.

Then, on the twenty-sixth, based on Stimson's memorandum, the United States, the United Kingdom, and China promulgated the Potsdam Declaration, which noted that "the full application of our military power, backed by our resolve, will mean the inevitable and complete destruction of the Japanese armed forces and just as inevitably the utter destruction of the Japanese homeland." The Japanese now had the opportunity to end the war. In order to do so, however, the Japanese would have to break the will of "those self-willed militaristic advisers whose unintelligent calculations have brought the empire of Japan to the threshold of annihilation." The declaration stated the following terms for the surrender of Japan: "the elimination of irresponsible militarism; temporary occupation of points in Japanese territory; limitation of Japanese sovereignty to the islands of Honshu, Hokkaido, Kyushu, Shikoku, and minor islands; the return of Japanese military forces to their homes; the punishment of war criminals; the maintenance of industries to sustain Japanese economy and permit the exaction of reparations in kind; eventual participation in world trade relations; and occupation by Allied forces until a peacefully inclined and responsible government had been established in Japan." The declaration then called upon Japan "to proclaim now the unconditional surrender of all Japanese armed forces, and to provide proper and adequate assurances of their good faith in such action. The alternative for Japan is prompt and utter destruction."[39] The Potsdam Declaration contained nothing about the potential employment of an atomic bomb. In late July, however, the Japanese Prime Minister Suzuki gave his answer to the Potsdam Declaration with a "mokusatsu" reaction: treating it "with silent contempt." It was unacceptable. Emperor Hirohito remained silent.

As far as use of the atomic bomb was concerned, Truman relied heavily on Marshall and Arnold. Leading up to Potsdam, the specific power and potential of the atomic bomb were not known; and the effect of its employment on the Japanese was also of course unknown. As we have noted, Truman had not known about the bomb until after he became president. Military planning for the invasion had gone forward without knowledge of the bomb's existence. Arnold was kept informed by Marshall and Stimson. After General Groves's report of the successful atomic experiment arrived at Potsdam, Arnold met with Marshall, Stimson, McCloy, and Bundy. "This did not come as a complete surprise to me," Arnold noted, "but I had thought the test was a week or two away. From the information we received, the scientists were very well pleased with the results. ... The results of that test proved conclusively that we had in our possession the means to wipe out completely large areas of an enemy country."[40] Thus, Arnold immediately grasped the revolutionary importance of the new weapon and its potential for a knock-out blow against Japan.

On July 22, Arnold and Marshall met with Stimson to discuss what Arnold termed "the big questions": When would the bomb be ready to use against Japan and what were the proper targets for optimum results? Arnold suggested leaving the issue of targets to General Spaatz, "who had planes ready and waiting out in the Pacific for the arrival of the bomb and who knew the cities chosen for the test."[41] On July 24, Arnold received a report from General Groves detailing the plan and schedule for employing the atomic bombs, termed "special bombs." The first bomb (gun type), "will be ready to drop between August 1 and 10 and plans are to drop it the first day of good weather following readiness." The report specified four targets: Hiroshima, Kokura, Niigata and Nagasaki. Hiroshima was described as an "Army" city, a major port of entry with large quartermaster and supply depots and industry and small shipyards. Nagasaki was a major shipping and industrial center on Kyushu. Industrialists and political figures were thought to have fled to all four cities. The report noted that the bomb would be "carried in a master airplane accompanied by two other project B-29s with observers and special instruments. The three B-29s will take off from North Field, Tinian, and fly via Iwo Jima."[42] Arnold then insisted that Spaatz, commanding the Strategic Air Forces in the Pacific, be given sufficient flexibility in timing and targeting to employ the bomb. This was accepted by Stimson and Marshall. Arnold then forthwith sent Spaatz a cable directing him to be ready to employ the bomb against Japan. On the twenty-fifth, the War Department order was signed in Washington by Gen. Thomas T. Handy, acting Army Chief of Staff:

> The 509 Composite Group, 20th Air Force, will deliver its first special bomb as soon as weather will permit visual bombing after about 3 August 1945 on one of the targets: Hiroshima, Kokura, Niigata, and Nagasaki. … Additional bombs will be delivered on the above targets as soon as made ready by the project staff. Further instructions will be issued concerning targets other than those listed above. … The foregoing directive is issued to you by direction and with the approval of the Secretary of War and the Chief of Staff, USA. It is desired that you personally deliver one copy of this directive to General MacArthur and one copy to Admiral Nimitz for their information.[43]

The directive was sent to Potsdam and approved by Stimson, Marshall, and Truman. In his memoir, President Truman wrote, "With this order the wheels are set in motion for the first use of an atomic weapon against a military target. I had made the decision. I also instructed Stimson that the order would stand unless I notified him that the Japanese reply to our ultimatum was acceptable."[44]

Spaatz's views on dropping the bomb and the potential invasion are of great interest here in light of Handy's directive to Spaatz, approved at the highest levels of the War Department. Spaatz in fact insisted on a written order and had carried Handy's directive with him to Guam. After the dropping of atomic bombs on Hiroshima and Nagasaki and the Japanese conditional surrender message of August 10, forwarded to the Swiss and Swedish, Spaatz wrote a memo dated August 11, 1945, not sent to anyone specifically, but apparently to get his thoughts on the record. In it he noted that prior to the Japanese message of the tenth, he had intended to write to Robert Lovett, "repeating my views toward invasion." Spaatz recounted that the atomic bomb was first discussed with him in Washington, apparently when he was transferring from command of the USSTAF in Europe to taking command of the Strategic Air Forces in the Pacific. "I was not in favor of it," Spaatz wrote, "just as I have never favored the destruction of cities as such with all inhabitants being killed."[45] According to Spaatz, it was pointed out to him, probably by Lovett and others—Arnold, Stimson, and Marshall being at Potsdam—that employment of the bomb would mean that an invasion would not be necessary and thousands of American lives would be saved. As of August 10, Spaatz noted that an invasion was still planned "and only the surrendering of the Japanese after attacks on their homeland by air will cancel the invasion." Spaatz always made the point well after the war that in the summer of 1945 the leadership of the Army Air Forces thought that an invasion was not necessary and that the dropping of the atomic bombs was a political decision; the military man followed through. This was clearly the view of the entire AAF leadership.

With the directive having gone out for the use of the atomic bomb, Arnold, Marshall, and Stimson at Potsdam continued to talk over the relevant issues and implications of its employment. In Arnold's mind, the key question revolved around which targets, if bombed, "would most speedily spell the destruction of industrial Japan." He was well aware of the race to force Japan to capitulate prior to the mounting of an invasion of the home islands. At the same time, Secretary Stimson, as noted, was much concerned about the potential for enormous civilian casualties. Arnold did not seem overly concerned about this question, returning time and again to the issue of targeting: "There was no doubt that the effect of the atomic bomb would be much severer if it were exploded over an area in a valley, with high ridges on both sides to concentrate the effect of the blast, than if dropped over a coastal plain or over a large, flat area inland."[46] Arnold also suggested to Stimson and Marshall the idea of dropping an atomic bomb in a harbor. He thought that such an explosion "sunk hundreds of feet in the mud beneath the water, might well destroy the surrounding area. I suggested that we evacuate a Japanese harbor after the war, put ships at dock and at anchor, and then try it. In that way we would learn what might happen to one of our land-locked harbors in case the same thing occurred to us when we least expected it. However, the test was never carried out."[47]

Arnold thought that Soviet Premier Stalin's promise at Potsdam to declare war on Japan was "good news," as it might result in air bases closer to Japan, "from which we could literally rip Japan to pieces."[48] Given the difficulty that the AAF had experienced in dealing with the Soviets over potential Siberian air bases, along with the progress of the incendiary bombing, this came as a most curious comment by Arnold. He then informed the Combined Chiefs that air supremacy over Japan was complete and that the bombing campaign was not meeting with air resistance. The Japanese air force was a shambles, had lost most of its pilots, and was short of fuel. In reply to Stalin's point that now that the war in Europe was over, the next meeting should be in Tokyo, Arnold emphasized to the Allied leaders "that if our B-29s continued their present tempo there would be nothing left of Tokyo in which to have a meeting."[49] This apparently was Arnold's oblique way of informing Churchill, Stalin, and Truman that the "present tempo" of B-29 conventional bombing could drive Japan out of the war. Again, Arnold was not about to make a flat prediction of when Japan would capitulate. Historian Michael Kort has pointed out that Arnold's emphasis upon strategic bombing concomitant with his reluctance to spell out a strategy or surrender date in fact provided support to King and Leahy's position: "While Army Air Force General Henry (Hap) Arnold declined to advocate a specific strategy openly, his emphasis on strategic bombing lent support to the overall naval strategy."[50]

Following promulgation of the Potsdam Declaration and the end of the conference, Arnold looked forward to continuing redeployment of air forces to the Pacific theater. He planned to operate B-17s and B-24s as well as medium bombers from Okinawa. He had an interim report of the U.S. Strategic Bombing Survey on the European theater in hand, which emphasized: "The strategic air offensive ... effectively paralyzed the German war economy and thereby contributed in a decisive measure to the early and complete victory which followed."[51]

Meanwhile, the Joint Target Group had been briefed by various Strategic Bombing Survey teams back from Europe. The Strategic Bombing Survey personnel emphasized that Japan's war-making capability was not comparable to Germany's in the summer of 1945; Japan was on the verge of collapse. As of late June, the Japanese were unable to stem the tide of air attack: "Japan's position as a strong military and industrial power is already terminated."[52] The U.S. Strategic Bombing Survey group recommended as top priority a sustained attack on the Japanese transportation system, the rail network, and shipping. In July 1945, such a campaign would in all probability force a Japanese surrender through starvation. As far as attacks on urban industrial concentrations were concerned, these were to be conducted only if "the most efficient method of destroying such precision targets is by area rather than precision attack."[53] Here was still more corroboration of the potential effectiveness of area bombing targeting civilian morale and the work force. Based on the Strategic Bombing Survey briefings, the Joint Target Group concluded that continued incendiary attacks would have the most significant effect on Japan, accelerating "the collapse obtainable eventually through the engagement of large land forces."[54]

In addition to the report of the Joint Target Group, Arnold's staff at Potsdam had reached some important conclusions about the incendiary campaign against Japan. Statistics as to the number of cities attacked or individual industrial plants destroyed failed to reflect either the strategic concept or the significance of the results. In July, the campaign had been extended to smaller cities. Gifu was cited as an area that included industry, a transportation nexus, aircraft production, and an "important residential area for the labor force." The staff pointed out that the B-29 attacks "must be evaluated on a qualitative as well as a quantitative basis." Destruction of specific, critical small industrial plants might be more important than smashing a large steel mill. More importantly, Arnold's staff thought that modern conflict equaled "total war in which the importance of the individual plant tends to be somewhat decreased while the aggregate importance of many plants, and in fact all economic resources, including the labor force, tends to be increased."[55] Here was corroboration that area incendiary attack resulting in enormous numbers of labor force evacuees continued to be the first priority of the B-29 campaign and required intensification.

Arnold followed up by proposing to the Joint Chiefs that operations against Japan should, first of all, place "complete emphasis" on the strategic air offensive, throwing everything into an intensive onslaught, complemented by the naval and air blockade. While present planning for strategic bombardment "is expected to create conditions favorable to invasion of the Japanese homeland on November 1st, it is believed that an acceleration and augmentation of the strategic air program culminating in a land campaign, will bring about the defeat of Japan with a minimum loss of American lives."[56] Here Arnold felt the need to reiterate to the Joint Chiefs that the Joint Target Group had estimated that the economic and military capacity of Japan could be destroyed by dropping 1,620,000 tons of bombs. This kind of air campaign, according to Arnold, could destroy the Japanese nation. At the very least, it would assure the success of an invasion, concomitantly reducing the loss of American lives.[57] There is little doubt what Arnold had in mind here: Japan could be forced to surrender without a ground assault on the homeland. And he was now stating this clearly to the Joint Chiefs.

At Potsdam, where urgent issues were being considered, Arnold convened his staff to present his vision of what needed to be accomplished in the future. "The war with Japan," Arnold announced, "is over as far as creative work is concerned. The die is cast. There is very little we can do other than see the planes and personnel with supplies get over there."[58] Arnold's eye was on the future, making certain that von Karman's Scientific Advisory Group, which he had established, could provide "a Buck Rogers program to cover the next 20 years."[59] He did not want to see the air forces ever again caught as unprepared as they had been at Pearl Harbor.

Well before the Potsdam conference, in the spring of 1945, under heavy pressure from the Navy, Arnold had reluctantly directed the Twentieth Air Force to initiate an aerial mining campaign of Japanese waters and harbors. Admiral Nimitz had requested that the campaign start in January, but Hansell was adamantly opposed to it; Arnold finally agreed to commence mining operations in April. Nimitz actually had pressed his case in the summer and fall of 1944, but Kuter and Norstad were against it, arguing it was time-consuming and a lower priority than the B-29 bombing campaign against the home islands.[60] Hansell agreed, stating that mining amounted to a misuse of the B-29s: "Mining is a tactical naval operation," he emphasized, "and I am opposed to sending B-29s singly on low-altitude night missions. I have always been opposed to night operations."[61] In line with AAF doctrine, the Superfortress was the weapon to pound Japan's war-supporting production rather than to be committed to a sideshow. Arnold, always alert and pre-emptive to real or imagined naval encroachments, may possibly have ordered the Twentieth to go ahead out of fear that the Navy otherwise might make its case yet again for land-based long-range aircraft.

However, back in August 1944, the XX Bomber Command in the CBI theater had dropped sea mines by parachute along enemy sea lanes in Sumatra, closing an important river link to Palembang.[62] Shortly after arriving on Guam, LeMay met with Nimitz, and although initially reluctant, LeMay was convinced by Nimitz to establish a joint task force for aerial mining operations. This became Operation Starvation, designed to shut down Japan's importation of food and raw materials by blockading the Inland Sea and Tokyo and Nagoya and mining the Shimonoseki Straits between Honshu and Kyushu. LeMay, who succeeded Hansell in January, selected the 313th Bombardment Wing to mine the Shimonoseki Straits, linking the Inland Sea with the Sea of Japan, beginning in late March 1945.

The mining was interrupted in April when the Twentieth supported the Okinawa campaign. In May however, more Japanese shipping was sunk by mines than by submarines. Between March and August 1945, B-29s flew thirty-four percent of all mine sorties by Allied aircraft, but laid sixty-three percent of all the mines. Of the two million tons of Japanese shipping sunk by mines, the B-29s were responsible for 1.25 million tons. During the campaign of four and a half months, the B-29s flew 1528 sorties and laid 12,053 mines, the heaviest aerial mining campaign ever conducted. Every major port and shipping lane in Japan and Korea was mined. Japan was effectively cut off, according to a Strategic Bombing Survey report, "virtually severed" from all water-borne supplies and raw materials, her shipping reduced to the status of "blockade runners." At the end of the war, huge quantities of raw materials and coal for Japan were stock-piled high in Korean ports due to the success of the blockade.[63]

Nimitz subsequently cabled LeMay: "The planning, operational and technical operation of aircraft mining, on a scale never before attained, has accomplished phenomenal results and is a credit to all concerned."[64] Even Hansell changed his mind, in retrospect noting that "The aerial mining campaign, as pushed by General LeMay, succeeded beyond anyone's expectation. His decision to launch a massive mining campaign was sound."[65] After the war, a captain in the Imperial Japanese Navy stated that "you probably could have shortened the war by beginning the air-dropping of mines earlier."[66]

In May and June 1945, after the B-29 campaign had turned around under LeMay's prosecution of the incendiary raids, Arnold's staff redoubled its efforts to find the key to knocking Japan out of the war. The staff focused on the connection between attacking the Japanese transportation network and the country's food supply. A successful outcome might result in starvation and thus force Japan to surrender. At the same time, Maj. Gen. Victor E. Bertrandias of the Air Technical Service Command at Wright Field proposed to General Arnold "a quick knockout" of Japan by a concentrated attack on its rice and fish supply. Once the home islands were isolated by blockade and bombardment, B-25s or A-26s would be employed in low level spraying missions against the rice supply of six major cities: Tokyo, Yokohama, Osaka, Nagoya, Kyoto, and Kobe, comprising one-fifth of Japan's population. The fish supply would be targeted by B-25s flying at low level along the coast from northern Hokkaido to southern Kyushu and the Sakhalin fishing banks. According to Bertrandias, "destruction of these two main sources of food, even for a short period of time, should reduce the Japs in the home islands to near-starvation and bring them to accept our terms of unconditional surrender."[67] General Arnold referred this proposal to the Joint Target Group. Brig. Gen. John A. Samford, the Group's director, and Norstad noted that it had previously been discussed in AAF headquarters and by other agencies. Their conclusion was that AAF resources would be better employed against targets having a more certain impact. The AAF and the Chemical Warfare Service also considered using gas against the Japanese. Arnold made the point in late May that the "strategic and tactical employment of gas by air" was under continuing study.[68]

It will be recalled that on May 14, 1945, the Joint Chiefs of Staff had directed the invasion of Kyushu (OLYMPIC) with a target date of November 1, 1945. In regard to the B-29 force, the Joint Chiefs stated, "The Commanding General, Twentieth Air Force, will cooperate in the plans, preparations and execution of Operation OLYMPIC and in the continuance of the campaign in Japan. At appropriate times, to be determined by the Joint Chiefs of Staff, the Twentieth Air Force will come under the direction of the appropriate commander for the support of operations directed above."[69] In the summer of 1945, the Allies' ability to decipher the Japanese military codes (ULTRA) and decrypt the enemy's Foreign Ministry communications (MAGIC) dramatically altered calculations for the Kyushu invasion and factors pertaining to employment of the atomic bomb. In late May, the Joint Chiefs concluded that "The Japanese know that successful Allied lodgement in Kyushu would result in effective interdiction of communications between Kyushu, Honshu, Shikoku, and the Continent. Therefore, the Japanese will use all available ground, sea, and air forces to resist a landing on Kyushu and will defend desperately to prevent Allied consolidation on the island."[70] Prior to the June 18 White House meeting, MacArthur's intelligence estimated that Japanese strength on Kyushu by about November 1 would number approximately 300,000, enabling the Allies to outnumber the Japanese defenders by three to one, indicating a high probability for a successful amphibious landing. This assumption formed a basis for Truman's discussion on the eighteenth with the Joint Chiefs.

At this meeting, Marshall informed Truman that he estimated that eight Japanese divisions or about 350,000 troops would defend Kyushu. Marshall also stated that it would be difficult for the Japanese to reinforce Kyushu. Admirals King and Leahy, and Lt. Gen. Ira Eaker representing Arnold, all supported the Army's position for an invasion (OLYMPIC). However, in late July, more Japanese divisions had deployed to Kyushu, possibly bringing the total to ten defending the southern third of the island where the OLYMPIC assault was to take place. Thus, the initial projections presented by Marshall and MacArthur turned out to be flat wrong. In fact, at the time of the June 18 meeting, the number of divisions on Kyushu had already reached the number that Marshall estimated on

November 1, still more than four months away. In mid-July, by the time Truman reached Potsdam, the original invasion calculus presented on the eighteenth had been shattered. Moreover, deciphered communications indicated that the Japanese were preparing a massive employment of suicide weapons to contest the Kyushu landing:

> Messages (decrypted) in late June described additional bases for piloted suicide torpedoes (Kaiten) and preparations for using oil and gasoline incendiary devices. Intercepted transmissions in July dealt with the deployment of a flotilla of 940 suicide aircraft to 18 concealed bases on Kyushu, as well as extensive efforts to reconfigure floatplanes for suicide missions.[71]

Also, it seemed clear that, according to intercepted communications, the number of Japanese divisions in southern Kyushu was more than double the number initially estimated for the southern part of the island. The Japanese had decided to vigorously contest the potential American landings on southern Kyushu. In early April 1945, the official Japanese Army directive for opposing the invasion—*Ketsu-Go* Operations—called for crushing the enemy "invading key areas of the mainland while the invasion force is still at sea. Enemy forces which succeed in landing will be swiftly attacked by resolute defenders in order to seek the decisive victory." The aim was to disrupt the landing by targeting the American convoys.

These intelligence estimates were being forwarded to the highest levels of the U.S. military in Washington. On August 4, two days prior to the atomic attack on Hiroshima, a Joint War Plans Committee memorandum to the Joint Planning Staff recommended that "The possible effects on OLYMPIC operations of this buildup and concentration" of Japanese forces should result in commanders reviewing "their estimates of the situation, reexamine objectives in Japan as possible alternates to OLYMPIC and prepare plans for operations against such alternate objectives."[72] The Joint Staff planners informed CINCPAC that "operations against extreme northern Honshu, against the Sendai area, and directly against the Kanto Plain are now under intensive study here."[73] The message here was that a fundamental re-examination of invasion plans was required. This had been favored by King, Leahy, and Arnold for some time, given their concern over heavy American casualties in any invasion.

The Japanese military believed that the *Ketsu-Go* strategy of contesting or even repelling the enemy invasion could in fact succeed. Field commanders thought that morale in their forces remained high for *Ketsu-Go*.[74] An assessment after the war by Major General Masakazu Amano, of the Imperial Headquarters, emphasized:

> We were absolutely sure of victory. It was the first and the only battle in which the main strength of the air, land and sea forces were to be joined. The geographical advantages of the homeland were to be utilized to the highest degree, the enemy was to be crushed, and we were confident that the battle would prove to be the turning point in political maneuvering.[75]

Leadership of the Imperial Army counted on success on the invasion beaches to foster a negotiated political settlement far short of unconditional surrender.

In fact, in light of the buildup on Kyushu, in early August 1945 the Joint War Plans Committee sought a more lightly defended target. This thrust was apparently supported by General Marshall, who nonetheless continued to insist on an invasion. The problems associated with invasion and the unconditional surrender policy were aptly drawn by Douglas J. MacEachin in his study of U.S. signals intelligence and invasion planning: "Achieving the surrender and unrestricted occupation of the entire national territory of an opponent steeped in a warrior tradition and a history as a great power, without having captured any portion of that territory, posed an extraordinary challenge."[76] The problem was whether unconditional surrender could be achieved without an invasion of the Japanese homeland. The enormous enemy buildup on Kyushu increased the pressure in July and August for an intensification of the bombing and blockade and perhaps a major departure in strategy. In fact, the Joint War Plans Committee in early August raised the possibility of placing the Kyushu invasion on hold while at the same time ramping up the air campaign from Okinawa. Even with overwhelming bombing support, the Joint Chiefs considered that the updated figure on the enemy's buildup resulted in a problematic ratio of invasion troops to defenders. Again, time was the key factor; it was possible that air and sea attacks could knock Japan out by December 1945 although this would not be soon enough to alter MacArthur's and Marshall's position favoring an invasion. In retrospect, Marshall stated that he had planned to use atomic bombs on the Kyushu beaches prior to an Allied invasion.[77]

Overall, the revised intelligence calculus was of great concern to the Joint Chiefs. It showed that the Japanese were prepared to inflict heavy, if not prohibitive, casualties on any invasion force. By the summer of 1945, the issue for Japan was what surrender terms might be acceptable. Even while Japan attempted to negotiate with the Soviet Union, it was preparing in the homeland for a fight to the finish. There is no doubt that Truman, Stimson, Marshall, and Arnold received this critical intelligence at Potsdam. Stimson, Secretary of the Navy Forrestal, and Arnold all noted in their diaries that they were privy to MAGIC communications. As it turned out, postwar reports emphasized the problematical nature of the proposed Kyushu invasion: "Judging by the difficult terrain; the scarcity and poor quality of the roads, the small size and capacity of the railroads and tunnels, and the prevailing weather conditions, it was fortunate that the invasion of Kyushu took place after the surrender and not before."[78] Even so, most historians believe that the decision to employ the atomic bomb had for all practical purposes been made by the start of the Potsdam conference. This view is sustained by archival documentation and the sequence of events. There is no doubt that President Truman and his advisers were influenced by their grave concern over potential invasion casualties and a quick end to war as a way of enforcing unconditional surrender terms.

According to the official history, on Tinian in the Marianas, the days preceding the Hiroshima mission were marked by secret meetings and conferences. On August 4, the crews were told details about the atomic bomb and its probable effects. Although the crew realized that this was some kind of special bomb, "the information that it would have a force equal to 20,000 tons of TNT seems to have been for almost all a complete surprise."[79] LeMay himself had not heard of the Manhattan District Project's development of the atomic bomb. "My job," he said, "had always been to get as many conventional bombs on enemy targets as it was possible to put there. Nothing more than that."[80] Once informed however, he described the atomic bomb project as "a magnificently kept secret. I had been told what it was about, yet still I didn't actually know what the bomb would do. ... Nor could those few of us now let into the secret take much time to sit around and speculate on what was going to happen. We had too much work to do."[81] On August 6, 1945, the B-29 *Enola Gay*, commanded by Col. Paul Tibbets and named after his mother, launched from Tinian with the uranium atomic bomb, "Little Boy." The *Enola Gay* was accompanied by weather and observation B-29s. Hiroshima, headquarters of the Second Army with numerous industries, was the primary target, Kokura, the secondary target. With a green light on Hiroshima from the weather planes, "this sealed the city's doom."[82]

The atomic bomb was dropped on Hiroshima from 31,600 feet, detonating 1900 feet above the ground, the crew undergoing two distinct shocks accompanied by a great ball of fire and a huge mushrooming cloud mass. After the explosion, Tibbets informed Tinian, "mission successful."[83] After Tibbets landed at Tinian, Spaatz greeted him and presented him with the Distinguished Service Cross, the second highest decoration that can be awarded by the U.S. Army for gallantry in combat.

On August 6, 1945, Truman was returning from the Berlin conference at Potsdam, aboard the cruiser USS *Augusta,* when Stimson cabled him that the U.S. had dropped an atomic weapon on Hiroshima. The president then approved release of a statement from Washington announcing to the world the dropping of an atomic bomb. The B-29 that "dropped one bomb on Hiroshima," Truman stated, "destroyed its usefulness to the enemy." The bomb released more power than 20,000 tons of TNT. He noted that "we have now added a new and revolutionary increase in destruction" to the military power already at hand.[84]

"It is an atomic bomb," Truman emphasized: "The force from which the sun draws its power had been loosed against those who brought war to the Far East." He noted that the nation had won "the battle of the laboratories," having spent two billion dollars on "the greatest scientific gamble in history." And he warned the Japanese: "We are now prepared to obliterate more rapidly and completely every productive enterprise the Japanese have above ground in any city. We shall destroy their docks, their factories, and their communications. Let there be no mistake; we shall completely destroy Japan's power to make war. ... If they do not now accept our terms, they may expect a rain of ruin from the air, the like of which has never been seen on this earth." Truman also noted that he would recommend to Congress "the establishment of an appropriate commission to control the production and use of atomic power in the United States."[85]

General Twining's Strategic Air Forces headquarters on August 8 reported on the first aerial reconnaissance taken over Hiroshima twenty-eight hours after the dropping of the atomic bomb, bringing "back the story of what happened in that one-tenth of a millionth of a second during which the first atomic bomb ever used in warfare delivered its concentrated wallop equivalent to 20,000 tons of TNT." This report to Spaatz's Strategic Air Forces headquarters began by noting that "Hiroshima is no more."[86] The report stated that Hiroshima "in that infinitesimal fraction of time, imperceptible to the most sensitive clock, during which the atoms of uranium 235 released a small fraction of their enormous energy, the city of Hiroshima was practically wiped off the map in a manner more devastating than if it had been hit by an earthquake of the first magnitude. The entire area within a radius of 10,000 feet from the heart of the city has been wiped clean as though it had never existed. Barring a few buildings that somehow miraculously escaped disaster, there is not even a sign that any buildings had ever stood on the site." So complete was the pulverization that not even debris of buildings was in evidence "as a reminder that only two days ago there stood here one the great cities of the empire of Japan." The most conservative estimate indicated that at least 100,000 Japanese "had been needlessly sacrificed by their military leaders through the insistence on continuing a war they knew they have already lost."[87] Unless the Potsdam terms were accepted, the report continued, even greater numbers of Japanese would be sacrificed in the near future.

Experienced B-29 pilots who had participated in the incendiary attacks on Tokyo and other Japanese cities stated that nothing even approached the effects of the atomic bomb that they had observed.[88]

Early in the war, the population of Hiroshima had surpassed 300,000, but due to government-ordered evacuation, it had slipped to about 255,000 at the time of the atomic attack. Because prior to the dropping of the atomic bomb, at 8:15 a.m. on August 6, 1945, the air raid alert over Hiroshima had been lifted—only a small number of B-29s had been sighted—the atomic attack came as a horrifying surprise. For hours, the Japanese were not certain as to exactly what had caused this cataclysm. Japan's first knowledge of what had happened came from the White House sixteen hours after the dropping of the bomb.[89]

Late in the afternoon of August 8 (Moscow time), Soviet Foreign Minister Vyacheslav Molotov summoned the Japanese ambassador Nautaki Sato, who thought Molotov was going to approve receiving the Emperor's special envoy, Konoye. Instead, Molotov gave Sato a statement that declared that the Soviet government considered that it was in a state of war with Japan. Although not a complete surprise, the Soviet entry amounted to a distinct shock to the Japanese, yet the government still did not surrender. Truman was informed by U.S. Ambassador to the Soviet Union, W. Averill Harriman. The president then called in the press: "I have only a simple announcement to make. I can't hold a regular press conference today, but this announcement is so important I thought I would like to call you in. Russia has declared war on Japan. That is all."[90]

Nagasaki was one of the largest seaports in southern Japan, of importance because of its war industries, including production of ordnance, ships, and military equipment. Nagasaki had never been under heavy bombing prior to the atomic attack. It was planned to drop the second bomb on August 11, but the weather factor accelerated the drop to August 9. The B-29 *Bockscar*, commanded by Major Charles Sweeney, 393rd squadron commander—who had piloted the observation plane *Great Artiste* over Hiroshima—had Kokura as its primary target, but the weather dictated Nagasaki instead. The plutonium bomb "Fat Man," twenty-two kilotons, detonated miles from the aiming point. Navy Commander F. L.

Ashworth, also aboard *Bockscar,* described the explosion: "The bomb burst with a blinding flash … a great swirling mushroom cloud of black smoke, luminous with red, flashing flame, that reached 40,000 feet in less than 8 minutes."[91]

The completion of the Nagasaki mission came close to disaster. Multiple problems began with an inoperative fuel pump and continued as *Bockscar* ran low on fuel. Sweeney's emergency landing on Okinawa bounced the aircraft twenty-five feet into the air, the plane landing ten feet from the end of the runway. To complete the almost disastrous mission, as *Bockscar* taxied in, two engines cut off due to lack of fuel.

After the war, a number of agencies and groups conducted surveys of the effects of the atomic bombings. These included the Manhattan Engineering District, the U.S. Strategic Bombing Survey, the Army, Navy, and the British Mission. All of the groups reached conclusions about the physical damage to Hiroshima and Nagasaki, but had more difficulty in determining the effects on the population. Due to differences in the topography of the two cities, more than five square miles of Hiroshima were totally destroyed while three square miles of Nagasaki were devastated. In Hiroshima, heavy damage occurred up to two miles from the blast and fifty percent or more up to three miles. In Nagasaki, severe damage could be seen for about three miles with partial damage about four miles from the blast center.[92]

It is also noteworthy that subsequently the Army determined—with corroboration from Japanese officials—that about twenty U.S. airmen who were POWs were killed in the bombing of Hiroshima. The difficulty of obtaining accurate data on the atomic bombings is reflected in the differing estimates of killed and injured in the atomic attacks. In Hiroshima, the Manhattan Engineer District estimated 66,000 dead, 69,000 injured. The U. S. Strategic Bombing Survey estimated 80,000 dead, 80,000–100,000 injured. In Nagasaki, the Manhattan Engineer District put the number of dead at 39,000 with 25,000 injured. The U.S. Strategic Bombing Survey estimated about 45,000 dead, 50,000–60,000 injured.[93] Both Hiroshima and Nagasaki were largely destroyed by the atomic attacks. For example, compared to the major incendiary raid on Tokyo in March, the impression, as the British Mission emphasized, "which both cities make is of having sunk, in an instant and without a struggle, to the most primitive level."[94] According to the Manhattan Engineer District report:

> Aside from physical injury and damage, the most significant effect of the atomic bombs was the sheer terror which it struck into the peoples of the bombed cities. This terror, resulting in immediate hysterical activity and flight from the cities, had one especially pronounced effect: persons who had become accustomed to mass air raids had grown to pay little heed to single planes or small groups of planes, but after the atomic bombings the appearance of a single plane caused more terror and disruption of normal life than the appearance of many hundreds of planes has ever been able to cause before. The effect of this terrible fear of the potential danger from even a single enemy plane on the lives of the peoples of the world in the event of any future war can easily be conjectured.[95]

As far as a prior demonstration of the bomb was concerned, U.S. officials were concerned that an atomic bomb demonstration might fail, encouraging the Japanese to even greater resistance. Also, a demonstration in a remote area would not exhibit the bomb's full destructiveness. Racism against the Japanese could also have been influential in this decision. Meanwhile, Japan in the summer of 1945 had been suffering from a severe food shortage and her cities were being destroyed by the B-29 attacks. Some Japanese officials were concerned that the people might blame the emperor for their situation. Yet, a negotiated peace that failed to allow Japan to keep the *Kokutai,* or emperor system, would be unacceptable, even to the peace party.

The unconditional surrender policy has been criticized in retrospect as inflexible and an impediment to a negotiated peace. However, once promulgated, it would have been difficult in 1945 for the Allies to turn the clock back and reverse it. Any amelioration of the unconditional surrender policy would have been seen as Allied weakness and a signal for the Japanese to redouble their efforts to inflict heavy casualties upon the Americans during an invasion. Unconditional surrender would ultimately be required to pave the way for Allied military government in Japan and to introduce reforms to prevent a revival of Japanese militarism.

The problem remained that the Imperial Japanese government was in the hands of militarists who opposed surrender. Army Minister Anami Korechika spoke for Japan's military chiefs when in late July and the early days of August he reiterated that plans were going forward to inflict a massive blow on the American invasion force, causing enormous casualties, and forcing a negotiated peace, the *Ketsu-Go* strategy.

After the war, MacArthur's own intelligence operation concluded that

> The strategists at Imperial General Headquarters believed if they could succeed in inflicting unacceptable losses on the United States in the Kyushu operation, convince the American people of the huge sacrifices involved in an amphibious invasion of Japan, and make them aware of the determined fighting spirit of the Japanese army and civilian population, they might be able to postpone, if not escape altogether, a crucial battle in the Kanto (Tokyo) area. In this way, they hoped to gain time and grasp an opportunity which would lead to the termination of hostility on more favorable terms than those which unconditional surrender offered.[96]

The three-to-three stalemate between the "peace party" (Suzuki, Togo, and Yonai) and the militarists (Anami, Umezu, and Toyoda) forced Emperor Hirohito's hand. On August 10, the Japanese cabinet unanimously ratified a decision to accept the Potsdam Declaration as long as it did not alter the prerogatives of the emperor. Of the full cabinet, thirteen ministers favored acceptance, three remained opposed (Anami, Umezu, and Toyoda). Japanese Navy Chief of Staff Toyoda noted that "it was the conviction of the Japanese people that the Emperor was a living god above whom there could be no earthly being. It was feared that the Japanese people would not readily accept the wording to the reply which placed the Emperor in a subordinate position."[97] The Emperor then made the "sacred decision" on August 10 to accept the Potsdam Declaration on the one condition of retaining the institution of the Emperor. The cabinet subsequently ratified this decision. Also on the tenth, the Japanese Foreign

Ministry forwarded the conditional message of surrender through the Swedish and Swiss governments to the U.S. government. The text of the Japanese government's communication to the Swiss and Swedish governments was as follows:

> The Japanese government today addresses the following communica-tions to the Swiss and Swedish governments respectively for trans-mission to the United States, Great Britain, China and the Soviet Union:
>
> In obedience to the gracious command of his majesty the Emperor, who, ever anxious to enhance the cause of world peace, desires earnestly to bring about an early termination of hostilities with a view to saving mankind from the calamities to be imposed upon them by further continuation of the war.
>
> Unfortunately, these efforts in the interest of peace having failed, the Japanese government, in conformity with the August wish of His Majesty to restore the general peace and desiring to put an end to the untold sufferings engendered by the war as quickly as possible, hav-ing decided upon the following:
>
> The Japanese government are ready to accept the term enumer-ated in the joint declaration which was issued at Potsdam on July 26, 1945, by the heads of the Governments of the United States, Great Britain and China and later subscribed by the Soviet Government, with the understanding that the said declaration does not comprise any demand which prejudices the prerogatives of His Majesty as a Sovereign Ruler.[98]

With the U.S. government's reply that the emperor shall be subject to the Supreme Commander of the Allied powers—"who will take such steps as he deems proper to effectuate the surrender terms"—it became necessary on August 14 for the emperor to again step in to resolve the deadlock. On the fourteenth, Suzuki requested the emperor to call an Imperial conference. Anami, Umezu, and Toyoda continued to state that the American position was unacceptable, and the war should be contin-ued. The others favored acceptance. The emperor himself then broke the standoff: "it is my belief that a continuation of the war promises nothing but additional destruction. I have studied the terms of the Allied reply and have concluded that they constitute a virtually complete acknowledgment of the position we maintained. ... In short, I consider the reply to be acceptable." The emperor then continued: "A continuation of the war would bring death to tens, perhaps even hundreds, of thousands of persons. The whole nation would be reduced to ashes."[99] This amounted to acknowledgment by Hirohito himself that the bombing, culminating with the atomic bomb, could destroy the entire nation. The emperor then requested an Imperial rescript to end the war, to broadcast to the country. The cabinet then accepted unconditional surrender. The key wording of Emperor Hirohito's rescript emphasized that "the war situation has developed not necessarily to Japan's advantage. ... Moreover, the enemy has begun to employ a new and most cruel bomb, the power of which to do damage is indeed incalculable, taking the toll of many innocent lives. Should we continue to fight, it would not only result in an ultimate collapse and obliteration of the Japanese nation, but also it could lead to the total extinction of human civilization."[100] On the fourteenth, Truman received the Japanese communication marking full acceptance of the Potsdam Declaration. Anami aggressively opposed accepting the U.S. terms and again called for a climactic battle against the invasion landing force. Hirohito thus intervened once more and on August 15 broadcast the surrender rescript. Recent scholarship however, suggests that Emperor Hirohito went along with the militarists throughout the war, fixated with his own survival while the great urban areas of the homeland were being smashed from the air.

The emperor's action in ending the war was a jarring departure from the norm, for he had no active role in the administration of civil government nor in military command. Japan's military, in fact, had maintained its iron control during the entire war. Consequently, despite Japan's militarily hopeless position in 1945, the militarists succeeded in prolonging the conflict and postponing the surrender. The emperor's decision to end the war in effect spurred the cabinet to endorse the "imperial decision." At the point that the emperor issued the rescript, the morale of the Japanese people had been thoroughly shattered. The Japanese nation, totally vulnerable to air bombardment, lay bereft of any way to stop the carnage. In the summer of 1945, the conflict in effect was basically a war to win air control over Japan. This was understood by Japanese leaders. It is noteworthy that in an interview in November 1945, Kido, the lord keeper of the privy seal, emphasized the psychological effect of the atomic bomb: "the feeling that the emperor and I had about the atomic bombing was that the psychological moment we had long waited for had finally arrived to resolutely carry out the termination of the war. ... We felt that if we took the occasion and utilized the *psychological* shock of the bomb to follow through, we might perhaps succeed in ending the war."[101] The Peace Party's efforts to end the war, Kido emphasized, were actually helped along by the shock impact of the atomic bomb. Recent scholarship based on Japanese sources corroborates the argument that the atomic bombing of Hiroshima and the entry of the Soviet Union in the war shocked Japan into capitulation. Japan's Navy Minister, Yonai, went so far as to argue that the atomic bomb and the Soviet entry were "gifts from Heaven," allowing the Peace Party to bring about the acceptance of the Potsdam Declaration.[102] Note that no use of the word "surrender" appears in the Japanese responses to the Potsdam Declaration.

The instrument of surrender, signed on September 2, 1945, at Tokyo Bay on behalf of the emperor, the Japanese government, and the Imperial General Headquarters, specified "the unconditional surrender to the Allied Powers of the Japanese Imperial General Headquarters and of all Japanese armed forces and all armed forces under Japanese control wherever situated."[103] There is also evidence to indicate that the emperor and Kido feared a potential internal uprising. There remains no doubt that Japanese morale had endured a collapse in the summer of 1945 primarily due to the bombing and blockade. Even after the dropping of an atomic bomb on Nagasaki, the Japanese continued to conduct military operations. However, in mid-August, after the emperor's rescripts, Japanese forces obeyed the emperor and terminated operations. "One may speculate," Drea noted, that this example of the emperor's authority, "was instrumental in the later American decision to retain the emperor and imperial institution as symbols of the Japanese state despite vociferous calls from other Allies for his indictment as a war criminal."[104] Further, the surrender document emphasized that the emperor and the Japanese government would

> issue whatever orders and take whatever action may be required by the Supreme Commander for the Allied Powers or by any other designated representative of the Allied Powers for the purpose of giving effect to that Declaration.
>
> We hereby command the Japanese Imperial Government and the Japanese Imperial General Headquarters at once to liberate all allied prisoners of war and civilian internees now under Japanese control and to provide for their protection, care, maintenance and immediate transportation to places as directed.[105]

And further:

> The authority of the Emperor and the Japanese Government to rule the state shall be subject to the Supreme Commander for the Allied Powers who will take such steps as he deems proper to effectuate these terms of surrender.[106]

Postwar interrogations of high-level Japanese officials underscored Arnold's opinion that the atomic bomb gave the Japanese "a way out," allowing them to save face. The militarists could claim that they were defeated by a scientific breakthrough and not by the enemy's force of arms on the battlefield. This concept also raises the question of whether, had Japan succeeded in its own atomic bomb project, the Japanese would have used it. Based on Japanese sources, there seems little doubt that the militarists would have employed the bomb. However, the Japanese were a very long way from producing an atomic bomb during the war.

Arnold thought that continued bombing and blockade could force Japan to surrender—certainly by the end of October—and the U.S. Strategic Bombing Survey concluded that Japan would have capitulated by the end of the year without the atomic bombs, the Soviet entry, or an invasion. Revisionist historians have also pointed to the Survey's counter-factual conclusion that Japan would have surrendered by the close of 1945 even without the atomic bomb, the invasion or the entry of the Soviet Union into the war. Historians have been arguing over the Survey for decades, some supporting parts of it that fit their agendas and others flatly discrediting it as unreliable at best, and "cooked up" at worst, to back up the case for an independent Air Force.[107]

Similarly, with interrogations, in the same vein historians cherry-pick interrogations of Japanese officials. It's true that some of the officials attempted to ingratiate themselves with their interrogators. This does not mean however, that all their testimony should be discounted. For example, Prof. Barton Bernstein, a renowned historian of the atomic bomb and the end of the war, argued that modification of the unconditional surrender policy "combined with other strategies would have speeded up Japan's capitulation—before the scheduled November invasion and without the use of the atomic bomb."[108] Such counter-factual opinions are interesting but purely speculative. On the other hand, historians who support the dropping of the atomic bomb as critical to ending the war and saving American lives, claim that there is no evidence to support the Survey's conclusion and thus it has been discredited. These criticisms, however, do not negate the usefulness of many of the Survey's comprehensive reports on topics such as the bombing effects on Japan's economy, war production, and morale.

What is certain is that we do *not* know whether Japan would have capitulated by the close of December 1945. What we *do* know is that the incendiary campaign had taken a terrible toll: Japan's cities were being burned out, her shipping was choked off, and with the coming B-29 campaign against transportation, the menace of starvation loomed on the horizon. It is reasonable to assume that the end for Japan was very close as recognized by Emperor Hirohito even prior to the dropping of atomic bombs. The island nation was isolated, dying from blockade with her cities being reduced to rubble. One does not need to agree with the Strategic Bombing Survey to realize that even without the dropping of atomic bombs, Japan would have surrendered *at some point*. This argument of course becomes counter-factual, purely speculative, when the attempt is made to estimate at what point the Japanese would have surrendered. It seems reasonable to assume that the emperor would have stepped in to call a halt to his people's suffering by the end of 1945 or by early 1946. Again, this is speculation, but it is supported by postwar interviews with a significant number of Japanese officials. It is well to remember that the blockade had in effect thrown an immovable fence around Japan and LeMay's incendiary campaign destroyed over two million houses and left thirty percent of the Japanese population homeless.

Arguments over the Survey at times reflect the contagion of interservice rivalry. It is certainly true that the Survey is at times unclear or contradictory and thus must be used judiciously, in combination with many additional sources from the massive amount of documentation on the war. Such being the case, it is difficult to avoid the conclusion that the defeat of Japan was due to a combination of factors. The island campaign drove the Japanese sphere backward; the anti-shipping offensive choked Japan from needed supplies and materials; the air and sea blockade had significant effects; the entry of the Soviet Union into the war was a factor in Japan's capitulation; and the conventional B-29 strategic bombing offensive brought home a terrible price to Japan's home islands. Given all of the above, it was the shock of the atomic bombs—a "cruel" weapon according to Emperor Hirohito—that drove Japan into surrender. Thus, one of the most reliable sources on the surrender rationale is Hirohito's own words. It is clear from his rescript that the atomic bomb resulted in a shock effect that had a major impact on his decision to end the war.

Recent scholarship based on Japanese source materials indicates that the atomic bombs and the Soviet entry into the war convinced the anti-military faction in the government (the "peace party") and finally, the emperor, that the time had arrived to end the war. Basically, the Hiroshima bomb, and then the Soviet attack, were the initial psychological shocks. This raises the question of whether or not the atomic bombing of Nagasaki was necessary. It certainly had an effect on the Japanese officials who wanted to end the war, as well as the emperor, for it raised in their minds the possibility, if not the probability, that the U.S. had additional atomic bombs ready to destroy Tokyo and the Japanese nation. The questions raised by the timing of Japan's surrender will forever engage the human mind. There is much to be learned from this continuous analysis and introspection. However, nothing falls out in neat packages. It remains a complex web to be rebuilt and studied.

Aside from the atomic bomb attacks, there is little doubt that certainly by June and July, there were many in the high echelons of the Japanese government who thought that termination of the war was on the horizon. Postwar interrogations revealed that a major part of this feeling was due to the B-29 attacks. Unquestionably also, the blockade had a significant effect on Japan's war production industry, choking off much-needed materials that now could not reach the homeland. Premier Konoye expressed the opinion that the loss of Saipan signaled that the war was a "hopeless cause." Konoye ventured the opinion that had the atomic bombs not been dropped the war would have gone on for the remainder of 1945. As to the B-29 attacks, Konoye emphasized that "there was bound to be a limit" to how long Japan could hold on. Japan was "nearing the limit," according to Konoye, "but the Army would not admit it. They wouldn't admit they were near the end."[109] He stressed the B-29 raids had a pulverizing effect, convincing the emperor by late July that it was time to terminate the war. And officials realized that those attacks would intensify in August and September.[110] Prime Minister Kantaro Suzuki, who was appointed in April, noted that the Supreme War Council, up to the point that the atomic bomb was dropped, thought that the U.S. would attempt an invasion, while "there were many prominent people who did believe that the United States could win the war by just bombing alone."[111] The Supreme War Council, Suzuki noted, continued to prepare for Ketsu-Go until the dropping of the atomic bomb, which convinced the Council that the United States possessed a war-ending weapon.

After the war, a U.S. Army General Staff intelligence group concluded that the OLYMPIC invasion would have been delayed about a month and a half by a powerful October typhoon. The typhoon of October 9, 1945, with 140-mile-per-hour winds, struck Okinawa and Japan near Osaka. The resulting losses and damage to planes and ships would surely have delayed any invasion by one to two months.[112] The group proceeded on the assumption that the atomic bomb would not have been used, stating that Soviet declaration of war on August 9 would have by itself forced Japan to capitulate. Now, more than sixty years after the end of the war, the great weight of evidence is that the Soviet entry alone, although important, was not sufficient in itself. It took the dramatic shock value of the atomic bomb, as described in the emperor's rescript, to force the surrender. Also, had the atomic bomb not been employed, the Army intelligence analysts failed to account for potential results from the massive strategic transportation bombing campaign that the Strategic Air Forces was to commence. Historian John Ray Skates concluded that American casualties in OLYMPIC would have hit sixty to seventy-five thousand—"high but tolerable"—in the range of Okinawa or Normandy.[113] These were the kind of "tolerable" casualties that Truman considered unacceptable and wanted to avoid. Enter the atomic bomb. An estimate of sixty to seventy-five thousand casualties, as noted, is certainly not insignificant. Truman was highly sensitive to casualty estimates, as he should have been, and even a much lower figure of twenty-five thousand would have made an impact upon him. As historian J. Samuel Walker noted:

> The casualty estimate issue is not of central importance in understanding Truman's decision to drop the bomb. It is probable if not certain that the president would have authorized use of the bomb even if the number of American lives saved was relatively small, at least compared with the figures that he and others cited after the war. One should not lose sight of the fact that the 25,000 deaths that the Joint War Plans Committee estimated for the invasion of Kyushu was a very large number that no policymaker could and no historian should dismiss lightly.[114]

Had an invasion proved to be necessary, it would have resulted in an enormous bloodbath. It is possible that additional atomic bombs would have been employed, Marshall having suggested the potential use of the atomic bomb as a tactical weapon supporting an invasion.[115] Historians have been arguing for decades over projected casualty figures anticipated in the Operation OLYMPIC invasion. In a real sense, in my view, this amounts to a chimera, for it is all speculation, based on a dizzying array of estimates.[116] The seemingly never-ending controversy over the number of estimated casualties during Operation DOWNFALL, pitting revisionists against so-called traditionalists, has masked the essential point that no one can deny: Truman, in the wake of the Okinawa campaign, feared that an invasion would be accompanied by huge numbers of American killed and wounded. There is nothing to be gained by arguing that "only" 25,000 or 50,000 American casualties would have resulted. As opposed to counter-factual arguments, the fact is that, as we have seen, Truman convened the June 18, 1945, meeting at the White House primarily to discuss the cost in lives of an invasion. These discussions resulted in Truman's giving the green light to invasion planning and subsequently—with Japan's not accepting the Potsdam Declaration—to dropping the atomic bomb.

Despite the employment of the atomic bomb, MacArthur incredibly never missed a beat; he continued to press the case for an invasion abetted by heavy support from air forces. He emphasized the buildup of Gen. George Kenney's Far East Air Forces to approximately 3000 aircraft prior to the November 1 scheduled date for OLYMPIC. This did not include the B-29s and escort fighters based in the Marianas. These air forces, according to MacArthur, would quickly gain air superiority and "practically immobilize ground forces in their present positions." These enemy forces would be in a greatly weakened position prior to the invasion. As commander of Army forces in the Pacific, MacArthur cabled Marshall on August 9, the same day of the atomic attack on Nagasaki, stressing that "there should not be the slightest thought of changing the OLYMPIC operation."[117] "The plan is sound," MacArthur wrote, "and will be successful." Massive land-based air on Okinawa and subsequently Kyushu would be required to mount an attack on the Tokyo Plain. Moreover, MacArthur claimed that his experience in the Southwest Pacific showed that intelligence estimates frequently overstated the number of enemy forces. Consequently, he doubted the reported huge enemy buildup on Kyushu: "In this particular case, the destruction that is going on in Japan would seem to indicate that it is very probable that the enemy is resorting to deception."[118] Historian Edward J. Drea has observed, "Like the charismatic figure he was, MacArthur took greater heed of his own counsels than those of his staff. The notion of leading the greatest amphibious assault in history—fourteen divisions versus nine at Normandy—held overwhelming appeal to MacArthur's vanity. Fortunately, the general was not permitted to test this egotistical ambition against the realities of OLYMPIC."[119] Clayton James, MacArthur's biographer, wrote that long after the war MacArthur stated that it wasn't necessary to drop the atomic bomb.

However, in early August, the latest intelligence on the Japanese build-up on Kyushu again prompted a review by the Joint Chiefs. MacArthur informed Marshall that he did not believe that this intelligence was in fact accurate and that OLYMPIC should go forward.[120] Richard B. Frank notes that Admiral King, on the other hand, held an ace in the fact that Nimitz had changed his mind and now opposed the Kyushu invasion. Had atomic bombs not been dropped, and had King raised this point within the Joint Chiefs, a critical break between Marshall and King would have resulted, imperiling the planned invasion. As it stood in August, OLYMPIC was already being reconsidered due to the enormous reinforcements the Japanese had poured into southern Kyushu. Frank has speculated that in the light of the startling new intelligence on the enormous complement of enemy troops on Kyushu, it was probable that Truman in August would have withdrawn his support for OLYMPIC.[121] After the war, Leahy stated that the Army did not understand that the Navy and the Army Air Forces already had defeated Japan. King all along thought that the naval blockade and air bombardment could force Japan to capitulate prior to an invasion. Here Arnold and King came to the same conclusion except that the airman put the emphasis on bombing while the admiral emphasized the sea blockade.

Meanwhile, coordination procedures for OLYMPIC air operations were agreed upon by CINCAFPAC (MacArthur), CINCPAC (Nimitz), and CGUSASTAF (Spaatz). The primary objectives of the fast carrier task forces were to destroy the enemy's naval and air forces, shipping and coastal objectives, and to protect sea communications in the western Pacific. Particular attention would be given to enemy air bases that could not be effectively reached by Kenney's forces. Far East Air Forces under Kenney and naval air, Ryukyus, would target enemy forces in southern

Japan and those reinforcing Kyushu. Spaatz's strategic air forces out of the Marianas would concentrate on hostile strategic targets.[122]

The summer of 1945 marked the apex of Arnold's journey to build a long-range strategic air force that could make a decisive impact in modern conflict. In a mere five months, from March to August 1945, the Twentieth Air Force propelled itself to a dominating position in the war against Japan, culminating in the dropping of atomic bombs on Hiroshima and Nagasaki. With the Japanese having surrendered unconditionally, Arnold now asserted that

> The surrender of Japan was not entirely the result of the two atomic bombs. We had hit some 60 Japanese cities with our regular H. E. and incendiary bombs, and as a result of our raids, about 241,000 people had been killed, 313,000 wounded, and about 2,333,000 homes destroyed. Our B-29s had destroyed most of the Japanese industries and, with the laying of mines, which prevented the arrival of incoming cargoes of critical items, had made it impossible to carry on a large-scale war.[123]

In pointing to the impact of the "regular" high explosive and incendiary bombing, he expressed his opinion that "it always appeared to us that atomic bomb or no atomic bomb, the Japanese were already on the verge of collapse."[124] After the end of the war, Arnold's opinion was corroborated by Japanese leaders, such as Konoye, who stressed that Japan could not have stayed in the war much longer, even without the use of the atomic bomb. And Prince Naruhiko Hagashi-Kuni stated that the incendiary attacks had "disastrously undermined" the ability of Japan to continue the war.[125]

Thus, here was Arnold's instinctive view that the dropping of atomic bombs might well dilute what he saw as the decisive contribution of the B-29 conventional assault. The Japanese surrender was brought about "because air attacks, both actual and potential, had made possible the destruction of their capability and will for further resistance."[126] Ninety percent of the very heavy bombardment tonnage was accomplished with 165,000 tons of bombs and mines in addition to the two atomic bombs and delivered during the last five months of the war. According to the conclusion of the United States Strategic Bombing Survey, the volume on The Strategic Air Operation of Very Heavy Bombardment in the War Against Japan (Final Report): "During this period the B-29 force operated at continuous maximum capacity in an effort to knock Japan out of the war before invasion day."[127]

"The surrender of Japan," Arnold emphasized, "comes after the severest and most concentrated bombing campaign in history and without actual invasion of the homeland. Thus it is the first time a nation has capitulated with its major armies designed for defense of the homeland still intact."[128] Strategic bombing, he insisted, along with the sea and air blockade, crippled Japan's industrial, economic, and military capability. The successful operations of the XXI Bomber Command "had made clear to the world the full meaning of strategic bombardment." Nonetheless, Arnold made it clear that the victory in the Pacific was a combined effort: "We cannot over-emphasize the immeasurable contributions of our sister forces which preceded the sustained attacks by land-based bombers. The land battles up from Australia, Burma and China—the ability of the Navy to bridge unprecedented distances and join with its fast carrier and fleet strength in bombarding Japanese occupied islands, permitted air power to wield the maximum strength." Knocking Japan out of the war without an invasion saved countless lives. "This was done at great cost," Arnold stated, "but the cost and casualties were far less and fewer than a direct land assault would have entailed."[129] Here it should be noted that while in general naval officers stated that the B-29 campaign played a large role in bringing down Japan, they concomitantly emphasized that the sea blockade was crucial in bringing about the Japanese capitulation. Consequently, in the immediate postwar period friction between the Navy and the Air Force evolved over the strategic mission.

It seems reasonable to conclude that the incendiary attacks and the targeting of the Japanese transportation network would have killed more civilians during August–November than did the atomic bombs at Hiroshima and Nagasaki. By August 1945, with its coastal shipping in shambles, the rail transportation system in effect remained Japan's lifeline. The U.S. Strategic Bombing Survey noted that the system was "one

of the most vulnerable of any size to be found anywhere."[130] The Survey
concluded that had the Twentieth Air Force concentrated on attacking
the rail network, Japan might well have surrendered sooner due to massive starvation. As of mid-August 1945, prior to the strategic bombing
campaign against the rail system, Japan faced a dire food crisis, which by
November would have reached the point of catastrophe with an enormous number of civilian deaths. Historian Richard Frank concluded that
even without the atomic bombs,

> the destruction of the rail-transportation system, coupled to the
> cumulative effects of the blockade- and-bombardment strategy,
> would have posed a severe threat to internal order and subsequently
> thus impelled the Emperor to see to end the war.[131]

Former President Herbert Hoover had validated the food crisis and
MacArthur himself had warned since January 1945 of the peril of starvation to Japan. According to Frank, by November 1, 1945, the Japanese
government possessed only enough rice for four days of consumption.
The big question was whether this crisis would have forced a Japanese
surrender in late 1945.[132] It is also well to keep in mind that had the war
continued into late 1945, undoubtedly hundreds of thousands of non-
combatant Asians would have died in the nations under Japanese control. Many Allied prisoners of war would also have been lost. Arnold
then went to Potsdam, emphasizing to the Allied leaders that the incendiary attacks would "tear Japan apart," and leave it no choice but to
capitulate. Following the atomic attacks, it was Emperor Hirohito, ironically, who in effect came to the same conclusions as Arnold and
informed his cabinet and the Japanese people that the U.S. had a "cruel"
new weapon that would destroy the Japanese homeland. Surrender was
the only choice.

In the controversy over the dropping of atomic bombs, historians
should remember that neither Roosevelt nor Truman had the luxury of
decades of perspective. They had to struggle with issues and decisions
on a daily basis during a ferocious war that mortally threatened the
western democracies. FDR and Truman faced two holocausts, one by the
Nazis in Europe and the other committed in East Asia by the Japanese

Imperial Army. Far more Japanese were killed by "conventional" incendiary bombing than by the atomic bomb.

A clear continuity existed between FDR and Truman on strategic bombing policy. Long before December 7, 1941, Roosevelt had directed a massive buildup of the U.S. Army Air Forces. Long harboring a deep sympathy toward the suffering of the Chinese people at the hands of the Japanese military, FDR thought that in the event of war with Japan it would be most important that the United States be able to strike Japanese urban areas with land-based bombers.

Incendiary attacks against Japanese cities, which included military targets, were strongly advocated by FDR, Truman, and General Marshall. Roosevelt and Truman implored Marshall to do everything to end the war with Japan as quickly as possible with the least loss of American and Allied lives. With the ferocious fighting on Okinawa having lasted several months with a cost of 49,000 American casualties, and with 7000 Kamikaze planes and 600,000 troops ready to contest an American landing on Kyushu in November, Truman in July 1945 faced a critical decision.

Although defeated, Japan was unwilling to surrender. American ULTRA intelligence clearly showed that the Japanese military had no intention of surrendering. The Japanese military and government were holding their own people and American and Allied POWs hostage. Factions were calling for a fight to the finish, even inviting an invasion and planning to inflict enormous casualties on American forces. Had the atomic bombs not been dropped, and had the B-29 conventional attacks continued, even more Japanese would have been killed than at Hiroshima and Nagasaki.

Today, it is easy to look back and conclude that it was not necessary to drop the bomb. Harry Truman however, had a responsibility to the American military and to the people of the United States to bring the Pacific war to an end. For in the context of the time, it is clear that had Roosevelt lived, he would have undoubtedly made the same decision as Truman. Both presidents believed deeply that the United States should, whenever it was feasible, end the war and save American lives. Here Arnold had obviously been in tune with both U.S. Commanders-in-Chief.

7

Who Was Hap Arnold?

In the Pacific, a time compression evolved in the strategic bombing campaign.[1] Only two months of the incendiary campaign had passed between LeMay's Tokyo raid in March and the defeat of Nazi Germany in May 1945. With the intensive B-29 campaign, Arnold and the American airmen overcame Japan's will to continue in less time than was the case with Germany. Ironically, what Arnold hoped for in Europe evolved in the Pacific: the B-29 incendiary campaign crumbled Japan.

The evolution of the B-29—going back to the report of the Kilner board well before U.S. entry into World War II—perfectly followed the march of aircraft technology. General Arnold and the Army Air Forces specified the requirement for a very long-range bomber that far exceeded the B-17 in all important categories. Based on the AAF doctrine of high-altitude precision bombing, the B-29 would fly higher, farther, and with a greater bomb load. There was no doubt that from early on, and through the war, Arnold and the air leadership viewed the potential success of the revolutionary B-29 as proving the case for a postwar independent Air Force. Arnold went so far as to admonish Haywood Hansell, his

B-29 commander of XXI Bomber Command, that the results of his bombing campaign would determine the future of the Army Air Forces. The irony of the campaign was that LeMay, who succeeded Hansell, only had success when he area-bombed with incendiaries at low level at night over Japan, a stunning departure from the original specifications and doctrine. Thus, the strategy and tactics of strategic bombing clearly came to be based upon the dual impetus of technology and circumstance—what would work at the time and place. In this regard, as I have noted earlier, the AAF's early strategic bombing doctrine was found wanting in both Europe and the Pacific. Escort fighters proved to be a necessity in Europe where tactics and targeting evolved haltingly, leading to enormous frustration on Arnold's part. In the Pacific, as Norstad and Hansell pointed out, target data was at first somewhat scarce and constantly required modification, culminating in LeMay's area bombing offensive in the spring and summer of 1945. Just prior to the dropping of atomic bombs, the AAF had finally concluded that an eleventh-hour bombing campaign against the railroad system might bring Japan down.

The reasons for the Japanese surrender will always remain a matter of controversy. Early Allied war plans stipulated that top priority would be assigned to the defeat of Germany. And after Germany's capitulation in May 1945, it was anticipated, and emphasized by directives of the Joint Chiefs of Staff, that an invasion of the Japanese homeland would be necessary to bring about her defeat. In noting that Japan's surrender in August 1945 came about without an invasion, and with a home army of two million men intact, the official history of the Army Air Forces made the observation: "Something new had been added to America's experience with war—something that called for close study."[2] Whatever the rationale for Japan's surrender, the official history commented, "it seemed indisputable that the war's end marked one of the revolutionary turning points in the history of warfare itself."[3]

The "something new" that the official historians referred to was of course the prosecution of the strategic bombing campaign. It was a campaign, as we have seen, with no boundaries, either geographical or in intensity. Historian Michael Sherry has criticized the *carte blanche* given LeMay in the Pacific, but the record clearly indicates that there was plenty of pressure and guidance from Twentieth Air Force headquarters in Washington.[4] Historians have also long speculated over to what degree Arnold influenced operational commanders in the field. Conrad Crane, in his fine study of strategic bombing, suggests that "Arnold rarely wielded a great deal of direct influence especially in key operations late in the conflict."[5] Arnold's influence did not obtain through operational orders, but was nonetheless pervasive. He communicated directly with Hansell and LeMay, building the pressure on them. Norstad, as we have seen, informed LeMay that if he did not get results he would be fired. LeMay realized that "the turkey" was around his neck and that Arnold and Norstad supported incendiary attacks.[6]

The requirement for incendiary attacks went back to 1943 and 1944 and evolved with reports from the Committee of Operations Analysts and the Joint Target Group. The vulnerability of Japan's urban areas to incendiary strikes was well-known long before the start of World War II. Note that the Doolittle raid in April 1942 was designed as a low-level terror raid against the population. The success of strategic bombardment, along with the sea and air blockade, meant that in the final denouement the U.S. did not have to depend upon a significant redeployment of its forces from Europe. In the summer of 1945, air and naval power forced the surrender of Japan. Thus, to state the obvious does not downgrade the overriding importance, over the long stretch of the war, of the coordinated offensive of ground, sea, and air forces (land-based and carrier-based).

To Arnold, the war's major lesson was "the extent to which air, land and sea operations can and must be coordinated by joint planning and unified command."[7] Improved coordination and balance among the services remained essential to national security. Unity of command, he emphasized, "is not alone sufficient. Unity of planning, unity of common item procurement and unity of doctrines are equally necessary."[8]

In all of this one must keep in mind the wartime circumstances attending decisions. It is, of course, easier to judge the situation now, with knowledge accumulated more than half a century later. Wars are almost never fought according to plan and Arnold's air offensive over Japan was conducted under various limitations. Air strategy was governed by feasibility, by the existing conditions and forces available. Arnold, for all his bravado and impatience, was able to adjust—bringing in LeMay—and then prosecute the air attack on Japan's cities. As Hansell ironically emphasized to Arnold, much had to be learned by trial and error. This was certainly the case with strategic bombing over Japan.

World War II showed that—whatever their reasons—American airmen were not averse to area bombing if they thought it would shorten the war and save lives. In Europe the U.S. did not adopt a deliberate policy of area bombing, unlike the British; nonetheless, area attacks were made, sometimes forced by circumstances. Against Japan, the U.S. adopted a policy of area bombing. And after the war, air strategists usually included a provision in their plans for striking the enemy's population. It was almost never absent. Most airmen felt that the "morale strategy" would shorten wars, save battlefield lives, and thus prevent a repetition of the terrible attrition of World War I.

Consequently, the subject of strategic bombing, especially the incendiary bombing of Japan, will forever be controversial. In any discussion of the incendiary bombing of Japan, one must consider the "organizational" thesis. Ever since the end of the war, historians have argued that the all-out strategic bombing of Japan had as much to do with the AAF's desire to become an independent service as it did with the drive to force a Japanese surrender without the necessity of an invasion. In my view, Arnold's overarching objective was the defeat of Japan, which he came to believe could be accomplished by bombing and blockade, a view also held by Admirals King and Leahy, and certainly a goal of Roosevelt's. Beyond a doubt, however, Arnold thought that such a contribution to Japan's capitulation would cement the case for an independent Air Force.

It is well to remember that the drive for air independence goes back to the interwar period, long before the start of World War II. And during the war, in May 1944, the Joint Chiefs had appointed their own committee to study postwar defense organization. The JCS Special Committee for Reorganization of National Defense conducted a ten-month study. Its final report, issued in April 1945, recommended (with a dissent by the committee's naval member) creation of a separate United States Air Force, coequal with the Army and Navy.[9] In addition, during World War II, Congress maintained its interest in defense reorganization, including postwar establishment of an independent Air Force. Arnold, of course, was well aware of these developments. He knew that the demonstrated success of the B-29 campaign would influence the drive for independence. This duality remained clear in his own mind. The roots of the incendiary campaign however, go back to prewar studies and to wartime reports that emphasized the vulnerability of Japanese cities to fire-bombing.

During the war, Arnold remained sensitive to the connection between on-going operations and postwar planning, creating cells in AAF headquarters to start planning for postwar independence. Dwelling on the wartime experience, immediately after the war Arnold made the case for an independent Air Force as part of a defense establishment consisting of three coequal services, "each of which has an equal and direct share" of the total defense responsibility. In his thinking on postwar defense organization, he favored retaining the Joint Chiefs of Staff, albeit, as he put it, "presided over by the Chief of Staff to the President," a position held during the war by Admiral Leahy. According to Arnold, even though the JCS encountered rough going at times, they succeeded with coordinating among the services and with the allies. "This organization," he stated, "should be continued in time of peace when the absence of the compulsions of war make cooperation and coordination of effort much more difficult to achieve."[10]

The argument continues to be made, frequently without sufficient context, that racism made it easier for Americans to fire-bomb Japanese cities. Although racism was evident in the Pacific war, it had nothing whatever to do with devising technology, politics, strategy, and command. Arnold and the Army Air Forces had a huge and complex job to do. They were building technologies, bases, training, tactics, and strategy and trying to defeat the enemy. Similarly, at the highest levels of government, while racism against the Japanese was certainly apparent, as it was in the American populace, the driving, obsessive concern was to win the war as quickly as possible with the least loss of American lives.

A bit of historical context is most relevant here. It is well to remember that President Franklin D. Roosevelt, in his support of Arnold, was a strong advocate of strategic bombing. Although in the years preceding U.S. entry into the war, FDR denounced indiscriminate bombing, he also made clear long before Pearl Harbor that he was outraged by the Japanese rampage in East Asia and that bombing Japan from China would teach the Japanese a lesson. After the Nazis attacked Poland on September 1, 1939, Roosevelt emphasized that indiscriminate bombing of civilians "has sickened the hearts of every civilized man and woman and has profoundly shocked the conscience of humanity."[11] He called on all belligerents to stop such military action. In early August 1941, however, he informed Henry Morgenthau that he had told the British that the way to defeat Germany was to send "a hundred planes over Germany for military objectives that ten of them should bomb some of the smaller towns that haven't been bombed before. There must be some kind of factory in every town. That is the only way to break German morale."[12] Even prior to the German attack on Poland, prompted by Hitler's Nuremberg speech in 1938, FDR figured that German morale could be broken by strategic bombing.

Arnold's views on attacking civilian morale in a general sense can be seen as a holdover from the classrooms in the 1930s at the Air Corps Tactical School. Although Arnold did not attend the school, it will be recalled that air doctrine, as it evolved at the school, emphasized precision bombing of selective industrial facilities, but at the same time noted that attacks on civilian morale would be appropriate because "no barrier can be interposed to shield the civil populace against the airplane."[13] The underlying thrust of Tactical School doctrine always pre-supposed that if precision bombing failed to produce the anticipated results, it might well be necessary to attack civilian morale. Arnold certainly espoused the idea that no one wanted a repeat of the trench carnage of World War I.

However, Arnold during the war was not consulting a notebook of Tactical School doctrine. As noted, he did not attend this school. He has been criticized for being overly impatient, hectoring his field commanders, Eaker in Europe and Hansell in the Pacific. His impatience however, produced results with the evolution of the B-29 ("Battle of Kansas") and with LeMay's taking over for Hansell. The same was true when he ordered Eaker to the Mediterranean and Spaatz to Europe. Arnold required clear results so that the American people could have confidence in the AAF's "way of making war." He constantly emphasized to his operational commanders that the public must be kept informed of what the Army Air Forces was accomplishing. Arnold throughout the war maintained an acute ear on the populace, and it was true that he always gave a high priority to his "public relations." His acumen here was undeniable. He was under enormous pressure in Washington from Marshall and Roosevelt who were pouring resources into the AAF and expected commensurate results. Ethical considerations were not a priority with Arnold or his operational commanders. In late May 1945, in the wake of the giant raids on Tokyo, Stimson asked Arnold whether these attacks could be considered "precision bombing." Arnold replied that cottage industries supporting the Japanese war effort were scattered throughout urban areas, but that the AAF was being careful to limit damage to civilians. In the Pacific, LeMay emphasized, "I do not beam and gloat where human casualties are concerned ... no matter how you slice it, you're going to kill an awful lot of civilians. Thousands and thousands. But if you don't destroy the Japanese industry, we're going to have to invade Japan. And how many Americans will be killed in an invasion of Japan? We just weren't bothered about the morality of the question."[14]

The leadership of the Army Air Forces in fact could be seen as a microcosm of the American public. The air leaders were well aware of Japanese atrocities—especially the execution of captured flyers who bombed Japan in 1942 with Jimmy Doolittle, the rape of Nanking, and the Bataan Death March—although they did not condone firebombing per se because of any specific atrocities. The fact was that Japan conducted a holocaust in East Asia from 1931 to 1945, resulting in approximately 15 million people killed, the great majority of them civilians. Almost half died from brutality and forced-labor mistreatment. The Japanese also employed biological warfare, postwar research uncovering the grisly atrocities by Unit 731, headed by General Shiro Ishii, and termed "the death factory." It was one of the largest germ factories in the world. The Japanese used biological agents, including typhoid, anthrax, cholera, dysentery, and plague, against civilians and military. Unit 731 built a large germ production and experimentation facility in 1932 in the Harbin, Manchuria, area, operating under the guise of a water purification facility, and supported by the

Japanese high command in Tokyo. Additional locations were built in China and subsequently in Thailand, Burma, and Singapore. Japanese doctors and scientists conducted biological experimentation that according to Sheldon Harris, author of a book on Japanese biological warfare, even exceeded Nazi Germany's horrible experimentation. Japanese military doctors injected Chinese prisoners with botulism and dissected live prisoners.[15]

After the war, American intelligence uncovered the story of Unit 731, including plans for producing bacteria bombs. Incredibly, General Ishii and his band of criminals were never prosecuted by the United States although Germans were hauled into the dock for conducting experiments in the European concentration camps. The failure to prosecute the Japanese was surely one of the most outrageous omissions in the postwar prosecution of war criminals. After the war, instead of prosecuting these butchers, the U.S. government decided to cover up the story in exchange for the data on experiments and germ warfare that the Japanese criminals provided. In the mid-1950s, an FBI report stated that information on Japanese biological warfare was not used in war crimes trials because "as a political expedient, it was felt that public disclosure of such information would seriously prejudice the (American) occupying forces (in Japan).[16]

In the decades since the war ended, Japan has had a difficult time facing up to the holocaust in East Asia perpetrated by its Imperial Army. Japanese textbooks continue to describe the Army's barbarism in bland, general terms. The controversy over "comfort women," or sex slaves, continues unabated. Japanese scholars uncovered official archival documentation showing conclusively that tens of thousands of women from East Asian countries were tricked or coerced into sexual slavery. The Japanese military structured a system of military-run brothels that started in 1932 and continued throughout the war. The Japanese military maintained and expanded this system. This failure to reconcile with the historical record has poisoned Japan's relations with China, Korea, and other East Asian nations.[17] Japanese reluctance to come to terms with the war experience extended to the very cause of World War II. In October 2008, a former chief of the Japanese Air Force was forced to quit his post for writing an essay claiming that Japan was not an aggressor in World War II. Gen.

Toshio Tamogami wrote that Japan bombed Pearl Harbor because President Roosevelt "trapped" the Japanese into the attack. Tamogami insisted that Asian countries take "a positive view" of Japan's wartime role.[18]

As to the questions of morality as juxtaposed with Japanese atrocities, General Eaker emphasized: "I never felt that the moral issue in bombing deterred the leaders of the AAF. A military man has to be trained and inured to do the job. Otherwise you would never win a war. I always felt that the skilled workman was a high priority target. The business of sentiment never enters into it at all for a soldier."[19] And Spaatz noted that he had no difficulty ordering the dropping of the atomic bomb: "That was purely a political decision, not a military decision. The military man carries out the orders of his political bosses. So that doesn't bother me at all." Spaatz also stated that "we didn't hear any complaints from the American people about mass bombing of Japan: as a matter of fact, I think they felt the more we did the better. That was our feeling toward the Japanese at that time."[20] Indeed, protests in the U.S. against strategic bombing during the war were rare, even among clergy. As Spaatz noted, the prevailing view among the American populace was that the Nazis and the Japanese, as President Roosevelt emphasized, had "asked for it." There was rage in the American public, a context that is now mostly forgotten and frequently absent from today's debate.

"As a nation," Arnold emphasized, "we were not prepared for World War II. Yes, we won the war, but at a terrific cost in lives, human suffering, and material, and at times the margin of winning was narrow. History alone can reveal how many turning points there were, how many times we were near losing, and how our enemies' mistakes often pulled us through. In the flush of victory, some like to forget these unpalatable truths."[21] At the war's close, however, Arnold looked back with satisfaction at what had been accomplished, to be sure with great difficulty. Prior to war, the air forces were "practically a paper organization. We had few planes; no industry to speak of when quantity production was desired; a limited number of pilots; and our operating technique had never been tested."[22] President Roosevelt, Arnold emphasized, made the difference when, before the war, he called for a massive buildup of air power. "The principle was then accepted for the first time," Arnold recalled, "that more airplanes, no matter what the numbers, could never make an Air Force, nor give a nation Air Power. For any nation to have an Air Force there must be an air industry; a flexible training system for pilots, and for all other personnel, that could be expanded rapidly; depots for supplies and for reserve personnel; air bases from which the planes could operate; radio, navigational, weather and other equipment to give service to the planes over the airways and at the bases."[23]

Pearl Harbor, Arnold emphasized, was the catalyst: "That was the shock we needed to bring us together for a common purpose, to make us renounce our self-complacency and the smug doctrine of isolationism." The Japanese thought that they could deliver a death blow to the U.S. Navy at Pearl Harbor. According to Arnold, Japan could have then established Pacific outposts that would have given it immunity from attacks on the homeland. Under these circumstances, Arnold stated, "a compromise peace would be the worst condition that Japan would have to meet." Japanese strategists however, were proved wrong. "They could not conceive," Arnold emphasized, "of the United States building up an Army, Navy, and an Air Force as rapidly as we did. Almost before the smoke had cleared away from the debris in Pearl Harbor, the coordinated advance of our Army, Navy, and Air Force started across the Pacific."[24] Over the next several years, American and Allied forces pushed the Japanese back toward the homeland. Her fleet and air force were destroyed. Islands were captured for operations of the U.S. Army Air Forces. Consequently, the B-29 strategic bombing campaign decimated Japan, destroying Japanese industry and, along with the blockade, cut off materials being imported to Japan. Japanese morale collapsed and brought about an end to the war without an invasion. "The massive destruction, social dislocation, and psychological impact of the B-29 campaign," historian Conrad Crane has written, "perhaps made it key in the series of shocks that produced a surrender."[25]

Nonetheless, the strategic bombing campaign in the Pacific seems destined always to arouse controversy. Those critical of the B-29 campaign on moral grounds frequently tie themselves into contradictory knots. Max Hastings has written:

> The material damage inflicted upon Japanese industry by LeMay's offensive was almost irrelevant because blockade and raw-material starvation had already brought the economy to the brink of collapse. ... It seems essential to acknowledge the psychological impact of the B-29 campaign. ... It seems impossible to doubt that, when Japanese surrender eventually came, it was influenced in some degree by the U.S. bomber offensive which preceded and indeed followed Hiroshima. It remains unlikely that the Twentieth Air Force's contribution justified its huge moral and material cost to the United States. It seems absurd however, to deny its contribution to the collapse of Japan's will to resist.[26]

The fact was that LeMay's B-29s wrought such havoc over Japan's urban areas that the sheer number of evacuees resulted in an enormous diminution of industrial production. Absenteeism became rampant, hitting forty-nine percent in July 1945. And as Hastings observes, strategic bombing played a role in breaking Japan's will to resist and forcing a surrender. This is undeniable.

Arnold was surprised at the sudden end to the war, perhaps because he had been so focused on redeploying mighty air forces from Europe to the Pacific. He termed it an abrupt surrender, thinking that the U.S. would have to use more atomic bombs, or alternatively, to power up the incendiary campaign by the redeployment of heavy bombers from the European theater. Once air power was shifted to the Pacific, his conventional bombing forces could deal Japan a fatal blow. At Potsdam, after being informed of the successful atomic test in the New Mexico desert, he viewed the bomb not so much as a new type of weapon, but rather as one that could produce destruction on a much larger scale.

The B-29 program, Arnold emphasized, "represents the high point in the continually advancing technique of strategic destruction by air power." He termed the Twentieth Air Force "the new cataclysmic force," which delivered the atomic weapon in a decisive manner: "It is difficult to conceive of any instrument other than the airplane so readily suited to this purpose." "The foundation of the Twentieth Air Force," he emphasized, "has provided the Strategic Air Forces the best organized and most technically and tactically proficient military organization the world had seen to date."[27] Having witnessed the surrender of Japan in the face of the atomic attacks, Arnold became concerned that use of the atomic bomb—although dropped by his B-29s—"tended to over-shadow an important point." Japan's situation, even before Hiroshima and Nagasaki, was hopeless. "We have good reason to believe," Arnold wrote in retrospect, that use of the atomic bomb "provided a way out for the Japanese government. The fact is that the Japanese could not have held out long, because they had lost control of their air. They could offer effective opposition neither to our bombardment nor mining by air, and so could not prevent the destruction of their cities and industries and the blockade of their shipping."[28]

By the end of the war, the B-29 conventional bombing had resulted in more casualties—killed and injured—and destroyed more of Japan's urban areas, than the atomic bombs dropped on Hiroshima and Nagasaki. To illustrate the wide chasm between prewar precision bombing doctrine and the incendiary campaign, it is noteworthy that over two-thirds of the entire B-29 campaign comprised incendiary attacks. In the last six months of the war, fifty-seven percent of the B-29 tonnage were incendiaries.[29] According to the United States Strategic Bombing Survey, strategic bombing accounted for 330,000 killed, 476,000 injured, and a total of 2.5 million buildings destroyed. Some 8.5 million people were rendered homeless, one-quarter of the Japanese urban population.[30]

However, immediately after the war, while Arnold emphasized the achievements of the B-29 campaign from the Marianas, Lt. Gen. Ira Eaker, Deputy Commander of the Army Air Forces, serving directly under Arnold, pointed to the dramatic effects of three major factors: "Japan's sudden surrender as the result of our terrible pounding plus the atomic bomb and Russia's entry into the conflict has caught us in a state of incompletion with respect to our preparations."[31] Thus, Eaker became perhaps the first high-ranking AAF leader to attribute Japan's capitulation to the *combination* of the B-29 incendiary attacks, the dropping of the atomic bombs, and the entry of the Soviet Union into the conflict (which occurred between the dropping of the atomic bombs on Hiroshima and Nagasaki). Eaker also concluded, as Arnold had before him, that the AAF leadership was surprised and caught off-guard by Japan's surrender. The major difficulty now, according to Eaker, was the inability to procure advanced aircraft to support the seventy-eight-group program. He emphasized that the present (postwar) procurement schedule went back to emergency powers granted by President Truman in the spring of 1945. Since that time, noted Eaker, "we have run into difficulty because the Congress and the people are obviously unwilling to spend money for aircraft that do not represent a definite advance over existing types."[32] With few exceptions, he concluded that the AAF did not currently possess such advanced models to initiate further procurement "to subsidize the individual companies."[33] Eaker remained hopeful that the research and development program as funded would enable the aircraft industry to develop the required advanced model aircraft.[34]

After the war, Army Air Forces personnel interviewed numerous Japanese, the *Taro Keda,* or so-called average citizens as opposed to high governmental authorities, in regard to their thinking before the dropping of atomic bombs. It was clear from the interviews in October 1945 that up until the end the Japanese newspapers and radio continued to be optimistic about the outcome of the war. Yet, as time went on, citizens noted the loss of islands such as Guadalcanal, Saipan, Iwo Jima, and especially Okinawa. However, the major reason for defeatism was the B-29 bombings. Many Japanese felt that the war was lost prior to the dropping of the atomic bomb. Jiighi Tsuji, the police chief of downtown Tokyo's Maranouchi ward, noted, "At Okinawa, I felt the situation was then extremely critical, and practically without hope. No, it didn't take the atomic bomb to convince me. I knew it was over before that. And, this may surprise you—I think the people are extremely relieved that the war is over."[35]

Kimesaburo Shimizu, fire chief of the Maranouchi ward, stated that the great Tokyo earthquake of 1923 resulted in approximately one-tenth of the destruction caused collectively by the Tokyo fire raids. "From a fire-fighting standpoint," he noted, "our position was hopeless. ... We had no way of fighting the fires. We tried our best. With the numbers of B-29s however, it was impossible. ... It was like watching the slow creep of annihilation, ward by ward. Sooner or later Tokyo—and all the cities of Japan—would be razed. And we had nothing with which to fight back." In Shimizu's view, "the number one factor which lost the war for Japan was the destruction of morale, due to air raids. The intensification of the raids was felt far more than the loss of territory. The people feared the bombings more than anything."[36]

Iwajiro Noda, director of the Japan Cotton and Silk Trading Company, also pointed to the B-29 campaign: "Here on the home front, the number one factor in bringing the war to a conclusion has been a sentiment of war-weariness, caused perhaps 80% by aerial bombings, and 20% due to critical food shortages. I don't know how much longer the war could have gone on without the Atomic Bomb, but it would not have been much longer."[37] Ryozo Asano, president of the Japan Steel Tube Company, noted that if the war had continued, "millions" of Japanese would have died of starvation during the winter of 1945–1946, due to the aerial mine-laying blockade. Heavy industry had been crippled by bombing and lack of raw materials, which had been cut off by the blockade. Absenteeism in war industries was an enormous problem. "The decision to surrender," according to Asano, "came long before the Atomic Bomb gave the militarists a chance to quit. In order of importance, this decision was most affected by: B-29 raids; the Atomic Bomb; the Russian declaration of war; the threat of invasion."[38] Miss Masu Yumaki was Dean of the College of Nurses at St. Luke's International Medical Center, founded in 1930 by the American Episcopal Church Mission. When Okinawa fell, and the bombings intensified, she thought that "we were approaching a critical state of affairs. ... I do not think it is justifiable to bomb large cities, but I think I can appreciate your standpoint in bombing to save American lives, ultimately. That's war. ... I think you shortened the war by bombing our cities."[39]

Masvo Kato, a graduate of the University of Chicago, was a Domei News Agency correspondent in Washington at the time of Pearl Harbor. He was interned and then sent back to Japan in 1942 where he became Chief of the Domei Research Bureau in Tokyo. He felt that the war was lost long before the atomic bomb was dropped. Civilian morale had plummeted and might have collapsed altogether in the event of an invasion.[40]

Goro Murata, news editor of the *Nippon Times,* the English-language paper of the Foreign Office, thought that when the B-29s "came in flocks all over Japan, unmolested," it marked the beginning of the end: "It was enough to dishearten the most fanatical chauvinist."[41] Eiyo Ishikawa, Tokyo's chief engineer for city planning, noted that only one-fifth of Tokyo was destroyed during the 1923 earthquake, whereas the B-29 attacks were much more destructive: "Of the two million wooden homes in Tokyo before the war, only one-fourth are now standing. Our fire-fighting equipment was completely useless during the raids. Up until the March 10 raid I did not feel so pessimistic; after that my hopes steadily deteriorated. ... I felt that the war could end at any time."[42] The enormously destructive raid on Tokyo, March 9–10, 1945, tended to obscure the later attack of May 25–26, in which seventeen square miles of the city were burned out, most of northwest Tokyo. The imperial palace was set afire and the emperor and empress were forced to move to the underground library on the palace grounds. By late May, more than half of the urban area of Tokyo had been destroyed.

In October 1945, AAF personal also interrogated high-ranking Japanese officers, and other military and government officials, on the events that forced Japan into submission. Lt. Gen. Barney M. Giles, Commanding General, U.S. Army Strategic Air Forces, stated, "the destruction of industry, the cutting of supply lines, bottling of Japanese shipping, primarily through air power, so reduced Japanese capacity to wage war, that they were ready to sue for peace before the atomic bomb was dropped." He added that "there is no doubt that the suicide defense planned by the Japanese would have been extremely costly in American lives."[43] Gen. Masakazu Kawabe, Commanding General of the Air General Army, confirmed that the Japanese planned a "special attack" (Kamikaze) defense against the planned invasion of Kyushu, having pinpointed where the landing would take place. "We expected annihilation of our entire air force," he stated, "but we felt that it was our duty." Kawabe based planning on the Leyte and Okinawa experiences: For defense of the homeland, "It was contemplated that one out of four planes, of the eight to nine thousand planes available for special attack, would sink or damage an Allied ship ... the decision to use special attack was made because of lack of sufficient aircraft; lack of experienced pilots to attack surface vessels; inability of our Navy to stop attacks."[44]

Kawabe's thinking was typical of that of other high-ranking officers and government officials who thought that the Kamikaze defense would give Japan a last-ditch opportunity to "win the war," in the sense that an enormously costly Allied landing would ultimately provide Japan better terms for ending the war. Kawabe admitted that special defense tactics basically were not the best option to win the war, but "it was force of circumstances which caused the decision."[45] Both at Leyte and Okinawa it had become apparent to the Japanese that ultimately they would have to employ all aircraft for Kamikaze attacks. Some special attack planes were used against B-29s but the success rate was much lower than against ships. He also noted that in the late summer of 1945 the available pilots were insufficiently trained due to a serious lack of fuel. Many pilots had been lost in the battle of Okinawa and in the attempt to repel B-29 attacks. Because of the lack of fuel, pilots were able to fly training sorties only seven or eight hours per month. Pilots need a total of 500 flying hours to be considered combat pilots. They were getting only about 130 hours.

According to Rear Admiral Toshitane Takata: "The fire bomb raids destroyed most of the smaller factories making aircraft parts, thus causing serious loss in production. The many small plants scattered over the cities which were destroyed caused serious loss in the material and general production. Bombing attacks on engine plants, therefore, were very effective in limiting aircraft output. As B-29 raids became more intensive, it became almost impossible to continue production, so they started to transfer industry to underground shelters thus further reducing production. The dropping of pamphlets warning of impending raids caused conditions close to panic in some of the cities."[46]

Culminating in July and early August 1945, LeMay had conducted a concerted program of propaganda leaflet drops over Japanese cities to undermine the people's morale. Thus, this effort started after LeMay's low-level, incendiary attacks had turned the B-29 campaign around from Hansell's problematical operations. Prepared by psychological warfare specialists, the leaflets were dropped in July by LeMay's planes on eleven cities. Following these drops, most of these urban areas were struck with incendiaries. The leaflet drops, followed by attacks, were continued during the first week of August. The manager of the largest industrial plant in Nagoaka informed postwar interrogators that the leaflets had a great effect on the morale of the people. They figured that if the enemy could announce a raid beforehand, the enemy was superior. A Tokyo governmental official noted that once the people decided that these air raid warnings could be trusted, they began to believe the propaganda leaflets and their morale decisively declined.

Mr. Koizumi, chief of the Police Bureau, a long-term official of the Home Ministry, and a former governor of various prefectures, stressed the influence of the leaflet campaign. Certainly by July, according to Koizumi, the U.S. leaflets were given wide credence. Even considering the factor of Japanese officials after the war wanting to ingratiate themselves with their captors, a report written by Koizumi noted that "The leaflets grew in influence until they were widely believed in June and July 1945 and, coupled with the bombing, were very effective, particularly those announcing forthcoming specific bombings. ... "[47]

In retrospect, Arnold's fear that the atomic bomb would place the contribution of the conventional bombing assault in the background, has in fact been realized. The way in which the Pacific war ended has forever cast a long shadow over what the Army Air Forces B-29 campaign accomplished in the spring and summer of 1945. "We were never able," Arnold emphasized, "to launch the full power of our bombing attack. ... The power of those attacks would certainly have convinced any doubting Thomases as to the capabilities of a modern Air Force. I am afraid that from now on there will be certain people who will forget the part we have played. As a matter of fact, I see evidence of it right now in the writings of the columnists—probably inspired by interested people."[48] It's a fair guess that the "certain people" Arnold had in mind were leaders of the Navy, some of the national press, and potentially, historians.

Arnold's concern about people forgetting the role played by the Army Air Forces also manifested itself in Washington where he "had quite a time" fighting, as he saw it, a "noticeable attitude to ignore the Air Arm and forget its existence insofar as representation was concerned."[49] Arnold's concern pertained especially to the official surrender ceremony and in this regard he wanted to forward an official dispatch from Washington to the effect that General Spaatz would represent the Army Air Forces. However, MacArthur's chief of staff, Maj. Gen. Richard Sutherland, left Washington with the understanding that MacArthur would invite Spaatz. As it turned out, Spaatz was present on September 2 on the deck of the USS *Missouri*, for the formal Japanese surrender ceremony. He was, in fact, the only U.S. military officer to attend all three World War II surrender ceremonies: at Reims, the second in Berlin, and the last, in Tokyo Bay.

According to Eaker back in Washington, when reading the text of MacArthur's remarks on the *Missouri*, Arnold had been visibly moved. MacArthur hit the perfect note, calling upon his great command of language, occasion, and also magnanimity:

> We are gathered here, representatives of the major warring powers, to conclude a solemn agreement whereby peace may be restored. The issues, involving divergent ideals and ideologies, have been determined on the battlefields of the world and hence are not for our discussion or debate. Nor is it for us here to meet, representing as we do a majority of the people of the earth, in a spirit of distrust, malice or hatred. But rather it is for us, both victors and vanquished, to rise to that higher dignity which alone befits the sacred purposes we are about to service, committing all our people unreservedly to faithful compliance with the understanding they are here formally to assume.

It is my earnest hope, and indeed the hope of all mankind, that
from this solemn occasion a better world shall emerge out of the
blood and carnage of the past—a world dedicated to the dignity of
man and the fulfillment of his most cherished wish for freedom, tol-
erance and justice.[50]

After the formal ceremony, MacArthur had arranged to broadcast a
message to the world. "A new era is upon us," he stated: "Even the lesson
of victory itself brings with it profound concern, both for our future
security and the survival of civilization. The destructiveness of the war
potential, through progressive advance in scientific discovery, has in
fact not reached a point which revises the traditional concepts of war.

"Men since the beginning of time have sought peace. … Military alli-
ances, balances of power, leagues of nations, all in turn failed, leaving the
only path to be by way of the crucible of war. We have had our last chance.
If we do not now devise some greater and more equitable system, Armageddon will be at our door."[51]

Arnold, however, thought it strange that MacArthur had failed to
make any recommendations regarding postwar air organization: "Strange
as it may seem, we have never received MacArthur's recommendations
for post-hostility dispositions of air. In view of his intense interest in all
phases of air operations, I was a little surprised that he should have no
recommendations from him."[52] MacArthur however, did ask Arnold about
potential organizational and command plans for the B-29 force. To Spaatz,
Arnold noted that for the short term the B-29s should be turned over to
MacArthur for operational control: "It looks to me as if we would be smart
to do this because he will have them anyhow and there is nothing much
that we can do about it." Nonetheless, for the long term, Arnold emphasized to Spaatz his conviction that had guided command of the B-29s
during the Pacific War: "I do think that in the final organization the strategic bombers must and should be controlled from Washington; that the
Washington Command should farm them out to local commanders when
it becomes necessary to take care of conditions in various parts of the
world. … Certainly I do not think that the strategic bombers should be

placed under a local Ground Commander as a normal organization."[53] Hap Arnold's view certainly echoed that of Gill Robb Wilson, the insightful columnist for the *New York Herald Tribune* who wrote on April 18, 1945: "The 20th (Air Force) is still embryonic to its ultimate stature. ... We are watching the pioneering stages of a realistic world influence to represent the United States in the air ages ahead."[54] This proved to be correct, for the Strategic Air Command became the U.S. nuclear deterrent force for the long decades of the cold war with the Soviet Union, an age that now seems almost lost in the American memory.

Arnold planned to retire by the end of 1945: "I would get out sooner only I am interested in the future of the Air Forces and accordingly want to have a talk with the powers that be concerning who my successor should be." He indicated to Spaatz that he wanted to have a major voice in the selection of his successor and "to have an overlap of time with him in this office sufficient to give him the benefit of my experience here in Washington, if he should like to receive it." The officer that Arnold had in mind to succeed him was Carl "Tooey" Spaatz. Consequently, Arnold suggested to Spaatz that he return to Washington from the Pacific as soon as possible—"there are many things I want to talk over with you"—although not interfering with arrangements and representation for the surrender.[55] As it turned out, Arnold officially retired in February 1946; Spaatz took over at that time as Commanding General, Army Air Forces.

It should be noted that the strategic bombing offensive against the Japanese homeland was prosecuted by only a small part of the evolving B-29 force that was preparing for even heavier attacks against Japan in the autumn of 1945. Ultimately, thirty-three combat B-29 groups were to be engaged in the bombing campaign, but during the offensive in 1944–1945 the average available monthly force amounted to only 10.3 groups. Ninety percent of the bomb tonnage was delivered during the last five months of the war.[56] When the war ended, the Twentieth was just becoming fully operational, and the Eighth Air Force was starting to move into the Ryukyus, with its first combat sorties scheduled for mid-August. Planners estimated that operating the XXI Bomber Command from the Ryukyus would reduce by almost fifty percent the number of hours per sortie. With the attendant reduction in combat fatigue, the cost in combat crews for the heavy bomber force was expected to be less from the Ryukyus than from operations in the Marianas.

The U.S. Strategic Bombing Survey referred to the B-29 force under LeMay that carried out the campaign against Japan as "a token force." The full capability of very heavy bombardment "was never fully recognized and was not given adequate weight in the plans established for conduct of the war against Japan." Between June 1944 and August 1945, the Twentieth dropped 165,000 tons of bombs and mines, over routes in excess of 1500 miles from point of take-off. The full bomber force arriving in the theater however, was never available, even by August 1. The Twentieth destroyed approximately 180 square miles of urban area in 66 cities with a population of about 21 million people. As noted, not until March 1945 had the Twentieth been sufficiently built up to initiate an intensive urban incendiary campaign. By the end of the war, the Twentieth was able to deliver over 50,000 tons of bombs per month on Japanese targets.[57]

According to the Strategic Bombing Survey, "the Very Heavy Bombardment campaign against Japan was conceived in effect as a means to an end, namely invasion, rather than as a decisive force within itself."[58] As we have seen, this was true during 1943–1945 as the Joint Chiefs of Staff and the Combined Chiefs of Staff evolved their plans for the defeat of Japan. The primary mission of the Twentieth Air Force, as stated by the Joint Chiefs, was to achieve the dislocation of the Japanese military, industrial, and economic systems and to undermine the morale of the Japanese people to the point where their will to wage war was decisively weakened. The *secondary* mission was to support Pacific operations.

Arnold had staked everything including, as he saw it, the future of the Army Air Forces, on the B-29 campaign. LeMay was his man to organize, operate, and command this force. Although the Joint Chiefs and Combined Chiefs continued to view the bombing and invasion plans as not mutually exclusive, Arnold was convinced that the very heavy bombing offensive by itself could bring Japan down. Arnold's postwar analysis reflected a threat that could be tracked back to the late 1930s and the classrooms of the Air Corps Tactical School. He called it "the Strategic

Theory," emphasizing that it drove the major wartime air operations. It was not new, but its application "was new and in the course of the war the original concept was greatly extended."[59] Arnold's theory was vintage Tactical School; it could, for example, have been lifted straight from Maj. Muir Fairchild's 1939 lectures. Simply stated, it posited that air attacks on the enemy's industrial and economic fabric could shatter his ability to make war and to resist. Concomitantly, Arnold's emphasis upon "the will to resist" strongly implied attacks on the morale of the enemy nation, the civilian population. This thread, sometimes neglected by air historians, had been specifically delineated by Fairchild and other lecturers at the Tactical School in the late 1930s. It was a major part of their corpus.

Air Corps doctrine specified attacks on morale as a denouement following—or in concert with—the air offensive against selected industrial targets. The value of intelligence pertaining to the enemy's industry could not be over-emphasized. Massive destruction of the enemy's industrial fabric, according to Arnold, was simply wasted effort. The key remained selectivity, pinpointing industry without which a modern nation could not prosecute war, such as the German oil industry. The effect of strategic air warfare, Arnold emphasized, was rarely immediately apparent: "Its effect was more like that of cancer, producing internal decay ultimately resulting in death."[60] This was Tactical School doctrine, built upon the necessity of maintaining a global intelligence network, constantly updated, on potential enemy nations.

Organization was the key to recognition and control, all of which led to proper employment of air forces. This was fundamental, the backdrop for evolution of doctrine, strategy, and tactics. Arnold believed that air forces should be organized so that, for example, sufficient mass of strategic bombing could be applied to the appropriate target sets. And this meant not only proper organization, but even more importantly, *control* of these air forces. The marquee example here, of course, became formation of the Twentieth Air Force, the jewel in the AAF's crown. Arnold saw it as the *Global Strategic Air Force,* overflying multi-theaters, independent of theater commanders and their plans and agendas that failed to mesh with the mission and strategy of the independent Twentieth, and that took direction from the Joint Chiefs, through Arnold.

During the war, Arnold kept a close eye on the major theaters, dictating how air forces overseas would be organized, even down to designating units as, for example, pursuit or attack. He not only hectored operational air commanders, he at times over-ruled their descriptive designation of individual units. And once the various air forces began operations, Arnold followed through, closely eyeing sorties and bomb tonnage —sometimes on a daily basis.

Arnold was a doer, a fixer, a driver. His long suit was impatience, wait for nothing. His forte was vision, the ability to recognize what had to be done to build, organize, and control air forces. Air forces required control by airmen as opposed to Army officers with little or no understanding of how to employ aircraft. To his critics, he was a lightweight, bereft of heavy intellectual thought and strategic concepts. He was an easy target for those who fancied themselves as sophisticates, strategic thinkers. As for being constantly under-estimated, the chances are that Arnold did not care. He was the airman at the top, at the high policy table. Though not especially articulate, he made his points when he needed to before the Joint Chiefs. He possessed the instinctive ability to identify an important requirement and then energetically to nail it down and drive it home, sometimes through his trademark mode of organization and command: chaos.

He gave the Army air arm shape and drive, and built and organized the world's first Global Strategic Air Force. He knew how to work with Roosevelt, Marshall, Hopkins, Stimson, and others whom he absolutely needed to get the job done, as he saw it. To those who after the war charged that Arnold had no plan, he was not about to inform the president and Marshall that he disagreed with them on the invasion. What was to be gained? Arnold—and King and Leahy—handled it as he should have, pressing full-blower ahead with blockade and the incendiary campaign. He wanted results—and he got them.

In World War II in Europe, the fact is that the AAF engaged in plenty of area bombing for the simple reason that the technology was not available for sustained "precision" bombing. And over Japan, with the B-29s, the Twentieth Air Force shattered the home islands with a brutal incendiary campaign because that is what produced the kind of results Roosevelt,

Marshall, Arnold, and his airmen wanted. The major drive for strategic bombardment flowed from the very top of the command chain—from the commander-in-chief, the president of the United States. This is what Roosevelt and Truman wanted–full prosecution of all wartime capabilities and resources. Historians and journalists, ignoring the context of the time, continue to show amazement over the fact that neither Roosevelt nor Truman were consulted about tactics in the B-29 strategic bombing campaign. Max Hastings, in his book on the battle for Japan, observed: "There is no documentation to suggest that either Roosevelt or Truman was ever consulted about LeMay's campaign. Here was an extreme example of the manner in which the higher direction of American's was left overwhelming in the hands of the service chiefs of staff."[61] Extreme? The fact is that this was the way Roosevelt and Truman wanted it. In this regard, Roosevelt early on set the table. He gave his service chiefs tactical *carte blanche* and moreover, urged them to do everything possible to decimate the enemy. Franklin Roosevelt, during World War II, was the premier advocate of strategic bombing. The strategic bombing campaign experience over Japan over-turned a great deal of doctrinal thinking. The assumed credibility of the high-altitude precision daylight bombing doctrine was shattered. It did not work for reasons enumerated here—weather being a major factor. Also interestingly, the Japanese experience showed that the anger of the populace could in fact be directed at their own government in addition to at the attackers. Here was a situation in which the attacking force could bomb at will, the homeland forces unable to prevent mass incendiary bombing. So much for the prewar doctrine of high-altitude "precision" bombing. It was in fact shoved out the window early on over Japan, due to the Doolittle raid.

And when it came to unity of command, no member of the Joint Chiefs of Staff outgunned Arnold. Starting not long after the Pearl Harbor attack, he fought long and hard for unity of command in the Pacific—never attained due to the parochial views of theater commanders. He knew MacArthur and was careful with him. Sending Kenney out to the Southwest Pacific command had been a ten-strike, showing MacArthur that with the appropriate airman, missions could be successfully accomplished. As far as unified command was concerned, however, Arnold knew full well, from early 1942 on, that it would never come to pass in the Pacific. Consequently, though he continued to raise the issue, he wasted no excessive time on it, concentrating on applying air power globally. During the war, he visited the Pacific a number of times, conferred with both MacArthur and Nimitz, and generally found that they provided him with useful operational updates. Nimitz could be especially forthcoming and Arnold found that upon occasion he could be quite helpful. Late in the war, after talking with Nimitz, Arnold concluded that a major portion of the Army Air Forces' logistical and supply problems were due to poor work by his own people, rather than owing to some sort of naval cabal.

Arnold knew MacArthur's strategic views well, having learned plenty from Kenney, but of course also receiving them from Marshall within the Joint Chiefs system. He never expected MacArthur to be any kind of cheerleader for the Twentieth's mission, hoping instead that "the big man" (as Kenney put it) at the least would not attempt to short-circuit the Twentieth in any way. The success of Kenney's operations in support of MacArthur's forces was a big plus. Otherwise, Arnold made it a point to be an on-looker as far as MacArthur was concerned, since Arnold had no direct command authority in regard to the Southwest Pacific theater.

He succeeded in establishing the Twentieth Air Force because he was a man with a mission, anything but doctrinaire and rigid when it came to organizing and controlling air forces. He needed an air force to overfly theaters in order to batter the Japanese "to a pulp" in their homeland. Even prior to creation of the Twentieth, Arnold knew he had to quickly fix the B-29 production mess or the Very Long-Range bombers would not make it operational to the Pacific in early 1944. He drove himself like there was no tomorrow, as the distinguished Washington columnist Marquis Childs remarked: "He bullied the program [B-29s] through. He risked everything on its success. ... He drove himself too hard."[62]

Perhaps the most surprising element of Arnold's flexibility occurred after the war. In the wake of Japan's capitulation, as Arnold saw it, determined in large part by the Twentieth Global Air Force, the AAF commander laid out his vision for the future. It did not necessarily include air forces like the mighty air armadas that flew in the wartime skies. Air power itself, he proclaimed, might very well become obsolete. How many Navy commanders immediately after the war were talking of the demise of battleships and carrier task forces? Arnold envisioned unmanned vehicles and robots. Also, Eaker envisioned supersonic flight as well as development of unmanned vehicles. Echoing von Karman's ideas, Eaker observed, on June 5, 1947, "We know today as little about the air weapon which can pierce the sonic barrier as the Wright brothers knew about conventional type airplanes when they made their first flight." Eventually, the primary air weapon would be "a pilotless craft, probably of the nature of a long range guided missile."[63] In the future, the air arm would be a corps of technicians and scientists rather than "flying men."

Moreover, Arnold realized probably better than most of the victorious wartime commanders that total war itself had become not only obsolete, but unimaginable, a pox on civilization. For all his alleged lack of intellectual power and sophistication, it was Arnold who after the war sounded the bell for the need for clear-headed brainpower to make certain that total war could be eliminated once and for all. He was a strong supporter of the United Nations organization and he advocated international air contingents for world police duty. Although this never materialized, he was out front about its possibilities.

For years prior to World War II, Arnold had been concerned with the broad field of aviation technology and its application to military air power. Technical advances during the war had transformed combat aviation. Atomic bombs, electronic devices, radar, and mechanical aids provided increased range and destructive power and "made most of the archaic ideas of air power obsolete almost over night." These technological advances meant that "future wars will be staggering in their widespread, complete annihilation of objectives and the tremendous, wholesale loss of life resulting from air attacks." Because the atomic bomb had brought an end to the war, and according to Arnold had thus saved thousands of lives, "is it not possible for modern air power to so completely annihilate and destroy a community or military objective, including assembled fleets, that navies will never fire a hostile shot and armies will never meet armies on the field of battle?"[64]

Well before the end of the war, Arnold thought about future scientific developments and their application to aerial warfare. In 1944, he had asked his friend Dr. Theodore von Karman to develop a study of Nazi Germany's wartime aeronautical science. The resulting report, *Where We Stand,* prompted Arnold to request a forecast of what aerial warfare would look like well into the future. The result, *Toward New Horizons,* available late in 1945, stressed the importance of science and technology to the evolution of air power. Von Karman described the thirty-three volumes that comprised the report as "the first exhaustive report of its kind in the history of the American military." It recommended development of supersonic aircraft and guided missiles, and echoing Arnold's thought and experience, highlighted the importance of cooperation between scientists and the air arm.[65] This was a subject that Arnold continued to emphasize after the war. One of the major lessons of the recent conflict was "the integration into the war effort of the cumulative resources of the natural and social sciences" and the experience of the scientific community, which enabled the United States "to outwit and overwhelm the enemy." Arnold suggested "a central group of Army and Navy air people who will meet with top scientists to discuss overall guiding principles. ... We would have an interchange of scientific people and service people, by putting the former in uniform for extended periods of duty to learn Army techniques and by having the latter work with technical and scientific people. We must liberalize our ideas as to who are to be Army officers, to provide scientific post-graduate training thereby creating a corps of officers who can handle these scientific matters better."[66]

To Arnold, the evolution of the Strategic Air Force was the key. It operated hundreds of miles from areas controlled by Army or Navy forces and struck targets far beyond their reach. Thus, functions of the Strategic Air Force were in every way "truly strategic and its operations cause destruction which may not be felt by the Army in the field—as in the case of Japan—for many months—though the enemy homeland may, as a result of its activities, lose all zest for war."[67]

Thus, portrayed as parochial and narrow-minded, Gen. Hap Arnold was clearly more broad-minded and complicated than historians and observers have perceived him. For all his emphasis upon technology and increasing the range and destructive power of military aircraft, Arnold after the war exposed his idealistic bent. He was, after all, a dreamer and certainly a futurist, who could envision a time when, as he put it, the airplane itself "could become obsolete," paving the way for unmanned aircraft. Moreover, the postwar world demanded "the highest type of intellectual leadership" to lay the foundation for a secure America and to "contribute to the organization of a world in which law, and not force, will rule."[68]

Arnold cited the joint declaration in November 1945 by President Truman, British Prime Minister Clement Attlee and Canadian Prime Minister Mackenzie King to the effect that the only sure protection for the world "lies in the prevention of war." Destruction by air power, Arnold emphasized, "has become too cheap and easy. This was true even before the advent of the atomic bomb; even then, mass air raids were obliterating the great centers of mankind by fire and explosion." The consequence of "this cheapness of destruction ... is to make the existence of civilization as we know it subject to the good will and the good sense of the men who control the employment of air power. The greatest need facing the world today is for international control of these forces of destruction." The advent of the atomic bomb had decreased the cost of destruction by air power. "Complete destruction of cities by incendiaries and high explosive bombs had become an accomplished fact early in the war; the name of Coventry reminds us of that. In the course of the war, strategic bombing advanced enormously in effectiveness and efficiency and in the attack on the Japanese Empire had become highly profitable from a military point of view; but the atomic bomb by comparison dwarfs all other advances. A dollars and cents approach to this problem will clarify these facts." Arnold pointed out that now one B-29 dropping an atomic bomb would cause as much destruction "as three hundred planes would have done before." The Twentieth Air Force employing atomic bombs could now "in one day's raid" destroy more of Japan's industry than was done in the entire B-29 campaign. Consequently, emphasized Arnold, "the best protection from atomic weapons lies in developing controls and safeguards which will prevent their use." However, Arnold pointed out that the destruction of urban areas was not the objective of the Strategic Air Force. The goal was "to weaken the enemy's military strength and will to resist to the point where he can successfully be invaded by ground forces, as was Germany, or capitulates in the face of certain destruction, as did Japan."[68] The evolution of the B-29 was the apex in destruction by strategic air power.

Arnold saw the immediate postwar period as interim, a time in which the nation needed to evolve "a transcending moral force, supported by an armed force, effective in the judgement of foreign powers." At that time, the United States could "start to turn over" responsibility for the nation's security to an international police force. Such a policy was dictated by the terrible experience of World War II. The fact that air power could destroy great urban centers meant that the world required "international control of these forces of destruction and disaster." Arnold emphasized that under provisions of the United Nations charter, "the Air Forces must assume their full responsibility of holding immediately available national air force contingents for combined international enforcement action. These forces must be of sufficient strength, and their degree of readiness must be such as to make effective use of their inherent striking power and mobility."[70] In the event the UN or any other international instrument proved not be to viable, the United States, the most powerful nation in the world, would have to rely on its own power: "Our possession of power which, in a just proportion, we can make available to the United Nations in the maintaining of peace, is the best guarantee of maintaining this collective peace. If the nations of the world find that they cannot act in concert, our possession of power will be our only resource. Therefore, we must at all costs maintain it."[71] This was the idealistic Arnold and he subsequently appointed Gen. George C. Kenney to serve on the United Nations Military Staff Committee. The fact that a UN police force was never established does not detract from Arnold's postwar vision, which truly set him apart from other postwar military leaders.

Yet his self-professed idealism about the UN was tempered by reality. He pointed to the failure of the League of Nations and noted that theoretically the United Nations organization should prevent future wars and iron out disagreements between nations. However, Arnold stated, "there was still the big question: Would it? Or would it be another organization with no power or teeth with which to enforce its decisions?"[72] The retaliatory power of atomic weapons, he stressed, might prevent their use. In a future war, neither side may want to employ atomic weapons and thus visit destruction upon its own cities and population. It is possible that area attacks, such as those conducted in World War II, might not be employed in a future war. Arnold noted that there existed historic precedent for withholding use of certain weapons. He pointed out that gas attacks had not been used in Europe. Consequently, looking to the future, Arnold surmised that atomic weapons would not be employed, thus bringing up the possibility of stalemate in war, and the necessity of development of advanced conventional weapons.[73]

Arnold emphasized that he did not "hold any brief" for a permanent Air Force. It was conceivable, he said, that a mighty Air Force, like that employed in World War II, would no longer be required. However, a well-trained, fully equipped force able to use the new technology would be needed. Most importantly, and following von Karman's prescription, the nation required a dynamic, well-financed research and development program: "If we fail to keep not merely abreast, but ahead of, technological development, we needn't bother to train any force and we needn't make plans for an emergency expansion: we will be totally defeated before any expansion could take place."[74]

Arnold held a clear vision of the future of weapons evolution which, from the retrospective of over sixty years, proved remarkably prescient. He predicted pilotless aircraft would roam the skies at supersonic speeds, doing away with aerial combat as we know it. He saw the evolution of guided and ballistic missiles, hitting targets in any part of the world. There would be "improved" atomic bombs, "destructive beyond the wildest nightmares of the imagination." On the other hand, fantastic developments in defense would obtain, against both aircraft and missiles, through evolution of target-seeking anti-aircraft missiles. Arnold called for evolution of "defensive" technology: "We must make sure that no potential aggressor out-distances us in his defensive developments. Once more this means strategic bases for warning, detection and interception of bombers for the near future and later for pilotless weapons to whatever extent is possible."[75]

Scientific and technological advances, Arnold emphasized, had changed the nature of war and placed the United States in a dominant strategic position. Concomitantly, the nation no longer possessed geographical security: "The conquest of space, which differentiated the late struggle from all other wars, has now progressed so that even the vast oceans ... present no effective security. Reliance can no longer be placed on geographical security, which, together with the help of our allies, gave us in the past the time to build our military machine after the outbreak of war."[76] Our security, he noted, can in the future be threatened suddenly and with terrific destructive power.

In a future war, it was possible that U.S. cities would be attacked first, possibly by rockets or guided missiles. This scenario naturally led Arnold to his emphasis upon preserving U.S. leadership in the aeronautical sciences. One of the major lessons of the war was the need for cooperation between the armed forces and science and industry: "I cannot help but reflect with sadness on the fact that we as a nation did not develop this cooperation voluntarily, but that the enemy himself by his attack on Pearl Harbor became the great catalyst. That was the shock we needed to bring us together for a common purpose, to make us renounce our self-complacency and the smug doctrine of isolationism. Only war—the ultimate challenge to a nation's ability to live—made us adopt a practice which common sense should have told us long before was necessary for protecting the security of the nation."[77]

In October 1945, Arnold testified to the Senate Committee on Military Affairs:

> it is unfortunately true that each new crisis in our history has found our armed services far from effectively efficiently or economically organized. With each crisis modernization and coordination have been hammered out under war pressure at great waste of resources, to be allowed in large measure to lapse when the crisis is over.
>
> The question of effective, efficient and economical organization comes before the country after every war, as each succeeding generation seeks—hitherto unsuccessfully—to profit to the full from the lessons learned in war. Today that question is with us again and this time more urgently than ever before.[78]

Characteristically, Arnold took a long view when pondering the immediate past and the future. Wars were no longer fought solely by armed forces, "but by all citizens united in a joint effort which touches every phase of national and private life. The danger zone of modern war is not restricted to battle lines and adjacent areas but extends to the innermost parts of a nation. No one is immune from the ravages of war."[79] The experience of World War II showed the enormous destructive power of modern war. And warfare, he was certain, would continue to undergo "radical" evolution. The cost of modern war in lives and resources made war "unthinkable." The military establishment of the United States must be structured with one thought uppermost: the maintenance of peace.

As noted, Arnold always maintained a keen sensitivity to the voice of the American public. It was not just a matter of public relations on which he placed great emphasis, but Arnold had a genuine appreciation for the democratic process:

> It is the American people who will decide whether this Nation will continue to hold its air supremacy. In the final analysis, our air striking force belongs to those who come from the ranks of labor, management, the farms, the stores, the professions, the schools and colleges and the legislative halls.
>
> Air Power will always be the business of every American citizen.[80]

Coming from other military leaders, these words may have struck an off-key note, but Gen. Hap Arnold really believed them.

Endnotes

The following abbreviations will be used in the Notes.

ACTS: Air Corps Tactical School
Cllctn: Collection
FDRL: Franklin D. Roosevelt Library
FRUS: Foreign Relations of the United States
GPO: Government Printing Office
L.C.: Library of Congress
N.A.: National Archives
PSF: President's Secretary File
RPTS: Reports

Introduction

1. Ray S. Cline, *Washington Command Post: The Operations Division* (Washington, D.C.: Office of the Chief of Military History, 1951), 1.
2. See Maj. Gen. John W. Huston, *American Airpower Comes of Age: General Henry H. "Hap" Arnold's World War II Diaries,* Two vols. (Maxwell Air Force Base, AL: Air University Press, January 2002).
3. Eaker, interview by author, Washington, D.C., 27 August 1974.
4. R. Cargill Hall, ed., *Case Studies in Strategic Bombing* (Washington, D.C.: Air Force History and Museums Program, 1998).

5. United States Strategic Bombing Survey, Final Report, 1 September 1945.

Chapter 1
1. Lt. Col. Edgar S. Gorrell, "The American Proposal for Strategic Bombing," *The Air Power Historian*, April 1958.
2. Quoted in Air Vice-Marshal E. J. Kingston-McCloughry, *Global Strategy* (New York: Frederick A. Praeger, 1957), 216.
3. Giulio Douhet, *The Command of the Air* (Rome: Air Ministry, 1921), translated by Dino Ferrari and published in New York by Coward-McCann, 1942; Edward Warner, "Douhet, Mitchell, Seversky: Theories of Air Warfare," in Edward Mead Earle, ed., *Makers of Modern Strategy* (Princeton: Princeton University Press, 1959), see especially Chapter 3. The most comprehensive recent work on air doctrine is Col. Phillip S. Meilinger, ed., *The Paths of Heaven: The Evolution of Power Theory* (Maxwell AFB, AL: Air University Press, 1997).
4. Douhet, especially Chapters 3 and 4.
5. Quoted in Wesley Craven and James L. Cate, *The Army Air Forces in World War II*, Vol. I, *Plans and Early Operations* (Chicago: University of Chicago Press, 1948), 42.
6. Thomas H. Greer, *The Development of Air Doctrine in the Army Air Arm, 1917–1941* (Washington, D.C.: New Imprint by Office of Air Force History, 1985), 42.
7. The standard work on Mitchell is Alfred F. Hurley, *Billy Mitchell: Crusader for Air Power* (Bloomington: Indiana University Press, 1975).
8. For an expansion of this concept see Herman S. Wolk, *The Struggle for Air Force Independence, 1943–1947* (Washington. D.C.: Air Force History and Museums Program, 1997); and Wolk, "Who's in Control? A Century of Organizing for Air War," in Michael Robert Terry, ed., *Winged Crusade: The Quest for American Air and Space Power* (Chicago: Imprint Publications, 2006).
9. *Aircraft in National Defense*, 69th Congress, Session 1, Senate Documents, pp 2–29.
10. Greer, 80.
11. Greer, 80–81. For a history of the Tactical School, see Robert Finney, *History of the Air Corps Tactical School, 1920–1940*, USAF Historical Study #100 (Maxwell AFB, AL: USAF Historical Division, 1955), 80.
12. For a well-researched biography of Arnold, see Dik Alan Daso, *Hap Arnold and the Evolution of American Air Power* (Washington, D.C.: Smithsonian Institution Press, 2000).
13. Thomas M. Coffey, *Hap: The Story of the U.S. Air Force and the Man Who Built It*, New York: The Viking Press, 1982, p117.
14. Fairchild, lecture, Air Warfare, Air Corps Tactical School, October 1939, General Muir S. Fairchild Cllctn, Container #5, Mss. Div, L.C.

15. Fairchild, lecture, Air Power and Air Warfare, ACTS, 27 October 1939, Fairchild Cllctn, Container #5, Mss. Div, L.C.
16. Fairchild, lecture, ACTS, 28 October 1939, in Fairchild Cllctn, Container #2, Mss. Div, L.C.
17. Ibid.
18. See Chapter V of this work.
19. Eaker, interview by Alfred Goldberg and Charles Hildreth, May 1962, in Office of Air Force History, Washington, D.C.
20. Arnold to Trenchard, 30 March 1943, Special Official File, 1941–1945, Arnold Cllctn, Container #39, Mss. Div, L.C.
21. Fairchild, lecture, Strategic Offense and Strategic Defense, ACTS, 1 November 1939.
22. Quoted in Greer, 111.
23. Fairchild, lecture, 28 October 1939.
24. Greer, 113.
25. Ibid.
26. Hansell, lecture, "The Development of the United States Concept of Bombardment Operations," Air War College, Air University, 19 September 1951.
27. See Greer, Chap 5.
28. Fairchild, lecture, 28 October 1939.
29. Mark S. Watson, *Chief of Staff: Prewar Plans and Preparations* (Washington, D.C.: Center for Military History, 1950), 132.
30. Ibid., 133.
31. Chief of the Air Corps for Asst Sec of War, memorandum, 10 November 1938, Strength of Army Air Corps, cited in Watson, 136.
32. Ibid.; See Watson, Chap. 5, for a consideration of the administration's new production goals.
33. Watson, 136; In his memoir, Arnold writes that the date for this meeting was 28 September 1938, possibly confusing it with Munich.
34. H. H. Arnold, *Global Mission* (New York: Harper and Brothers, 1949), 177.
35. Ibid.
36. Ibid., 177–79.
37. Ibid., 179.
38. Ibid.
39. Ibid., 179–80.
40. DeWitt S. Copp, *A Few Great Captains: The Men and Events that Shaped the Development of U.S. Air Power* (McLean, VA: EPM Publications, 1980), 458.
41. Carl Berger, *B-29: The Superfortress* (New York: Ballantine Books, 1970), 27.
42. Under Brig. Gen. Walter G. Kilner, the board included reserve Lt. Col. Charles A. Lindbergh, Lt. Col. Carl A. Spaatz, Lt. Col. E. L. Naiden, and Maj. A. J. Lyon.
43 . Berger, 27.

44. Ibid., p37.

45. Jeffrey S. Underwood, *The Wings of Democracy: The Influence of Air Power on the Roosevelt Administration, 1933–1941* (College Station: Texas A&M University Press, 1991), 166.

46. *Global Mission,* 184.

47. Ibid., 259.

48. Ibid.

49. Henry Morgenthau Diaries, #247, Roll 67, in FDRL.

50. *Global Mission,* 195.

51. Arnold to Lovett, memorandum, Aircraft Production for 1943, 20 October 1942, RG 107, File 452.1(7), Production, Item 11A, NA, quoted in George M. Watson, Jr., *The Office of the Secretary of the Air Force, 1947–1965* (Washington, D.C.: Center for Air Force History, 1993), 21.

52. Ibid.

53. Jonathan F. Fanton, "Robert A. Lovett: The War Years," (Ph.D. Dissertation, Yale University, 1978), available from University Microfilms Int'l, 81. For a discussion of Lovett's problems with Arnold's production goals, see Watson, 21–23 and Herman S. Wolk, "Lovett," Air Force Magazine, September 2006.

54. Forrest Pogue, George C. Marshall: Ordeal and Hope, 1939–1942, (New York: The Viking Press, 1965), 63.

55. *Industrial Mobilization for War, History of the War Production Board and Predecessor Agencies, 1940–1945,* Vol. I, Program and Administration (Washington, D.C.: U.S. Government Printing Office, 1947), 47, 50.

56. Arnold to President, memorandum, Dr. Soong's Proposal, 15 June 1942, File War, Gen Arnold, 1-42, PSF, in FDRL; Roosevelt to Arnold, memorandum, 19 May 1942, Safe File, Japan: in PSF, Box 82, FDRL; Arnold to President, memorandum, Dr. Soong's Proposal re Shanghai, 20 May 1942, Safe File, Japan, in PSF, FDRL.

57. For the detailed story behind the plan to send B-17s and American air crews to China, see Alan Armstrong, *Preemptive Strike: The Secret Plan that Would Have Prevented the Attack on Pearl Harbor* (Guilford, CT: Lyons Press, An Imprint of the Globe, Pequot Press, 2006). Armstrong has used original source material, but his argument that implementation of the plan to bomb Japan would have prevented the attack on Pearl Harbor is vastly overdrawn.

58. FDR to Marshall and Arnold, memorandum, 23 March, 1943, File War Dept-1941, in PSF, FDRL.

59. Watson, 5.

60. Arnold to Eaker, message, 19 June 1943, CMOUT8090, cited in Cline, 250.

61. Cline, 253.

62. Cline, 249.

63. *The Public Papers and Addresses of Franklin D. Roosevelt,* Vol. 1942 (New York: Harper and Brothers, 1950), 33.

64. Stimson to the President, 12 April 1942, File Stimson folder, in PSF, FDRL.
65. FDR to Stimson, 14 October in File, War Dept-1941, in PSF, FDRL.
66. Stimson to the President, 12 April 1942, in Stimson Folder, PSF, FDRL.
67. Ibid.
68. Ibid.
69. Arnold to President, memorandum, 8 October 1942; Nelson to the President, 3 October 1942, File A16/Gen, in PSF, FDRL.
70. *Global Mission,* 606–7.
71. Cline, 106.
72. See Maj. Gen. John W. Huston, *American Airpower Comes of Age: General Henry H. "Hap" Arnold's World War II Diaries,* Vol. 2 (Maxwell AFB, AL: Air University Press, 2002), 9.
73. FDR to Arnold, memorandum, 6 October 1942, File War Dept-1941, in PSF, FDRL.
74. Ibid.
75. FDR to Marshall and Arnold, memorandum, 23 March 1943, File War Dept-1941, in PSF, FDRL.
76. FDR to the Sec of War and the Sec of the Navy, memorandum, 16 March 1942, in PSF, FDRL.
77. Arnold to President, memorandum, 20 May 1942, Dr. Soong's Proposal re Shanghai, Safe File, Japan, in PSF, FDRL.
78. Arnold to the President, memorandum,11 June 1942, in PSF, Arnold File, Container # 82, FDRL.
79. Werner Gruhl, Imperial Japan's World War II (London: Routledge, 2007), 8.
80. Ibid., 137.
81. Ibid., 139.
82. Statement by the President, 21 April 1943, in Harry L. Hopkins Papers, Official File, Container #4, in FDRL.
83. *Global Mission,* p298.
84. This brief account of the Doolittle raiders is based on Bernard C. Nalty, ed., *Winged Shield, Winged Sword: History of the United States Air Force,* Vol. I, *1907-1950* (Washington, D.C.: Air Force History and Museums Program, 1997), 217–18.
85. Arnold to Roosevelt, quoted in Samuel Rosenman, ed., *The Public Papers and Addresses of Franklin D. Roosevelt, 1942 Volume* (New York: Harper and Brothers, 1950), 216.
86. Ibid., viii.
87. Eaker, interview by author, 27 August 1974.
88. Stimson to President, memorandum, Japanese Atrocities—Reports by Escaped Prisoners in Harry L. Hopkins Papers, Official File, Container #4, FDRL.

89. Leahy to President from Adm. William D. Leahy, 22 September 1943, Japanese Atrocities—Rpts of Escaped Prisoners, in Hopkins Papers, Official File, Container #4.

90. Statement by the President, 24 March 1944, in Hopkins Papers, Official File, Container #4.

91. Chennault to FDR, 26 January 1944, Safe File, AAF, Container #1, in PSF, FDRL.

92. FDR to Chennault, 15 March 1944, Safe file, AAF, Container #1, in PSF, FDRL.

93. Alexander B. Downes, *Targeting Civilians in War* (Ithaca: Cornell University Press, 2008), 132.

94. See George C. Kenney, *General Kenney Reports* (Repr., Washington, D.C.: Air Force History and Museums Program, 1997), 215–17, 343–44, 532–34.

95. *First Report of the Commanding General of the Army Air Forces to the Secretary of War,* by General of the Army H. H. Arnold, 4 January 1944.

Chapter 2

1. U.S. Serial ABC-4/cs-1, Washington War Conference, no date, memorandum by U.S. and British Chiefs of Staff, American-British Strategy, in PSF, American-British/JCS, Container #1, Franklin Delano Roosevelt Library, Hyde Park, hereafter abbreviated FDRL.

2. Ibid.

3. Arnold to Chief of Staff, memorandum, Employment of Army Air Forces, 3 March 1942, Special Official File, Container #39, Arnold Collection, Mss. Div, L.C.

4. Ibid.

5. Arnold to Chief of Staff, memorandum, Comparison of Bombing Capabilities of 8th Air Force and R.A.F., 22 August 1942, in Arnold Cllctn, Container #39.

6. Stratemeyer to Dep Ch of the Air Staff, et al., memorandum, Gen Arnold's Opinion on How to Win the War, 2 December 1942, in Arnold Cllctn, Container #39; Craven and Cate, Vol II, p. 277.

7. Lt. Gen. H. H. Arnold to the President, memorandum, 8 October 1942, File A16/Gen, PSF, FDRL.

8. Ibid.

9. FDR to the Secretary of War, Chief of Staff, Gen Arnold, Secretary of the Navy, Adm King, and Harry Hopkins, memorandum, 6 May, 1942, in PSF, War Dept File, Marshall Folder, Container #83, FDRL.

10. FDR to Marshall, King and Hopkins, memorandum,15 July, 1942, in PSF, War Dept File, Marshall Folder, Container #3, FDRL.

11. JCS 287/1, Strategic Plan for the Defeat of Japan, Rpt by the Joint Staff Planners, 8 May 1943, in PSF, File Current Strategic Studies, Container #2, FDRL.

12. See Alfred F. Hurley, *Billy Mitchell: Crusader for Air Power* (Bloomington: Indiana University Press, 1975). This is the standard work on Billy Mitchell.

13. Cited in DeWitt S. Copp, *A Few Great Captains: The Men and Events that Shaped the Development of U.S. Air Power* (McLean, VA: EPM Publications, Inc., 1980).

14. Arnold to Hopkins, memorandum, 15 July, 1942, Supreme Commander of Armed Forces of United Nations, in Harry L. Hopkins Papers, Container #131, FDRL.

15. JCS 263/2/D, Unified Command for U.S. Joint Operations, 20 April 1943, in PSF, File Current Strategic Studies, Container #2, FDRL.

16. Grace Person Hayes, *The History of the Joint Chiefs of Staff: The War Against Japan* (Annapolis: Naval Institute Press, 1982), 264–65.

17. Ibid.

18. Clayton James, *The Years of MacArthur: The War Years, 1941–1945,* Vol. II (Boston: Houghton Mifflin Co., 1975), 212–13; Hayes, 265.

19. Hayes, 265.

20. Ibid., 266.

21. *Global Mission,* 562–63.

22. Robert J. C. Butow, *Japan's Decision to Surrender* (Stanford, CA: Stanford University Press, 1954), 136.

23. Ibid., p137.

24. Hayes, p 358.

25. CCS 168, 22 January 1943, Conduct of War in Pacific Theater in 1943; cited in Cline, 336.

26. Carl Berger, *B-29: The Superfortress* (New York: Ballantine Books, 1970), 41.

27. CCS 170/2, "SYMBOL," Final Rpt to the President and Prime Minister, 23 January 1943, subj: Casablanca; cited in Hayes, 298.

28. Craven and Cate, *Vol. 5,* 26–29.

29. Ibid.

30. Hull to Handy, memorandum, 17 July 1943, with SS 111 in ABC 381, Strategy Sec Papers; quoted in Cline, 335.

31. Hayes, 470–71; see also Cline, 222–26.

32. Berger, 45.

33. Hayes, 342–48.

34. Berger, 47.

35. SS 282, 24 April 1944, Operations in the Pacific, ABC 381, Strategy Sec Papers, 7 January 1943; cited in Cline, 337.

36. JPS 476, 6 June, 1944, Operations against Japan, Subsequent to Formosa; see Cline, 338.

37. Minutes of the 167th meeting, CCS, 14 July 1944; cited in Cline, 339.

38. Ibid.

39. CCS 776/3, 9 February 1945, Rpt to President and Prime Minister; CCS 417/11, ARGONAUT, 22 January 1945, Operations for Defeat of Japan.

40. JIC 266/1, 18 April 1945, Defeat of Japan by Blockade and Bomb; quoted in Cline, 343.

41. Ibid.

42. CCS 900/3, TERMINAL, 24 July 1945, Rpt to President and Prime Minister; see Cline, 346.

43. CCS 894, TERMINAL, 16 July 1945, Rpt of Army Air Operations in War Against Japan; quoted in Cline, 346.

Chapter 3

1. On Arnold's role in the early development of the B-29 and its attendant problems, see Herman S. Wolk, "General Arnold, the Atomic Bomb, and the Surrender of Japan," in Gunter Bischof and Robert L. Dupont, eds., *The Pacific War Revisited* (Baton Rouge: Louisiana State University Press, 1997), 163–78.

2. Arnold to the Asst. Sec. of War, memorandum, 17 October, 1940, in Container #114, Arnold Cllctn, Mss. Div, L.C.

3. Wolfe, interview by Alfred Goldberg, 6 September 1952, Center for Air Force History, Washington, D.C.

4. Wolfe, no interviewer specified, June 1966, K105.5, Air Force Historical Research Center, Maxwell AFB, Alabama.

5. Historical Documentation of Maj. Gen. K.B. Wolfe, in Hqs Air Force Logistics Command Historical Office, Wright Patterson AFB, Ohio.

6. Norstad, interview by Murray Green, 15 July 1969, in H. H. Arnold Cllctn, Call #168.7316-249, Reel 43825, in Office of Air Force History, Washington, D.C.

7. See Wolk in *The Pacific War Revisited.*

8. Ibid.

9. Arnold to the Chief of Staff, memorandum, ca. May 1943, Initial Employment of the B-29 Airplanes.

10. Berger, 41.

11. JCS 287/1, 8 May 1943, Strategic Plan for the Defeat of Japan, Rpt by the Joint Staff Planners, in PSF, War Dept File, Marshall Folder, Container #83, FDRL.

12. Grace Person Hayes, *History of the Joint Chiefs of Staff: The War Against Japan* (Annapolis, MD: Naval Institute Press, 1982), 470–71.

13. Kenney to Arnold, 29 October 1943, in Kenney diaries, Vol. VI, Center for Air Force History, Washington, D.C.

14. Kenney was given the word by Brig. Gen. Kuter that he would not receive B-29s. See *General Kenney Reports*, 341–42, 378. See also Kenney to Arnold, 4 December 1943, in Kenney diaries, Vol VI, Center for Air Force History, Washington, D.C.

15. Berger, 45.

16. The White House (initialed FDR) to Marshall, memorandum, 15 October 1943, cited in Alvin D. Coox, "Strategic Bombing in the Pacific, 1942–1945," in R. Cargill Hall, ed., *Case Studies in Strategic Bombing* (Washington, D.C.: Air Force History & Museums Program, 1998), 277.

17. Arnold to the President, memorandum, B-29 Project, 11 October 1943, in PSF, War Dept File, Chiang Kai-shek File, Container #2, FDRL.

18. Roosevelt to Marshall, memorandum, 15 October 1943, B-29 Project, 11 October 1943, in PSF, War Dept File, Chiang-Kai shek File, Container #2, FDRL.

19. Arnold to President Roosevelt, 18 October 1943, in PSF, War Dept File, Chiang Kai-shek File, Container #2, FDRL.

20. Patterson to Harry Hopkins, memorandum, B-29 Program, 24 October 1943, in PSF, War Dept File, Container #22, FDRL.

21. Hopkins to Leahy, memorandum, 19 November 1943, in PSF, War Dept File, Container #22, FDRL.

22. Arnold to Deane, Priority Msg, Personal, 8 February 1944, in Map Room Files, Special Files, Container #35, MR 530, in FDRL.

23. JCS to Deane, cable, U.S. Military Mission, Moscow, # WAR 60689, in Map Room Files, Special Files, Container #35, MR 530, Japan (1), February–September 1944, in FDRL.

24. Berger, 55–57.

25. Ibid., 57–58.

26. Ibid., 59.

27. *Gen Arnold's Second Rpt to the Sec of War,* February 1944.

28. Eric C. Larrabee, *Commander-in-Chief: Franklin Delano Roosevelt, His Lieutenants, and Their War* (New York: Harper and Row, 1987), 580.

29. See Jacob Vander Meulen, Building the B-29 (Washington, D.C.: Smithsonian Institution Press, 1995), 9.

30. Hansell, interview by Murray Green , 2 January,1970, in H. H. Arnold Cllctn, Call #168.7326.184, Reel 43822, in Office of Air Force History, Washington, D.C.

31. LeMay interview by Green, 26 January 1965 in H. H. Arnold Cllctn, #168. 7326-217, Reel 43824, in Office of Air Force History, Washington, D.C.

32. Chennault to the President, 26 January 1944, in PSF, Safe File, AAF, Container #1, FDRL.

33. Chennault to Arnold, 26 January 1944, in PSF, Safe File, AAF, Container #1, FDRL.

34. Ibid.

35. Arnold to Spaatz, 29 September 1944, quoted in Craven and Cate, The Army Air Forces in World War II, Vol 5, 104.

36. For a provocative view of unity of command in the Pacific, see Phillip S. Meilinger, "Unity of Command in the Pacific During World War II," *Joint*

Forces Quarterly, Issue 56, 1st Quarter, 2010. Meilinger's thesis is that "unity of command" worked more efficiently in the Pacific under the existing three-theater commander setup—plus Twentieth Air Force commander Arnold —than it would have under one Supreme Commander. Depending upon the definition of "Europe," Meilinger argues that there was no unity of command in Europe.

37. Arnold, untitled manuscript, ca. October 1945, Speeches and Addresses, Reel #238, Mss. Div, L.C.

38. Ibid.

39. See Haywood S. Hansell, Jr., *The Strategic Bombing Campaigns Against Germany and Japan* (Maxwell, AL: Maxwell AFB, 1980), 156; Hansell, interview by author, 7 October 1974.

40. *Global Mission*, 550.

41. Ibid., 563.

42. Ibid., 550.

43. See Hansell, 156–57.

44. Ibid.

45. SACSEA to British Chiefs of Staff, 26 February 1944, in RG18, Records of the Hqs, Twentieth Air Force, Decimal File 1944–1945, Container #113, NA II.

46. British Chiefs of Staff, memorandum, Method of Control, 20th Bomber Command, 28 February 1944, in RG18, Records of Hqs, Twentieth Air Force, Decimal File 1944–1945, Container #113, NA II.

47. Ibid.; Giles to Chief of Staff, Administrative Responsibilities of Commanding General, Twentieth Air Force, 12 September, 1944, in RG18, Records of Hqs Twentieth Air Force.

48. U.S. Chiefs of Staff, to Chief of Staff, Control of the Strategic Air Force, 28 February 1944, in RG18, Records of the Hqs, Twentieth Air Force, Decimal File 1944–1945, Container #113, NA II.

49. Ibid.

50. See note 35 above.

51. Norstad to Joint Army-Navy Staff College, address, 27 September1944, in RG18, Records of the Hqs, Twentieth Air Force, Speeches, Decimal File, RAG350.001, 1944–1945, Container #14, NA II.

52. Ibid.

53. Ibid.

54. Arnold to MacArthur, 4 October 1944, in RG 18, Records of the Hqs, Twentieth Air Force, Decimal File 1944–1945, Container #2, NA II.

55. Ibid.

56. Giles to Chief of Staff, memorandum, 12 September 1944, Administrative Responsibilities of Commanding General, Twentieth Air Force, RG 18, Records of AAF, Records of Hqs, Twentieth Air Force.

57. Ibid.

58. Gen. Curtis E. LeMay with MacKinlay Kantor, *Mission with LeMay: My Story* (Garden City, NJ: Doubleday, 1965), 341.
59. Larrabee, 580.
60. Arnold to Hansell, 10 November 1944, in Records of the Hqs. Twentieth Air Force, File 201, Hansell, Container #7, NA II; Arnold to LeMay, 17 November 1944, in Arnold cllctn, Reel 107, Mss. Div., L.C.; Arnold to Hansell, 27 December 1944, in RG18, Records of Hqs, Twentieth Air Force, File Rag 201-Hansell, NA II; Hansell, interview by author, 7 October 1974; LeMay, interview by author, 14 November 1974.
61. Cleveland Plain-Dealer, 2 December 1944; copy in RG18, Records of the Hqs, Twentieth Air Force, Decimal File 1944–1945, File Media, Container #115, NA II.

Chapter 4

1. Arnold to Hansell, 27 December 1944, in RG18, Records of Hqs, Twentieth Air Force, File Rag 201-Hansell, NA II.
2. LeMay to Arnold, 19 October 1944, in LeMay Cllctn, Mss. Div, L.C.
3. Ibid.
4. Ibid.
5. Arnold to LeMay, 17 November 1944, in Arnold Cllctn, Reel 107, Mss. Div, L.C.
6. Ibid.
7. Arnold to Eaker, 10 April 1943.
8. Ibid.
9. Arnold to Trenchard, 30 March 1943, in Arnold Cllctn, Special Official File, 1941–45, Container #39, Mss. Div, L.C.
10. Maj. Gen. Haywood S. Hansell, Jr., "Balaklava Redeemed," *Air University Review*, September–October 1974, 94–106.
11. Eaker, interview by Lt Col Joe B. Green, Military History Institute, Carlisle Barracks, Pa.: 11 February 1967.
12. Craven and Cate, *Vol. 2*, 749.
13. Cable W8550, Eisenhower to Marshall, 25 December 1943, in Alfred D. Chandler, Jr., ed., *The Papers of Dwight David Eisenhower: The War Years*, Vol. 3 (Baltimore, MD: The Johns Hopkins University Press, 1970), 1611–14.
14. Eaker, interview by Lt Col Joe B. Green, 11 February 1967; Eaker, interview by author, 27 August 1974; Maj. Gen. Haywood S. Hansell Jr., "Balaklava Redeemed," 94–106; Hansell, interview by author, 7 October 1974; for a penetrating personal analysis see Ralph H. Nutter *With the Possum and the Eagle: The Memoir of a Navigator's War Over Germany and Japan* (Denton: University of North Texas Press, 2005), especially 121–23, 136–43, 149. Nutter served under both Hansell and LeMay.

15. Arnold to Hansell, 10 November 1944, in RG18, Records of the Hqs, Twentieth Air Force, File 201, Hansell, Container #7, NA II.

16. Ibid.

17. Norstad to Hansell, 13 November 1944, in RG18, Records of the Hqs, Twentieth Air Force, File 201, Hansell, NA II.

18. Norstad, interview by Murray Green, H. H. Arnold Cllctn, Office of Air Force History, Washington, D.C.: 15 July 1969, Call #168.7326-249, Reel 43825, hereinafter referred to as H. H. Arnold Cllctn by Murray Green.

19. Norstad to Hansell, 7 December 1944, in RG18, Records of the Hqs, Twentieth Air Force, File 201, Hansell, in NA II.

20. Kenneth P. Werrell, *Blankets of Fire: U.S. Bombers over Japan during World War II* (Washington: Smithsonian Institution Press, 1996), 138; Hansell, interview with author, 7 October 1974.

21. Berger, 119.

22. Report to the Committee of Operations Analysts, 4 September 1944, Economic Effects of Successful Area Attacks on Six Japanese Cities, in RG18, Records of Hqs Twentieth Air Force, Decimal File 1944-45, Container #7, File Ops Analysis, in NA II.

23. Ibid.

24. Berger, 106.

25. Draft manuscript (memoir), Hansell to author, October 1974.

26. See Nutter.

27. Ibid., 208.

28. Hansell to Arnold, 14 January 1945, in RG18, Records of the Hqs, Twentieth Air Force, File 201, Hansell, Box 1, NA II.

29. Ibid.

30. Draft manuscript, Hansell to author, October 1974; Hansell, interview by author, 7 October 1974.

31. Conrad C. Crane, *Bombs, Cities, and Civilians: American Airpower Strategy in World War II* (Lawrence: University Press of Kansas, 1993), 141.

32. LeMay, interview by author.

33. Draft manuscript, Hansell to author, October 1974.

34. Ibid.

35. Ibid.

36. Ibid.; Hansell, interview by author, 7 October 1974.

37. Hansell, interview by author, 7 October 19 1974.

38. Ibid.

39. Norstad; interview by Ahmann, 13-16 February and 22–25 October 1979, K239,0512-116, USAF Oral History Interview, Maxwell AFB, Ala.

40. Norstad, interview by Green, 15 July 1969, in H. H. Arnold Cllctn, Office of Air Force History, Washington, D.C.

41. LeMay, interview by Green, 14 March 1970, in H. H. Arnold Cllctn, #168.7326-217, Reel 43824, Office of Air Force History, Washington, D.C.

42. Norstad, interview by Green.
43. Hansell, interview by Green, 19 April 1967, in H. H. Arnold Cllctn, Call #168.7326-184, Reel 43822, Office of Air Force History, Washington, D.C.
44. LeMay, interview by author, 14 November 1974.
45. Norstad to LeMay, 19 January 1945, in File, Letters LeMay & Norstad, 1944–45, Official Correspondence, Container 11, LeMay Cllctn, Mss. Div, L.C.
46. LeMay, interview by Green.
47. Ibid.
48. *Mission with LeMay*, 346.
49. Ibid.
50. Ibid., 338.
51. Quoted in Richard B. Frank, *Downfall*, 60.
52. Marshall to King, 13 March 1945, in RG18, Records of Hqs, Twentieth Air Force, File RAF 201, LeMay, NA II.
53. *Mission with LeMay*, 347.
54. Ibid., 348.
55. LeMay interview by Green, 14 March 1970.
56. Ibid.
57. Ibid.
58. Transcript of (Verbatim) Press Conference by Brig. Gen. Lauris Norstad; Chief of Staff, Twentieth AF, Pentagon, 23 March 1945, in RG18, Records of the Hqs. Twentieth Air Force, Decimal File 1944-45, File Norstad, Box 2, NA II.
59. Frank, 335.
60. See note 48 above.
61. Norstad to Joint Army-Navy Staff College, address, 18 September 1944, in RG18, Records of Hqs Twentieth Air Force, Decimal File 1944-45, File Norstad, Box 2, NA II.
62. Huston, telephone interview by author, 8 May 2008.
63. "1,000 Superforts to Hit Japs at One Time, Arnold Assures," Washington Times Herald, 29 March 1945, copy in Arnold Cllctn, Reel 155, Mss. Div, L.C.
64. David Lawrence, "Air Power Now Seen in Proper Perspective, *The Washington Star,* 14 March 1945, in RG18, Records of the Hqs, Twentieth Air Force, Decimal File 1944–1945, File Media, Box 115, NA II.
65. Arnold to LeMay, 21 March 1945, in File, Letters LeMay & Arnold Folder, 1944–45, Container 11, LeMay Cllctn, Mss. Div, L.C.
66. Ibid.
67. Giles to LeMay, 20 April 1945, in RG18, Records of Hqs, Twentieth Air Force, File Rag 201, C. E. LeMay, NA II.
68. Norstad to LeMay, 3 April 1945, in File Personal, Letters LeMay & Norstad, 1944-45, Official Correspondence, LeMay Cllctn, Mss. Div, L.C.
69. Ibid.

70. *Mission with LeMay,* 373.
71. *The New York Times,* 15 May 1945, in RG18, Records of the Hqs Twentieth Air Force, Box 115, NA II.
72. Norstad, memorandum, Recommended Intensification of Attack on Japan Immediately Following V-E Day, 10 April 1945, in RG18, Records of Hqs, Twentieth Air Force, Readers File, NA II.
73. Lt Col Hartzel Spence to Norstad, memorandum, Public Relations Twentieth Air Force, 22 May 1945, in RG18, Records of the Hqs, Twentieth AF, Box 13, NA II.
74. Hoito Edoin, *The Night Tokyo Burned* (New York: St. Martin's Press, 1987), quoted in Stephen L. McFarland, *America's Pursuit of Precision Bombing, 1910–1945* (Washington, D.C.: Smithsonian Institution Press, 1995), 204.
75. Draft, 17 July 1945 Presentation, in RG18, Records of the Hqs, Twentieth Air Force, Special File, Box 126, NA II.
76. Ibid.
77. Ibid.

Chapter 5

1. D. Clayton James, *The Years of MacArthur,* Vol. II, *1941–1945* (Boston: Houghton Mifflin Co., 1975), 723. James's work remains a standard on MacArthur in World War II and is especially insightful on command relations.
2. Quoted in Grace Person Hayes, *The History of the Joint Chiefs of Staff in World War II: The War Against Japan* (Annapolis, MD: Naval Institute Press, 1982), 688.
3. Ibid., 689.
4. Ibid., 686–695.
5. Msg. Marshall to MacArthur, CM-OUT 67098, 12 April 1945, quoted in "Entry of the Soviet Union into the War Against Japan," Dept. of Defense, 1956, 54, in Air Force Historical Studies office.
6. MacArthur to Marshall, CM-IN 19089, 20 April 1945, in "Entry of the Soviet Union into the War Against Japan," 55.
7. Ibid., 56.
8. Ibid.
9. Ibid., 57.
10. JCS 1313/2, Revision of Policy with Relation to Russia, 23 April 1945, quoted in "Entry of the Soviet Union into the War Against Japan," p61.
11. "Entry of the Soviet Union," 64.
12. JCS WARX 87938, to MacArthur, Nimitz and Arnold, 25 May 1945, in RG 218, Records of the Joint Chiefs of Staff. Adm. Leahy's File, Box 10, Pacific Area File, in NA II.
13. Enclosure, Memorandum for the President, Campaign Against Japan, to JCS 1388, 16 June 1945, Details of Campaign Against Japan, Joint Staff Planners.

14. Ibid.

15. Ibid.

16. *Global Mission,* 548–49.

17. Ibid.

18. See note 13 above.

19. Leahy to Joint Chiefs of Staff, memorandum, 14 June 1945, in RG 218, Adm. Leahy's File, quoted in Douglas J. MacEachin, *The Final Months of the War with Japan: Signals Intelligence, U.S. Invasion Planning and the A-Bomb Decision,* Center for the Study of Intelligence, December 1998.

20. Enclosure, Memorandum for the President, Campaign Against Japan, to JCS 1388, 16 June 1945, Details of Campaign Against Japan, Joint Staff Planners; quoted in MacEachin.

21. Ibid.

22. Ibid.

23. Ibid.

24. Ibid.

25. Secretary of the Joint Chiefs of Staff (McFarland), memorandum, Minutes of Meeting Held at the White House on Monday, 18 June at 1530. The text of the minutes can be found in the "Entry of the Soviet Union into the War Against Japan," DOD, 1956. See also MacEachin.

26. Ibid.

27. Ibid.

28. Ibid.

29. Ibid.

30. Ibid.

31. Ibid.

32. Ibid.

33. Ibid.

34. Arnold, *Global Mission,* 566.

35. D'Olier to Secretary of War, memorandum, Preliminary Review of Effectiveness of the Combined Offensive in the European Theater of Operations, 11 June 1945, in Arnold Cllctn, Reel #5, Mss. Div, L.C.

36. Ibid., Atch, "Rpt on USSBS and Joint Target Grp Conferences," in Arnold Cllctn, Reel #5, Mss. Div, L.C.

37. Rpt on USSBS and Joint Target Group Conferences, in Arnold Cllctn, Reel #5, Mss. Div, L.C.

38. Ibid.

39. *Global Mission,* 566.

40. LeMay, interview by author, 14 November 1974.

41. Minutes of 18 June 1945 meeting.

42. Eaker, interview by author, 27 August 1974; Eaker, letter to author, 22 October 1974.

43. Eaker, interview by author, 27 August 1974.

44. Maj. Gen. John W. Huston, ed., *American Airpower Comes of Age: General Henry H. "Hap" Arnold's World War II Diaries*, Vol. 2 (Maxwell AFB, Alabama: Air University Press, January 2002), 6.

45. Arnold to JCS, memorandum, U.S. Army Strategic Air Force in the Pacific, ca. 15 June 1945, in Arnold Cllctn, Reel #5.

46. Joint Target Grp, Estimate of Air Bombardment Necessary to Devastation of Japan, June 1945, in Arnold Cllctn, Reel #5.

47. Enclosure, Memorandum for President, Campaign Against Japan, to JCS 1388, 16 June 1945, Details of Campaign Against Japan, Joint Staff Planners; quoted in MacEachin.

48. Ibid.; JTC 191/7, 16 May 1945; quoted in MacEachin.

49. Ibid.

50. Enclosure, Memorandum for President, Campaign Against Japan, to JCS 1388, 16 June 1945, Details of Campaign Against Japan, Joint Staff Planners; quoted in MacEachin.

51. Huston, 330; Commanding General, Army Air Forces, to Joint Chiefs of Staff, Memorandum, U. S. Army Strategic Air Force in the Pacific, June 1945.

52. See note 44 above.

53. *Global Mission*, 568.

54. Ibid.

55. Eaker with Wolk, interview, 27 August 1974. For MacArthur's views on bombing cities, see Richard B. Frank, MacArthur, 168.

56. Ibid.

57. Msg, JCS to CINC, Army Forces, Pacific; CINC, Pacific Fleet; CG, USAS-TAF, WARX 29978, Msg to MacArthur, Nimitz and Spaatz for Action, 19 July 1945, Reel #219, Arnold Cllctn.

58. *Mission with LeMay*, 387.

59. Ibid.

60. *Global Mission*, 563.

61. Ibid., 564.

62. Ibid., 565.

63. Brig. Gen. John A. Samford, to Chief of the Air Staff, memorandum, Discussions Between D'Olier Committee and JTB, June 1945, Reel #219, Arnold Cllctn.

Chapter 6

1. Stimson, "Memo Discussed with President," 25 April 1945, Manhattan Engineer District Records, RG 77, NA; cited in Norman Polmar and Thomas B. Allen, Code-Name Downfall: The Secret Plan to Invade Japan and Why Truman Dropped the Bomb (New York: Simon and Schuster, 1995), 125.

2. Polmar and Allen, 127.

3. Arnold to LeMay, 5 July 1945, Container #11, LeMay Cllctn. Mss. Div, L.C.

4. Ibid.

5. LeMay to Arnold, 20 July 1945, Container #11, LeMay Cllctn, Mss. Div, L.C.

6. CCS 880/4, Development of Operations in the Pacific, 29 June 1945, in FRUS, The Berlin Conference, Vol. I, 910–11.

7. Ibid., 911.

8. CCS 643/3, 8 July 1945, Estimate of the Enemy Situation (as of 6 July 1945), in Michael Kort, *The Columbia Guide to Hiroshima and the Bomb* (New York: Columbia University Press, 2007), 254.

9. Enclosure, Memorandum for the President, Campaign Against Japan, to JCS 1388/4, 11 July 1945, Details of the Campaign Against Japan, Report by the Joint Staff Planners.

10. Ibid.

11. Ibid.

12. Eric Larrabee, *Commander in Chief: Franklin Delano Roosevelt, His Lieutenants, and Their War* (New York: Harper and Row, 1987), 10.

13. I am indebted to historian Eric Bergerud for his insightful comments on the unconditional surrender policy.

14. Butow, 137–38.

15. Harry S. Truman, *Memoirs*, Vol. I, *Year of Decisions* (Garden City, NJ: Doubleday & Co., 1955), 10.

16. Ibid., 415.

17. Einstein to F.D.R., 2 August 1939, in PSF, Box #5, File Outline Plans for Specific Optns, FDRL. Also see Walter Isaacson, *Einstein: His Life* and Universe (New York: Simon & Schuster, 2007), 474.

18. Einstein to F.D.R., 2 August 1939, in PSF, Box #5, File Outline Plans for Specific Optns, FDRL.

19. Leo Szilard, interview by author, Airlie House Conference, Warrenton, Va., ca. June 1962.

20. Isaacson, 474–75.

21. Ibid., 476.

22. Kort, 26.

23. See Leslie R. Groves, *Now It Can Be Told: The Story of the Manhattan Project* (New York: Harper & Brothers, 1962), 254; Craven and Cate, *Vol. V*, 705.

24. Groves, 266–67.

25. Ibid., 267.

26. Ibid., 273; Craven and Cate, *Vol. V*, 710.

27. Groves, 275.

28. Ibid., 258–59.

29. FRUS, Diplomatic Papers, *The Conference of Berlin*, 1945, Vol. II (Washington, D.C.: US Government Printing Office, 1960), 1462–63.

30. Harry S. Truman, *Year of Decisions.*

31. Eaker, interview by author, 22 October 1974; Eaker, interview by author, 27 August 1974; Eaker to author, 19 October 1974.

32. See Margaret Truman, *Harry S. Truman* (New York: William Morrow & Co., 1973), 273; Eaker, interview by author, 27 August 1974.

33. CCS 894, TERMINAL, 16 July 1945, Rpt on Army Air Operations in War Against Japan, cited in Cline, p346.

34. Stimson to the President, memorandum, Proposed Program for Japan, 2 July 1945, in FRUS, *The Berlin Conference (Potsdam)*, Vol. I, p890.

35. Ibid.

36. Ibid., 892.

37. Ibid.

38. Quoted in "Entry of the Soviet Union into the War Against Japan," 104.

39. Proclamation by the Heads of Governments, United States, China, and the United Kingdom, 26 July 1945, Potsdam, in *FRUS, Berlin Conference*, Vol. II, 1474–76.

40. *Global Mission*, 585.

41. Ibid.

42. Col. John N. Stone to Arnold, memorandum, 24 July 1945; Groves Report, quoted in Kort, 258–59.

43. General Handy Directive to General Spaatz, 25 July 1945, in Kort, 259.

44. Truman, *Year of Decisions*, 421.

45. Spaatz, memorandum for record, 11 August 1945, in Spaatz Cllctn, Mss. Div, L.C.

46. *Global Mission*, 590.

47. Ibid., 589–90.

48. Ibid., 590.

49. Ibid.

50. Kort, 104.

51. Quoted in *Global Mission*, 590.

52. Atch, Rpt on USSBS and Joint Target Group Conferences, to Memo for Gen Spaatz from Col R. T. Proctor, Exec to CG.AAF., D'Olier Committee Rpt, 20 July 1945, Arnold Cllctn, Reel #5, Mss. Div, L.C.

53. Ibid.

54. Ibid.

55. Draft Presentation for General Arnold, 17 July 1945, in RG 18, records of Hqs, Twentieth Air Force, Decimal File, 1944–1945, Container #126, NA II.

56. Ibid.; *Global Mission*, 595–96.

57. Commanding General, Army Air Forces to Joint Chiefs of Staff, memorandum, U. S. Army Strategic Air Force in the Pacific, June 1945.

58. Arnold Diary Note, 13 July 1945, in "Terminal Conference," in Arnold Cllctn, Reel #185, Mss. Div, L.C.
59. Ibid.
60. Craven and Cate, *Vol. V,* 663.
61. Nutter, 250.
62. Coox, p343.
63. *USSBS, Final Rpt, The Strategic Air Operation of VHB, in War Against Japan, Twentieth AF,* GPO, September 1946, p6.
64. Nutter, 251.
65. Ibid.
66. Coox, 345.
67. Maj. Gen. Victor E. Bertrandias, Air Technical Service Command to Arnold, 29 May 1945, in Arnold Cllctn, Reel #114, Mss. Div, L.C.
68. Arnold to Chief of Staff, memorandum, 30 May 1945, Comments on Air Aspects of Gen Stilwell's Memo Relative to Invasion of Japan, in Arnold Cllctn, Reel #114, Mss. Div, L.C.
69. JCS/331/3, Directive for Operation OLYMPIC, 25 May 1945, Encl., Directive to CINC, U.S. Army Forces, Pacific, CINC, U.S. Pacific Fleet, CG, Twentieth Air Force, quoted in MacEachin, 10.
70. MacEachin, 36.
71. Ibid., p17.
72. JWPC 397, "Alternatives to OLYMPIC," 4 August 1945, RG 165, ABC 384 Kyushu, Sec 1-B, Entry 421, Container 434, NA II.
73. Messages to CINCPAC, quoted in Kort, 264.
74. Frank, 195.
75. Ibid., 196.
76. MacEachin, 36.
77. Frank, 312.
78. Rpt by Adm. Deyo, U.S. Navy Task Force 550, Surrender of Japan, February 1946.
79. Craven and Cate, *Vol.V,* p 716.
80. *Mission with LeMay,* 379.
81. Ibid., 385.
82. Ibid.
83. Ibid., 717; also see Kenneth P. Werrell, *Blankets of Fire: U.S. Bombers Over Japan during World War II* (Washington: Smithsonian Institution Press, 1996), 215.
84. Statement by President H.S. Truman, 6 August 1945.
85. Ibid.
86. Msg FN-08-21, COMGENAAF 20 to COMGENUSASTAF (Rear), Hiroshima Mission, 8 August 1945, papers of Gen Carl A Spaatz, Container I-73, Mss. Div, L.C.

87. Ibid.

88. Ibid.

89. Manhattan Engineer District, The Atomic Bombings of Hiroshima and Nagasaki, October 1945, Reel #192, Arnold Cllctn, Reel #192.

90. Quoted in Herbert Feis, *Japan Subdued: The Atomic Bomb and the End of the War in the Pacific* (Princeton: Princeton University Press, 1961), 116.

91. Quoted in Werrell, 216.

92. See Vincent Jones, *MANHATTAN: The Army and the Atomic Bomb* (Washington, D.C.: Center of Military History, 1985), 545–46.

93. Ibid., 547.

94. Ibid.

95. Ibid.

96. MacArthur quoted in Thomas B. Allen and Norman Polmar, "Was Truman Right to Drop the Bomb?" *Insight on the News* 2, no. 28 (24 July 1995).

97. See General Umezu and Admiral Toyoda Rpt to the Emperor, 12 August 1945, in Kort, 302–3.

98. Japanese Surrender Note, 10 August 1945, The Swiss Charge (Grassli) to the Secretary of State, in Kort, 324–25.

99. Emperor Hirohito's Surrender Statement to the Imperial Conference, 14 August 1945, in Kort, 327–28.

100. Imperial Rescript, 14 August 1945, in Kort, 330–31.

101. See Sadao Osada, "The Shock of the Atomic Bomb and Japan's Decision to Surrender—A Reconsideration," in Robert J. Maddox, ed., *Hiroshima in History: The Myths of Revisionism* (Columbia: University of Missouri Press, 2007).

102. Ibid.

103. The Instrument of Surrender is reproduced in Butow, 249–50.

104. Edward J. Drea, *MacArthur's ULTRA: Codebreaking and the War Against Japan, 1942–1945* (Lawrence: University Press of Kansas, 1992), 225.

105. Butow, 250.

106. The End of the War in the Pacific: Surrender Documents in Facsimile, The National Archives, No. 46-6, USGPO, Washington, D.C., 1945.

107. See Gian Peri Gentile, "Advocacy or Assessment? The United States Strategic Bombing Survey of Germany and Japan," in Maddox, ed., *Hiroshima in History: The Myths of Revisionism*, 120–45.

108. Barton J. Bernstein, "Was Truman Right to Drop the Bomb?" *Insight on the News* 2, no. 28 (24 July 1995).

109. Interview with Konoye is published in Kort, 345–49.

110. USSBS Interrogation #373, Prince Fumimaro Konoye, 9 November 1945, in Kort, 345–49.

111. USSBS Interrogation #531, Prime Minister Kantaro Suzuki, 26 December 1945, in Kort, 358.

112. John Ray Skates, *The Invasion of Japan: Alternative to the Bomb* (Columbia: University of South Carolina Press, 1994), 256.

113. Ibid., 265.

114. J. Samuel Walker, *Prompt and Utter Destruction: Truman and the Use of Atomic Bombs Against Japan* (Chapel Hill: University of North Carolina Press, 2004), 118.

115. Frank, 312.

116. See Michael Kort, "Casualty Projections for the Invasion of Japan, Phantom Estimates, and the Math of Barton Bernstein," in *Passport*, The Newsletter of the Society for Historians of American Foreign Relations 34, Issue 3 (December 2003).

117. Msg, C31897, COMAFPAC (MacArthur) to Marshall, info Arnold, Bissell, in RG 218, Records of JCS, Chairman's (Leahy) File, Container 10, File Pacific Areas, in NA II.

118. Ibid.

119. Drea, 223.

120. Ibid.

121. See Richard B. Frank, *Downfall: The End of the Imperial Japanese Empire* (New York: Penguin Books, 1999).

122. Msg, USASTAF to War Dept, 1448, 7 August 1945, in RG 218, Records of JCS, Chairman's File, Box 10, Pacific Area File, in NA II.

123. *Global Mission*, 598.

124. Ibid.

125. Quoted in Arnold's *Third Report to the Secretary of War,* 12 November 1945.

126. Ibid.

127. This report is found in the LeMay Collection, Container #41 File-Strategic Air Operations Against Japan.

128. Msg, AFACG 1468, Arnold to LeMay, 15 August 1945, LeMay Cllctn, Official Correspondence, Container #11, Mss. Div, L.C.

129. Cable, Msg 15-17, Arnold to Spaatz, Strategic Bombing Guidance, 14 August 1945, Gen Carl A. Spaatz Cllctn, in File July 1945, Diary, Container I-21, Mss. Div, L.C.

130. Quoted in Frank, 352–53.

131. Frank, 354.

Chapter 7

1. See Wolk, *Reflections on Air Force Independence* (Washington, D.C.: Air Force History and Museums Program, 2007), Chapter III.

2. Craven and Cate, *Vol V,* 736.

3. Ibid., 737.

4. See Michael S. Sherry, *The Rise of American Air Power: The Creation of Armageddon* (New Haven: Yale University Press, 1987), especially 282–83.

5. Conrad C. Crane, *Bombs, Cities, and Civilians: American Airpower Strategy in World War II* (Lawrence: University Press of Kansas, 1993), 6.

6. LeMay, interview by author, 14 November 1974.

7. Arnold's *Third Report to the Secretary of War,* November 1945.

8. Ibid.

9. See Wolk, *The Struggle for Air Force Independence, 1943–1947* (Washington, D.C.: Air Force History and Museums Program, 1997), 91–92.

10. Arnold's *Third Report to the Secretary of War,* November 1945.

11. Crane, 32.

12. Ibid.

13. Lecture by Maj. Muir Fairchild, "Air Warfare," ACTS, October 1939, Fairchild Cllctn, Container #5, Mss. Div, L.C.

14. Curtis E. LeMay, *Mission with LeMay,* 352.

15. For data on Unit 731, see Gruhl, 81–84 and the landmark study by Sheldon H. Harris, Factories of Death: Japanese Biological Warfare, 1932–1945 and the American Cover-up (London: Routledge, 1994).

16. "War Crime," Produced by Joseph Wershba, CBS Network, "60 Minutes," Vol XIV, #27, 4 April 1982, in Hopkins Papers, Official file, Container #4; FDR Library; Gruhl, 81–86.

17. *The New York Times,* 1 April 2007; 25 April 2007; 12 May 2007.

18. *The Washington Post,* 12 November 2008.

19. Eaker, interview by Goldberg and Hildreth, Washington, D.C., May 1962; Eaker, interview by author, 27 August 1974.

20. Spaatz, interview by Goldberg and Parrish, 21 February 1962.

21. *Third Rpt of the CG, AAF to the Secretary of War,* 12 November 1945.

22. Draft paper, "The Past Predicts the Future," by Arnold, ca. 1946, Arnold Cllctn, Reel #238, Mss. Div, L.C.

23. Ibid.

24. Ibid.

25. Crane, 141.

26. Max Hastings, *Retribution: The Battle for Japan, 1944–1945* (New York: Alfred A. Knopf, 2008), 318.

27. Arnold, Draft mss., "The Air Force in the Atomic Age," undated, in Arnold Cllctn, Reel #238, Mss. Div, L.C.

28. Ibid.

29. These figures are from Werrell, 226.

30. USSBS, "The Strategic Air Operation of Very Heavy Bombardment in the War Against Japan," Final Rpt, USGPO, 1 September 1946, File Strategic Air Operations Against Japan, LeMay Cllctn, Container #41, Mss. Div, L.C.

31. Eaker to Maj Gen Oliver P. Echols, Asst Deputy, Military Governor, U.S. Group Control Council (Germany), 7 September 1945, in RG 165, Records of War Dept General and Special Staffs, Patch-Simpson Bd. Files, NA II.

32. Ibid.

33. Ibid.

34. Ibid.

35. Undated mss., ca..Oct 1945, "The Bomb is Mightier than the Sword," by Maj. Ben Zion Kaplan, U.S. Army Air Forces intelligence, Arnold Cllctn, Reel #238, Mss. Div, L.C. This document consists of interviews with Japanese officials.

36. Ibid.

37. Ibid.

38. Ibid.

39. Ibid.

40. Ibid.

41. Ibid.

42. Ibid.

43. *Nippon Times,* 20 October 1945; copy in Arnold Cllctn, Reel #238, Mss. Div, L.C.

44. Ibid.

45. Ibid.

46. Ibid.

47. Records of the USSBS, Roll 5, Pacific Survey Intelligence Branch, Koizumi (4), Factors in Decline of Morale, Serial No. 158, NA II.

48. Arnold to Spaatz, 19 August 1945, in Spaatz Cllctn, File August 1945, Container #21, Mss. Div, L.C.

49. Ibid.

50. Clayton James, 790.

51. Ibid., 791.

52. Arnold to Spaatz, 19 August 1945.

53. Ibid.

54. Gill Robb Wilson, "The Air World," *New York Herald Tribune,* 19 April 1945; copy in RG18, Records of the Headquarters Twentieth AF, Container #115, NA II.

55. Arnold to Spaatz, 19 August 1945.

56. USSBS, "The Strategic Air Operation of Very Heavy Bombardment in the War Against Japan," Final Rpt, USGPO, 1 September 1946, File Strategic Air Operations Against Japan, Container #41, in LeMay Cllctn, Mss.Div, L.C.

57. Ibid.

58. Ibid.

59. "Air Power and the Future," in Arnold's *Third Rpt to the Sec of War,* November 1945.

60. Ibid.

61. Hastings, 298.

62. Marquis Childs, "Arnold's Air Victory," *The Washington Post.* 8 May 1945; copy found in RG 18, Records of the Hqs, Twentieth AF, Container #115, NA II.

63. Remarks by General Eaker, "The Army Air Forces, Its Status, Plans and Policies," to the National War College, 5 June 1947, in archives, Office of Air Force History, Bolling, AFB, D.C.

64. Arnold, Undated mss., "Air Forces—Their Destructive Power and Where Do We Go From Here?" Arnold Cllctn, Reel 238, Mss. Div, L.C.

65. For a consideration of Arnold and von Karman, see Dik A. Daso, *Architects of American Air Supremacy: Gen. Hap Arnold and Dr. Theodore von Karman* (Maxwell AFB, AL: Air University Press, 1997).

66. Arnold, interview (off the record), by unknown interviewer, 18 September 1945, Arnold Cllctn, Reel 238, Mss. Div, L.C.

67. Arnold, Draft address, "The Past Predicts the Future," ca. October 1945, Arnold Cllctn, Reel 238, Mss. Div, L.C.

68. Ibid.

69. Arnold, Draft, "The Air Force in the Atomic Age," Arnold Cllctn, Reel 238, Mss. Div, L.C.

70. Ibid.

71. Ibid.

72. Ibid.

73. Ibid.

74. Ibid.

75. Ibid.

76. Ibid.

77. Arnold, Draft address, "The Past Predicts the Future," Arnold Cllctn, Reel 238, Mss. Div, L.C.

78. Statement by General of the Army H. H. Arnold before the Committee on Military Affairs of the U.S. Senate Concerning the Unification of the War and Navy Depts, 19 October 1945, in RG 165, 320 (September–December 1946), NA II.

79. Arnold's Third Report to the Secretary of War, November 1945.

80. Ibid.

Glossary

AAF	Army Air Forces
ABC	American-British Conversations
ACTS	Air Corps Tactical School
ARCADIA	U.S.–British staff conference at Washington, December 1941–January 1942
ARGONAUT	Conference at Malta/Yalta, January–February 1945
AWPD	Air War Plans Division
CCS	Combined Chiefs of Staff
CBI	China-Burma-India Theater
CGUSASTAF	Commanding General, U.S. Army Strategic Air Forces in the Pacific
CINCAFPAC	Commander-in-Chief, Army Forces in the Pacific
CINCPAC	Commander-in-Chief, U.S. Pacific Fleet
CINCPOA	Commander-in-Chief, Pacific Ocean Areas
CG	Commanding General
COA	Committee of Operations Analysts
CORONET	Codename for 1 March 1946 planned invasion of the Kanto (Tokyo) Plain
DOWNFALL	Overall war plan to invade Japan
GHQ	General Headquarters
JCS	Joint Chiefs of Staff

MAGIC	Decrypted Japanese diplomatic communications
OCTAGON	International conference in Quebec, 12-16 September 1944
OLYMPIC	Codename for 1 November 1945 planned invasion of Kyushu
OPD	Operations Division
ORANGE	Prewar plan to be used should war with Japan occur
OVERLORD	Plan for the invasion of western Europe in 1944
POW	Prisoner of War
QUADRANT	International Conference at Quebec, 14-24 August 1943
SAC	Strategic Air Command
SACSEA	Supreme Allied Commander, Southeast Asia
SEXTANT	International conference at Cairo, 22-26 November and 3-7 December 1943
SWPA	Southwest Pacific Theater
TERMINAL	International conference near Potsdam, 16–26 July 1945
TRIDENT	International conference at Washington, 12–25 May 1943
RAF	Royal Air Force
UN	United Nations
ULTRA	Deciphered Japanese military codes
USASTAF	U.S. Army Strategic Air Forces in the Pacific
USSBS	United States Strategic Bombing Survey
USSTAF	U.S. Strategic Air Forces in Europe
VLR	Very Long Range

Bibliographic Note

The enormous documentation on the end of the war in the Pacific presents a challenge to the historian. It becomes necessary to concentrate primary research on the topic at hand and at times to rely on the work of others to provide background and context.

For this work on General Arnold, the primary source material resided in a number of archives. The Manuscript Division, Library of Congress, holds a number of relevant collections. The huge General H.H. Arnold collection formed a bedrock for this work. Navigating through this collection demands patience and rigorous selectivity. The collection is comprehensive and includes correspondence, mission, and logistical reports; personnel actions; minutes of conferences; and copies of Arnold's addresses, wartime and postwar.

The General Curtis E. LeMay collection provided important material for this work, including correspondence and reports on LeMay's B-29 commands in both the CBI and the Marianas. Although centered on the air war in Europe, the General Ira C. Eaker collection included material covering his time as deputy commander, AAF, under Arnold in Washington, from May to September 1945. Similarly, the General Carl A. Spaatz collection contains some source material relevant to the Pacific although its concentration is on the air war in Europe. The small Maj. Gen. Muir Fairchild collection includes his lectures in the late 1930s at the Air Corps Tactical School, important for doctrinal issues.

Cataclysm

At the National Archives II, College Park, Maryland, a number of record groups proved key to this study, as follows:

- Record Group 18, Records of the Army Air Forces
- Record Group 218, Records of the U.S. Joint Chiefs of Staff
- Record Group 107, Records of the Office of Secretary of War
- Record Group 243, Records of the United States Strategic Bombing Survey
- Record Group 165, Records of the War Department General and Special Staffs

The Franklin D. Roosevelt Library in Hyde Park, New York, contains a trove of archival material on Roosevelt and Arnold and air policy during the war years. The most important groups proved to be the President's Secretary File and the Map Room records. The papers of Harry Hopkins at the FDR Library proved valuable as did the diary of Henry Morgenthau.

I was fortunate to have the opportunity to interview Generals Ira C. Eaker, Curtis E. LeMay, and Haywood S. Hansell, Jr. Each made important contributions to the U.S. air effort in World War II. As operational commanders in the Pacific, LeMay and Hansell framed the doctrinal and strategic issues in the air war against Japan. General Eaker, a long-time associate of Arnold's, and the Deputy Commander of the Army Air Forces in the summer of 1945, provided the author with relevant insights into the functioning of AAF Headquarters and the evolution of doctrine and strategy.

The Murray Green collection includes 240 oral history transcripts of General Arnold's contemporaries compiled by Dr. Green. The original collection is at the U.S. Air Force Academy Library in Colorado Springs. Microfilm copies of the collection reside at the Office of Air Force History, Bolling AFB, Washington, D.C. and the Air Force Historical Research Agency, Maxwell AFB, Montgomery, Alabama. The Historical Research Agency at Maxwell AFB is the official repository for records of the U.S. Air Force. Many of these records are also available on microfilm in the Office of Air Force History at Bolling AFB in Washington, D.C.

The following interviews proved most useful to this work:

- Author with Maj. General Haywood S. Hansell, Jr., October 7, 1974
- Author with General Curtis E. LeMay, November 14, 1974
- Author with General Ira C. Eaker, August 27, 1974
- Brig. Gen. Noel Parrish and Alfred Goldberg with General Carl A. Spaatz, February 21,1962
- Charles Hildreth and Alfred Goldberg with General Ira C. Eaker, May 1962
- Alfred Goldberg with Maj. Gen. Kenneth B. Wolfe, September 6, 1952

- Hugh Ahmaan with General Lauris Norstad, February 13-16 and October 22-25, 1979

Interviews by Murray Green in the H. H. Arnold Collection, Office of Air Force History, Washington, D.C. (Microfilm); original collection at the United States Air Force Academy Library, Colorado Springs, Colorado.

- Gen. Lauris Norstad, July 15, 1969
- Gen. Curtis LeMay, January 12, 1965; January 26, 1965; March 14, 1970
- Maj. Gen. H. S. Hansell, April 19, 1967; January 2, 1970

The following letters to the author proved to be most useful:

- Lt. Gen. Ira C. Eaker, October 22, 1974; February 18, 1975; December 10, 1976
- Maj. Gen. Haywood S. Hansell, Jr., June 17, 1974; October 24, 1964; February 11, 1975
- General Jacob E. Smart, February 19, 1983

The following unpublished manuscript proved most helpful:

- Maj. Gen. Haywood S. Hansell, Jr., to H. S. Wolk, October 1974

Selected Bibliography

Alperovitz, Gar. *Atomic Diplomacy: Hiroshima and Potsdam.* New York: Simon & Schuster, 1965.

Arnold, General Henry H. *Global Mission.* New York: Harper and Brothers, 1949.

Armstrong, Alan. *Preemptive Strike: The Secret Plan that Would Have Prevented the Attack on Pearl Harbor.* Guilford, CT: The Lyons Press, 2006.

Berger, Carl. *B-29: The Superfortress.* New York: Ballantine Books, 1970.

Bess, Michael. *Choices Under Fire: Moral Dimensions of World War II.* New York: Alfred A. Knopf, 2006.

Bischof, Gunter, and Robert L. Dupont, eds. *The Pacific War Revisited.* Baton Rouge: Louisiana State University Press, 1997.

Bix, Herbert P. *Hirohito and the Making of Modern Japan.* New York: Harper Collins, 2000.

Brodie, Bernard. *Strategy in the Missile Age.* Princeton, NJ: Princeton University Press, 1959.

Burns, James MacGregor. *Roosevelt, The Soldier of Freedom: 1940–1945.* New York: Francis Parkman Prize Edition, History Book Club, 1996.

Butow, Robert J. C. *Japan's Decision to Surrender.* Stanford, CA: Stanford University Press, 1954.

Cameron, Rebecca H., and Barbara Wittig, eds. *Golden Legacy, Boundless Future: Essays on the United States Air Force and the Rise of Aerospace Power.* Washington, D.C.: Air Force History and Museums Program, 2000.

Chandler, Alfred D., Jr., ed. *The Papers of Dwight David Eisenhower: The War Years, Vol. 3,* Baltimore: The Johns Hopkins University Press, 1970.

Churchill, Winston S. *The Hinge of Fate.* Boston: Houghton Mifflin, 1950.

Cline, Ray S. *Washington Command Post: The Operations Division.* Washington D.C.: Center for Military History, 1951.

Coffey, Thomas M. *Hap: The Story of the U.S. Air Force and the Man Who Built It, General Henry H. "Hap" Arnold.* New York: The Viking Press, 1982.

Copp, Dewitt S. *A Few Great Captains: The Men and Events That Shaped the Development of U.S. Air Power.* McLean, VA: EPM Publications, 1980.

Crane, Conrad C. *Bombs, Cities, and Civilians: American Airpower Strategy in World War II.* Lawrence: University Press of Kansas, 1993.

Craven, W. F., and J. L. Cate, eds., *The Army Air Forces in World War II, Vol 2, 5.* Chicago: University of Chicago Press, 1953.

Crowl, Philip. *Campaign in the Marianas.* Washington, D.C.: Office of the Chief of Military History, Department of the Army, 1960.

Daso, Dik Alan. *Hap Arnold and the Evolution of American Airpower.* Washington, D.C.: Smithsonian Institution Press, 2000.

_____. *Architects of American Air Supremacy: Gen. Hap Arnold and Dr. Theodore von Karman.* Maxwell AFB, AL: Air University Press, 1997.

David, Richard G. *Carl A. Spaatz and the Air War in Europe.* Washington D.C.: Center for Air Force History, 1993.

Douhet, Giulio. *The Command of the Air.* Trans. Dino Ferrari. New York: Coward-McCann, 1942. Originally published in Italian by the Air Ministry, 1921.

Dower, John W. *War Without Mercy: Race and Power in the Pacific War.* New York: Pantheon Books, 1986.

Downes, Alexander B. *Targeting Civilians in War.* Ithaca: Cornell University Press, 2008.

Drea, Edward J. *MacArthur's ULTRA: Codebreaking and the War against Japan, 1942–1945.* Lawrence: University Press of Kansas, 1992.

Earle, Edward Mead, ed. *Makers of Modern Strategy.* Princeton, NJ: Princeton University Press, 1944.

Fanton, Jonathan F. "Robert A. Lovett: The War Years." Ph.D. diss., Yale University, 1978. Available from University Microfilms International.

Feis, Herbert. *Japan Subdued: The Atomic Bomb and the End of the War in the Pacific.* Princeton, NJ: Princeton University Press, 1961.

Finney, Robert T. *History of the Air Corps Tactical School, 1920–1940.* Washington, D.C.: Air Force History and Museums Program, 1998.

Foreign Relations of the United States, Diplomatic Papers: The Conference of Berlin (The Potsdam Conference), 1945, Volume II. Washington, D.C.: U.S. Government Printing Office, 1960.

Frank, Richard B. *Downfall: The End of the Imperial Japanese Empire.* New York: Penguin Books, 1999.

_____. *MacArthur.* New York: Palgrave MacMillan, 2007.

Futrell, Robert Frank. *Ideas, Concepts, Doctrine: Basic Thinking in the United States Air Force, 1907-1960.* Maxwell AFB, AL: Air University Press, 1989.

Gordin, Michael D. *Five Days in August: How World War II Became a Nuclear War.* Princeton, NJ: Princeton University Press, 2007.

Grayling, A. C. *Among the Dead Cities: The History and Moral Legacy of the World War II Bombing of Civilians in Germany and Japan.* New York: Walker and Company, 2006.

Greenfield, Kent Roberts. *American Strategy in World War II: A Reconsideration.* Baltimore: Johns Hopkins University Press, 1963.

Greer, Thomas H. *The Development of Air Doctrine in the Army Air Arm, 1917–1941.* Washington, D.C.: New Imprint by Office of Air Force History, USAF, 1985.

Griffith, Thomas E., Jr. *MacArthur's Airman: General George C. Kenney and the War in the Southwest Pacific.* Lawrence: University Press of Kansas, 1998.

Gruhl, Werner. *Imperial Japan's World War Two 1931–1945.* New Brunswick: Transaction Publishers, 2007.

Hall, R. Cargill, ed. *Case Studies in Strategic Bombing.* Washington D.C.: Air Force History and Museums Program, 1998.

Hansell, Haywood, S., Jr. *The Air Plan That Defeated Hitler.* Atlanta: Higgins-MacArthur/Longino and Porter, 1972.

_____. *Strategic Air War Against Japan.* Alabama: Maxwell AFB, 1980.

Hasegawa, Tsuyoshi. *Racing the Enemy: Stalin, Truman, and the Surrender of Japan.* Cambridge, MA: The Belknap Press, 2005.

Hastings, Max. *Retribution: The Battle for Japan, 1944–45.* New York: Alfred A. Knopf, 2008.

Hayes, Grace Person. *The History of the Joint Chiefs of Staff: The War Against Japan,* Annapolis, MD: Naval Institute Press, 1982.

Hewlett, Richard G., and Oscar E. Anderson, Jr. *The New World, 1939–1946: A History of the United States Atomic Energy Commission.* University Park: Pennsylvania State University Press, 1962.

Holley, I. B. Jr. *Ideas and Weapons.* Washington, D.C.: Air Force History and Museums Program, 1997.

Hurley, Alfred F. *Billy Mitchell: Crusader for Air Power* Bloomington: Indiana University Press, 1975.

Huston, Maj. Gen. John W., ed. *American Airpower Comes of Age: General Henry H. "Hap" Arnold's World War II Diaries, Vols. 1 and 2.* Maxwell AFB, AL: Air University Press, 2002.

Isaacson, Walter. *Einstein: His Life and Universe.* New York: Simon & Schuster, 2007.

James, Clayton. *The Years of MacArthur: The War Years, 1941–1945.* Vol 2. Boston: Houghton Mifflin Company, 1975.

Jones, Vincent C. *Manhattan: The Army and the Atomic Bomb.* Washington, D.C.: Center of Military History, United States Army, 1985.

Kenney, George C. *General Kenney Reports: A Personal History of the Pacific War.* Washington, D.C.: Air Force History and Museums Program, 1997.

Kort, Michael. *The Columbia Guide to Hiroshima and the Bomb.* New York: Columbia University Press, 2007.

Kozak, Warren. *LeMay: The Life and Wars of General Curtis LeMay.* Washington, D.C.: Regnery Publishing, 2009.

Lane, Peter B., and Ronald E. Marcello, eds. *Warriors and Scholars: A Modern War Reader.* Denton: University of North Texas Press, 2005.

Larrabee, Eric C. *Commander in Chief: Franklin Delano Roosevelt, His Lieutenants, and Their War.* New York: Harper and Row, 1987.

LeMay, Curtis E., with MacKinlay Kantor. *Mission with LeMay, My Story.* Garden City, NY: Doubleday, 1965.

_____. and Bill Yenne. *Superfortress: The Story of the B-29 and American Air Power.* New York: McGraw-Hill Book Company, 1988.

McClendon, R. Earl. *Autonomy of the Air Arm.* Washington, D.C.: Air Force History and Museums Program, 1996.

McCullough, David. *Truman.* New York: Simon & Schuster, 1992.

MacEachin, Douglas J. *The Final Months of the War with Japan: Signals Intelligence, U.S. Invasion Planning and the A-Bomb Decision,* Center for the Study of Intelligence, December 1998.

McFarland, Stephen L. *America's Pursuit of Precision Bombing, 1910–1945.* Washington, D.C.: Smithsonian Institution Press, 1995.

MacIsaac, David. *Strategic Bombing in World War II: The Story of the United States Strategic Bombing Survey.* New York: Garland Publishing, 1976.

Maddox, Robert J., ed. *Hiroshima in History: The Myths of Revisionism.* Columbia: University of Missouri Press, 2007.

Malloy, Sean L. *Atomic Tragedy: Henry L. Stimson and the Decision to Use the Bomb Against Japan.* Ithaca: Cornell University Press, 2008.

Matloff, Maurice, and Edwin Snell. *Strategic Planning for Coalition Warfare: 1941–1942.* Washington, D.C.: Office of the Chief of Military History, Department of the Army, 1953.

Meilinger, Phillip S. *The Paths of Heaven: The Evolution of Airpower Theory.* Maxwell AFB, AL: Air University Press, 1997.

Miller, Donald L. *Masters of the Air: America's Bomber Boys Who Fought the Air War Against Nazi Germany.* New York: Simon & Schuster, 2006.

Morison, Elting E. *Turmoil and Tradition: A Study of the Life and Times of Henry L. Stimson.* Boston: Houghton Mifflin Co., 1960.

Morton, Louis. *Strategy and Command: The First Two Years.* Washington, D.C.: Office of the Chief of Military History, Department of the Army, 1962.

Murray, Williamson, and Allan R. Millett. *A War to Be Won: Fighting the Second World War.* Cambridge, MA: The Belknap Press of Harvard University Press, 2000.

Nalty, Bernard, C., ed. *Winged Shield, Winged Sword: A History of the United States Air Force: Volume I, 1907–1950.* Washington, D.C.: Air Force History and Museums Program, 1997.

Neufeld, Jacob, William T. Y'Blood, and Mary Lee Jefferson, eds. *Pearl to V-J Day: World War II in the Pacific.* Washington, D.C.: Air Force History and Museums Program, 2000.

Nutter, Ralph. *With the Possum and the Eagle: The Memoir of a Navigator's War Over Germany and Japan.* Denton: University of North Texas Press, 2005.

O'Reilly, Charles T. and William A. Rooney. *The Enola Gay and the Smithsonian Institution.* Jefferson, NC: McFarland & Company, 2005.

Overy, R. J. *The Air War: 1939–1945.* New York: Stein and Day, 1980.

Parton, James. *Air Force Spoken Here: General Ira Eaker and the Command of the Air.* Bethesda, MD: Adler & Adler, 1986.

Perret, Geoffrey. *There's a War to Be Won: The United States Army in World War II.* New York: Random House, 1991.

Pogue, Forrest. *George C. Marshall: Ordeal and Hope, 1939–1942.* New York: The Viking Press, 1965.

_____. *George C. Marshall: Organizer of Victory, 1943–1945.* New York: The Viking Press, 1973.

Polmar, Norman, and Thomas B. Allen. *Codename Downfall: The Secret Plan to Invade Japan and Why Truman Dropped the Bomb.* New York: Simon & Schuster, 1995.

Rosenman, Samuel I., comp. *The Public Papers and Addresses of Franklin D. Roosevelt: 1943 Volume, The Tide Turns.* New York: Harper and Brothers, 1943.

Schaffer, Ronald. *Wings of Judgement: American Bombing in World War II.* New York: Oxford University Press, 1985.

Sherry, Michael S. *The Rise of American Air Power: The Creation of Armageddon.* New Haven, CT: Yale University Press, 1987.

Sherwood, Robert E. *Roosevelt and Hopkins: An Intimate History.* New York: Harper and Brothers, 1948.

Skates, John Ray. *The Invasion of Japan: Alternative to the Bomb.* Columbia: University of South Carolina Press, 2000.

Spector, Ronald H. *Eagle Against the Sun: The American War with Japan.* New York: Free Press, 1985.

_____. *In the Ruins of Empire: The Japanese Surrender and the Battle for Postwar Asia.* New York: Random House, 2007.

Stimson, Henry L., and McGeorge Bundy. *On Active Service in Peace and War.* New York: Harper and Brothers, 1948.

Tillman, Barrett. *LeMay.* New York: Palgrave Macmillan, 2007.

Trest, Warren A. *Air Force Roles and Missions: A History.* Washington D.C.: Air Force History and Museums Program, 1998.

Truman, Harry S. *Memoirs: Years of Decisions,* Garden City, NY: Doubleday, 1955.

_____. *Memoirs by Harry S. Truman.* Vol. 2, *Years of Trial and Hope.* Garden City, NY: Doubleday & Company, Inc., 1956.

_____. *Public Papers of the Presidents of the United States,* April–December 1945. Washington, D.C.: U.S. Government Printing Office, 1961.

Truman, Margaret. *Harry S. Truman.* New York: William Morrow, 1973.

Underwood, Jeffrey S. *The Wings of Democracy: The Influence of Air Power on the Roosevelt Administration 1933–1941.* College Station: Texas A&M University Press, 1991.

Vander Muelen, Jacob. *Building the B-29.* Washington, D.C.: Smithsonian Institution Press, 1995.

Walker, J. Samuel. *Prompt and Utter Destruction: Truman and the Use of Atomic Bombs Against Japan.* Chapel Hill: University of North Carolina Press, 2004.

Waller, Douglas. *A Question of Loyalty: Gen. Billy Mitchell and the Court-Martial That Gripped the Nation.* New York: Harper Collins Publishers, 2004.

Watson, Mark S. *The War Department, Chief of Staff: Prewar Plans and Preparations.* Washington, D.C.: Historical Division, U.S. Army, 1950.

Weintraub, Stanley. *The Last Great Victory: The End of World War II, July/August 1945.* New York: Truman Talley Books/Dutton, 1995.

Weller, George. *First into Nagasaki: The Censored Eyewitness Dispatches on Post-Atomic Japan and Its Prisoners of War.* New York: Crown Publishers, 2006.

Werrell, Kenneth P. *Blankets of Fire: U.S. Bombers Over Japan during World War II,* Washington, D.C.: Smithsonian Institution Press, 1996.

_____. *Death from the Heavens: A History of Strategic Bombing.* Annapolis, MD: Naval Institute Press, 2009.

Wolk, Herman S. *Fulcrum of Power: Essays on the United States Air Force and National Security.* Washington, D.C.: Air Force History and Museums Program, 2003.

_____. *Reflections on Air Force Independence.* Washington, D.C.: Air Force History and Museums Program, 2007.

_____. *Strategic Bombing: The American Experience.* Manhattan, KS: MA/AH Publishing, 1981.

_____. *The Struggle for Air Force Independence, 1943–1947.* Washington, D.C.: Air Force History and Museums Program, 1997.

Index